Observing Children in Their Natural Worlds

A Methodological Primer

Second Edition

Observing Children in Their Natural Worlds
A Methodological Primer

Second Edition

Anthony D. Pellegrini

with

Frank J. Symons

John Hoch

University of Minnesota

2004

LAWRENCE ERLBAUM ASSOCIATES, PUBLISHERS

Mahwah, New Jersey London

CONTENTS

PREFACE

Writing a second edition of a textbook is in many ways easier than the first edition. In some ways it is more difficult. It is easier, as most writers know, because the organizational ideas of the book are already there. For me at least, the most difficult part of writing is organization, or knowing what it is I want to say. At a simple level, then, all the writer must do is to add new information to the extant template. The difficulty of revision is related to the ease, as strange as that might sound. Specifically, in the second edition I had to decide what to keep, what to expand, and what to cut.

My decisions were guided by having used the first edition in classes at both the University of Georgia (where I taught until 1998) and at the University of Minnesota. At Minnesota, I have used the book as part of a general research methods course I teach in the Department of Educational Psychology. The class has MA and PhD students from varied backgrounds, such as Special Education, School Psychology, and Psychology. Consequently, I received feedback on the book from a variety of different perspectives, from groups of very conscientious and competent students.

I have also based my revision decisions on feedback I received from colleagues around the world who have used the book. (The first edition has Korean and Japanese translations.) Dave Bjorklund, my friend and colleague, deserves special thanks.

By consensus, the most popular aspect of the first edition was the organization of the book, in which the student or researcher is guided through conceptualizing, designing, implementing, and writing the research project. So, this basic organization is the same as in the first edition.

Within this organizational frame, things have changed. For example, the discussion of the place of direct observational methods in relation to different qualitative and quantitative research traditions has been kept, but expanded. I have extended discussions of the use of direct observations in naturalistic setting (drawing from research methods in ethology and ethnography) and in more contrived settings (drawing from experimental psychology). The assumptions guiding research in these different areas is especially relevant as debate (and

(e.g., number and composition of the group being observed) of the observational setting. Certainly these factors influence behavior. For example, female-preferred toys influence the behavior of males and females to the extent that boys might be less engaged than the girls (Pellegrini & Perlmutter, 1989). However, it is also important to recognize that the distal forces also influence the proximal forces. For example, that boys are biased toward higher levels of physical activity may influence their choice of toys and, in turn, their behavior with them.

Although this very general definition of context is useful in understanding the interrelations between individuals' behavior and the situation in which they are embedded (see Hinde, 1976, for an exhaustive description of context), it is also important to recognize that two behaviors may have similar features but have very different meaning, depending on context. For example, the play face and gentle push of a popular child (a dimension of the social context) is typically interpreted as playful. For an aggressive child, on the other hand, the exact same behavior is typically interpreted as aggressive. Thus, one dimension of context, the participants, relates to the meaning of the behaviors exhibited.

Although the methods discussed in this book are generic, that is, they can be applied to the observations of ground squirrels, rhesus monkeys, shoppers in a super market, or children on playgrounds, I will be concerned, primarily, with children embedded in the context of schools, neighborhoods, and families. These methods can be applied to describing children in the many contexts they inhabit. I agree fully with the concerns expressed by Herbert Wright (1960), more than 40 years ago, when he noted that we have very limited knowledge of children. Our knowledge now, as was the case 40 years ago, is mostly based on descriptions of children in preschool settings or in laboratories. Although this concern was echoed by Bronfenbrenner (1979) 25 years after Wright, we still know very little about children outside of school settings. For example, we know virtually nothing about who children interact with after school and on weekends. Given today's demographics of increasing instances of dual career families, single parents, and paternal custody it seems important to generate such descriptions. After all, some of our educational intervention strategies, such as joint book reading between parents and their children, assume that this is

FIG. 1.1.

still the primary dyad in children's lives. Observational methods applied to children's natural worlds can be very helpful in answering these sorts of applied and policy questions.

GOOD DESCRIPTIONS: OR, MAXIMIZING RELIABILITY AND VALIDITY

While I suggest that the methods considered here are useful for observing children in their everyday worlds, it must be noted that these same observational methods can be used in experimental laboratories, as well. In both cases the aim of good description is the same. *Good* descriptions meet criteria of being reliable and valid. Generally, reliable observations are those in which one observer records in a consistent manner and there is agreement between different observers. Valid observations, on the other hand, are those that actually measure what they purport to measure. Although much more will be said about these issues in subsequent chapters, suffice it to say for now that in both the laboratory and in the field reliability between and among observers is necessary, but not sufficient, for validity. Simply put, before we can claim anything about the truthfulness of our descriptions (i.e., validity) we must agree on what it is we see (i.e., reliability).

With validity we have the usual trinity of concerns: internal validity, external validity, and ecological validity, as well as the overarching issue of construct validity. Construct validity refers to the degree to which that we are observing represents a psychological construct, or an abstract representation of a phenomenon

FIG. 1.2.

such as aggression or intelligence. While we cannot have direct measures of a construct because it is abstract, we can have indirect indicators (e.g., punch, bite, and kick, are indicators of aggression).

Added to this, construct validity must be concerned with any policy or social implications of using the measure as part of a decision-making process (Cronbach, 1971, 1980; Moss, 1992). For example, if we are using a measure of aggression to evaluate students' placement into special classes, we must also consider our confidence in our measurement in relation to the impact on students' lives.

It is, however, on these first three dimensions of validity (internal, external, and ecological) that laboratory and field methods diverge, and often the divergence is abrupt. Laboratory procedures are concerned primarily with internal validity, and less concerned with external validity. By manipulating and controlling variables experimentalists can make internally valid statements about the effects of independent variables (e.g., the nature of toys that children are exposed to) on dependent variables (e.g., children's play behavior). That is, we can be sure that variation in independent variable is affecting the dependent measures. Experimentalists are often less concerned with external validity, or generalizing laboratory results to relevant field settings, and ecological validity, or the comparison of results across a number of different settings.

Field studies (or studies of people in their everyday environments), on the other hand, are primarily concerned with describing behavior as it occurs in its natural habitat and recognize limited internal validity. Imbalances in both laboratory and field approaches result in incomplete knowledge. Obviously, descriptions of laboratory behavior with minimal ties to its field analogue are of limited use and interest. Similarly, descriptions of behavior in the field, without clear limits on alternative explanations, do not advance our understanding of the ways in which variables affect each other. Alternatives to these two approaches include designing *ecologically valid* experiments, such as comparisons of children's behavior in laboratory and classroom settings (e.g., Bronfenbrenner, 1979) or taking advantage of natural experiments.

Examples of natural experiments include examining the effects of androgens (a male hormone) on female fetuses and subsequent sex-typed behavior. More specifically, there are cases in which female fetuses are exposed to excessive amounts of male hormone (the syndrome is known as Congenital Adrenal Hyperplasia [CAH]). Research has shown that CAH girls, relative to control girls, prefer to play with male toys and male playmates (Hines, 1982; Hines & Kaufman, 1994). In this case we have an intervention (in the form of excessive amounts of male hormones) in nature, that we would not be able to experimentally manipulate (for ethical reasons). In short, field experiments and natural experiments represent a rapprochement, of sorts, between the lab and the field. At a minimum, field work should precede experimental analogues.

If we do not work toward some sort of rapprochement between experimental and field approaches disciplines such as early education and child and educational psychology are sure to atrophy, and probably with good cause. I say with good cause because our experiments should aspire to explaining the ways in which organisms live and develop in their natural world. Similarly, we need some level of explanation and causal inferences so that we can begin to understand these processes more clearly and then use this information to design educational environments. So, my bias is that description is an important, and necessary first step, of any scientific enterprise.

MERE DESCRIPTION?

Frequently descriptive research, in which observational methods play an indispensable part, is considered merely descriptive, implying that description is either an unimportant or an atheoretical enterprise. Mere descriptions are often contrasted with research designs that are explanatory, to the extent that the latter proffers causal statements for the interrelation among variables. I, along with others (e.g., Blurton Jones, 1972; Hinde, 1980) believe that thorough descriptions are a necessary and very important first step in conducting research that aims to explain. Correspondingly, descriptions, as seen later in this chapter, are important aspects of most educational programs.

Good descriptions are neither atheoretical nor less scientific than approaches offering causal explanations. The ability to adequately describe a phenomenon, especially in complex organisms like humans, requires some theory. The complexity of the human organism interacting, even in the simplest ways, necessitates that observers make choices about who, what, and when to observe. For example, take the seemingly simple issue of classifying participants' roles. Kagan's (1994) simple but informative example clearly points to the importance of theory in description: "Zoologists classify cows as mammals, economists classify them as commodities, and some cultures regard these animals as sacred symbols" (p. 11). Further, theory guides us in terms of the levels of specificity of our categories. If we had a biological orientation, we might examine relations between hormones and behavior. If, on the other hand, we had a cultural anthropological perspective, we might examine the match between the cultures of school tasks and those indigenous to children's homes. Given the complexity of the phenomena that can be observed, a clear theoretical orientation is necessary because it guides decisions we make about observational methods.

It thus makes sense to foreground, or to make explicit, those decisions we make when we observe. In this way we know the paths we have traveled in making these decisions. It is naive and unrealistic for observers to think or state that they enter an observational field with no biases in terms of what they will observe or how the phenomena will be observed and categorized. Human observers have too many schema, or concepts about the ways in which the world works, in their heads to take such a stance. The best we can hope for is to make our biases explicit and to try to minimize them. Similarly, observers can not go out and observe everything for there is clearly too much to observe. With this in mind, we should then make explicit what it is we are interested in (i.e., our question). With an explicit question in mind (which may arise from making preliminary observations) we can then begin to consider what it is specifically we will observe.

USING OBSERVATIONAL METHODS IN EDUCATIONAL, CHILD, & DEVELOPMENTAL PSYCHOLOGY

The major focus of this book is on using observational methods with children and their families. Thus, observations can be conducted in the home, school, after-school program and anywhere else that children spend time. I follow the child study tradition (see Pellegrini & Bjorklund, 1998) whereby good descriptions of children are the bases for designing educational, as well as other sorts of intervention, programs. Thus, my basic assumption is that we must understand children before we can intervene. Observational methods are an indispensable tool used in understanding children.

There is a crucial need of good descriptions (i.e., reliable and valid descriptions) of children in settings where they spend substantial portions of their time. Descriptions of this sort are useful in a number of ways.

First, and most basically, good descriptions are the basis for accurate and valid category systems. As ethologists have shown us (e.g., Blurton Jones, 1972), detailed descriptions of individuals' behavior in their natural settings (or what ethologists call an *ethogram*) provide the basis for grouping behaviors together into categories. This orientation is contrasted with an intuitive approach to developing categories. In the latter case a research would come up with descriptors for a category system based on what he or she thinks should go there.

There is an interesting contrast of these two approaches in the child development literature. Ethologists, such as Blurton Jones (1972) and Smith (Smith & Connolly, 1980), developed ethograms for preschoolers' social behavior and developed separate categories for rough-and-tumble play (R&T) and aggression. R&T was comprised of play face, chase, soft hit, swipe, and grapple. Aggression included frown, punch, kick, and bite. More consistent with the intuitive approach, others have described the R&T of preschoolers in terms of both playful and aggressive behaviors. Empirically, the two do not seem to co-occur so to aggregate them is misleading and not valid.

Valid descriptions should provide the basis for the application of these categories in various arenas, such as program evaluation. They could provide bases for programs for children and families. For examples, models of successful adult–child and child–child interaction, derived from descriptive work, can be used to design programs for teacher–child and peer interaction in schools.

The assumption that programs for children and families should be based on good descriptions of children and their families is an old one and basic to the fields of educational, child, and developmental psychology, as well as to the child study movement (see Pellegrini & Bjorklund, 1998). The child study movement assumes that the child and his or her family are at the center of any educational program in which they are enrolled. Dimensions of the programs, such as curriculum materials and teacher strategies, as well as evaluation of the program are based on these descriptions.

My approach to programs for children can be contrasted with other approaches to education. For example, many educational programs base their programs on the nature of the subject matter being taught; that is, rather than basing mathematics or science lessons on the nature of the child, subject approaches typically present basic subject matter concepts in a manner consistent with the disciplines.

The approach I advocate involves using observations to describe children in various stages of their educational experiences. More specifically, observations provide the bases of generating curriculum and instruction as well as evaluation procedures. Descriptions of children in their everyday context, that is, school and nonschool settings, are particularly useful here. The importance of using children's relevant, everyday experiences for educational programs has been recognized from at least Dewey (1938) and more recently by Cole (1993).

Activities that are important in children's communities and family lives need to be identified and described so that they can be included in educational programs. For example, certain groups of children may experience specific interaction styles of reading and mathematics activities as important aspects of their culture (Pellegrini & Stanic, 1993). These specific activities, rather than others, are often motivating for children. The inclusion of such indigenous strategies and materials in educational curriculum is important, particularly when the children in those programs come from culturally diverse communities. Thus, observational methods form an important part of the curriculum planning cycle.

Evaluation of children and programs is another part of the curriculum cycle for which observational methods can be very useful. By *evaluation*, I mean the documenting the operation and impact of the program. Traditionally, children and teachers have been evaluated with various forms of paper-and-pencil tests. For example, to document a teacher's competence to teach, some schools use tests of teachers' knowledge of subject matter. Similarly, paper-and-pencil tests are typically used to determine the extent to which children have mastered the subject matter presented in the programs. The criticisms of such approaches are well recognized and have been more eloquently argued elsewhere (e.g. Shepard, 1993) so I will not restate them except to say, generally, that tests are less than perfect indicators of young children's competence.

The use of tests is particularly problematic with young children, as we have known for many years (see Messick, 1983 for a thorough discussion). One reason for this limitation is that tests are artificial and sometimes anxiety-producing events; this combination of factors, as well as numerous factors related to the design of tests per se, adversely affects children's test-taking behavior. The effect of these extraneous factors on children are probably responsible for the well-known fact that children are unreliable test takers (Messick, 1983). That is, their scores on different days tend to vary. Relatedly, when children and adults are placed in anxiety-producing situations they tend to exhibit lower, rather than higher, levels of competence. This may be due to the fact that they are unwilling to offer new or novel solutions in a threatening situation. With such unreliability we have no chance for validity.

In light of these many limitations of testing, the educational community has begun to consider alternative forms of assessment, such as authentic assessment. Observational methods fit quite nicely into this movement in that they are excellent for gathering information on children and teachers in authentic situations. Consequently, observational methods are useful for evaluation of children and teachers to the extent that they do not put them in anxiety-producing situations, thus, we have a higher likelihood of getting a truer measure of their competence.

An added benefit of observational methods relates to the fact that results from naturalistic observations do not have to generalize from one performance context to another. Tests often have difficulty making this transition from assessment to performance contexts. More specifically, reliable and valid test scores are indicators of how children and teachers might perform in the contexts from which the test items were generated. Thus, the scores should generalize or transfer to a performance (i.e., real) setting. Observational methods have the benefit of documenting competence in those relevant situations from the start. So, if we are interested in making inferences about teachers' ability to teach literacy lessons, we can observe him or her directly in those sorts of lessons. We do not have to test him or her on subject and instructional materials related to literacy and then make inferences about his or her teaching ability.

In order to use observational techniques effectively, however, observers must be careful to choose, or sample, behaviors and events that they see as important. A sure guide here is to observe those aspects of the program that are specified in the program goals and objectives. Based on specified program goals and objectives, the observer can, first, document the degree to which these program components are actually being implemented. Descriptions of program implementation are very important because there is often a mismatch between educational programs as they are stated in some policy manual and the actual implementation of the program. Thus, we must first describe the actual process and the degree to which it relates to the formal (or written) program. A second step in the evaluation process has the observer documenting the degree to which these program components relate to children's development. Thus, by matching specific program components with specific child outcomes, we can design effective programs.

As seen in later chapters, this is no quick fix because the use of observational methods to conduct evaluations is very time consuming. To make inferences about competence based on observations, requires numerous observations whereas less time is typically involved in testing. Thus, costs and benefits exist in both areas.

SUMMARY AND CONCLUSIONS

To conclude this introductory chapter, observational methods are general techniques for use in either experimental or field setting. In each setting investigators should be concerned with the dual concerns of reliability and validity; correspondingly, attention should be paid to internal, external, and ecological validity. If our goal is to use observational methods to understand the ways in which specific children and adults interact in the world, it is imperative that we attend to these issues of reliability and validity with the utmost vigilance.

The ways in which we choose to use the methods outlined in this book, of course, will vary depending on individuals' needs. Certainly this book should be useful to students of the scientific study of behavior, interactions, and relationships. It is the aim of this group to describe the interaction between organism and environment. Recollection of Wright's (1960) advice, however, should be kept in mind when we choose a problem to study. Recall, more than 40 years ago, he bemoaned the fact that we knew very little about children beyond the preschool period and outside of the confines of their preschool classrooms or outside the laboratory. Forty years later, things have not changed much. If we want to understand children's circumstances it seems that a very important first step is to describe what they spend their time doing and with whom they do it with. From an educational perspective, this information can be very useful in program design.

Relatedly, observational methods are useful in solving problems with which we are confronted in our everyday circumstances. For example, a teacher confronted with a noncompliant child could apply these methods to begin to identify the nature of the context and the behaviors that constitute noncompliance for this specific child. Correspondingly, these noncompliant behaviors could be paired with specific consequences in service of identifying possible motives. The work of Gerald Patterson (e.g., 1982) and colleagues is exemplary in its use of observational methods to describe the behaviors of problem children in their everyday lives. In short, this sort of "action research," in which a person studies a relevant problem in their real-world circumstances, is very useful. Given the rather idiosyncratic nature of most problems and concerns, it seems to me that teachers, social workers, labor organizers (see R. H. Tawney's biography by Ross Terrill [1973], for an interesting example), and the like, can most effectively solve work-related problems when they confront them themselves.

A basic starting point, no matter what type of research venture we plan, is a thorough description of that which we plan to study. As noted, descriptions are a necessary part of any scientific or intervention enterprise. Descriptions are needed to generate reliable and valid categories that help us to understand those who are being observed. Research of this sort can also be used to solve real problems people confront every day.

SOME THINGS TO THINK ABOUT

1. Regarding the interrelation between dimensions of context and their affect on behavior consider the following:

Sam and Jack playing together with blocks.

Sam and Jack playing together with dolls.

Sam and Anna playing together with blocks.

Sam and Anna playing together with dolls.

2. How do you think the children would act differently in each situation?

3. How do you think the behavior of children and their parents would differ if they were observed playing a monopoly game at home compared to playing the same game in an experimental room?

4. How might you find out?

5. Where and with whom do children that you know spend most of their out of school time?

6. How would you go about finding out?

to the goals of psychological research (i.e., description, explanation, prediction, and control). Third, I explicate the properties of the scientific methods as they are represented in experimental research.

WHAT IS SCIENCE?

In order to explore the nature of science in psychology we must take a brief foray into philosophy. Psychology, not so long ago, was a branch of philosophy, not a discipline in its own right. Indeed, even today the connection between psychology and philosophy is seen as vital at some universities. For example, at Oxford University in England the study of psychology is embedded in the study of philosophy and physiology. Undergraduate students study psychology in conjunction with either philosophy or with physiology. So, for guidance in exploring the meaning of science for psychologists, we initially turn to a philosopher from the other place (Cambridge), Bertrand Russell.

We begin by using Bertrand Russell's (1959) definition of science: "Science is primarily knowledge; by convention it is knowledge of a certain kind, the kind, namely, which seeks general laws connecting a number of particular fact" (p. viii). From Russell's view there are three main stages in arriving at a scientific law. These stages are displayed in Table 2.1.

Science, in its ultimate form (Russell, 1959) consists of a set of propositions (or formally stated declarations), in the form of significant facts, arranged hierarchically, with particular facts being the lowest level and scientific laws being the highest.

The first stage in establishing a scientific law involves observing significant facts and stating them in propositional, or formal, form. A significant fact is a single instance that is relevant to the current scientific debate. For example, a significant fact could be the observation that domesticated chimpanzees seem to engage in pretend play. Stated as a proposition, it is expressed as: Chimpanzees engage in pretend play.

In science, hypotheses are not isolated as they are viewed against the backdrop of the other facts in the research literature. Generally, hypotheses are educated guesses about what we expect to find in research. Thus, significant facts are viewed in terms of their relative importance to the *current* state of knowledge and their significance is viewed in terms of the extent to which it supports or refutes some general law.

This particular fact on chimpanzees engaging in fantasy play is significant to the extent that it informs the current debate on theories of mind research. One

TABLE 2.1
The Three Stages in Establishing Scientific Laws

1. Observing significant facts
2. Arriving at hypotheses
3. Deducting the consequences from the tested hypotheses

school of thought holds that only humans are capable of symbolic play because only humans are capable of that level of cognitive decentering (see Tomasello, 1999; Tomasello & Call, 1997). Another theory holds that nonhuman primates are capable of this level of decentering (see Bekoff, 1997). Thus, this observation is significant because of its use as an instance in supporting (or not supporting) a particular hypothesis.

Correspondingly, the same finding may not have been significant if it was observed at an earlier time when the question of primates' theory of mind was not part of the scientific discourse. So, the findings of Hayes and Hayes (1952) of a chimp exhibiting fantasy was not significant in 1951 but was in 2002 (see Pellegrini & Bjorklund, 2002).

A coherent collection of particular facts, taken together, suggests a law. These facts are connected upwardly toward the law by induction and downward from the law to the particular fact that we isolated earlier by deduction.

Interestingly, Russell (1959) suggested that the textbook view of science suggests a deductive process where the laboratory view of science is actually inductive. By this he meant that laws are built up from observations, not from laws down to predicted facts. *Induction* is defined as the logical process of reasoning from a specific to a more general level. *Deduction*, on the other hand, moves from a general statement to a specific event: from hypothesis to result.

The textbook view, especially as expressed in many research methods and statistics texts, holds this deductive view of science. According to Russell (1959), and more recently Bem (in press) science is not conducted primarily by deduction. So, scientists do not sit back and hypothesize, test hypotheses, and evaluate the results. They use the results to induce new hypotheses, and then test them deductively.

To make this more concrete, induction has us moving from the observation of specific facts, or the results of specific experiments, to a more general statement. Continuing with the case of fantasy, we could have a number of observations of chimpanzee fantasy and induce that nonhuman primates engage in fantasy. As I organize the facts to make an induction I also propose explanations for the ways in which individual facts are interrelated. These explanations serve as the basis for making predictions, or hypotheses, in which a hypothesis is an educated guess about what would happen given certain conditions. If our hypothesis accounts for all the facts observed, it leads us to have confidence in the hypothesis.

Induction alone, however, does not enable us to support our hypothesis as there may be a number of reasons accounting for our results. From this view, I move down the hierarchy to test the hypothesis. Hypothesis testing involves deductive logic, as deduction moves from a general statement, such as a hypothesis, to a specific observation. Our hypothesis is that nonhuman primates engage in fantasy. To test this hypothesis we either design an experiment or observe chimps across time to determine the extent to which our observations support or fail to support the hypothesis.

In short, scientific psychology involves both inductive and deductive processes as part of the scientific enterprise. Ideally, as Russell (1959) noted, the two

We begin by specifying that we will measure perspective taking on a specific test of this ability. By stating a problem in terms of specific measurement criteria we accomplish a number of things. First, we make clear exactly what it is we mean by perspective taking. This enables us to relate our findings to earlier research and theory in this area. It also allows other researchers to replicate our results if they so desire. By *replicate* I mean that other researchers can conduct the study in the same way as we did. If a study is replicated, the results are the same across different studies.

The measure of perspective taking might involve having an individual child sitting in a chair at a table with two other chairs, a red one and a blue one. The child would be presented with a standardized picture of three mountains. First, the child is asked: Tell me the things you can see. The child's responses would be audiorecorded. Next, the child would be asked: Now let's pretend that you are in the red chair. Tell me what you'd see if your were sitting there. The same procedure would be repeated for the blue chair.

This procedure must assess perspective taking in a reliable and valid manner. As I discuss reliability and validity in much greater depth in a subsequent chapter, I will offer only brief descriptions here. Both are necessary in scientific data.

Reliability, in this instance, refers to the stability of performance on the task. For example, children's performance on the task should be similar on Monday and Tuesday. Validity refers to the truthfulness of the measure. In short, does it really measure perspective taking?

Reliability is necessary but not sufficient for validity. That is, we need reliability, but we also need more for validity. In this case, a measure will give us the same information on Monday and Tuesday if it is a good measure of perspective taking. To be valid, however, it should relate to other measures of perspective taking.

As part of this process we try to maximize objectivity and minimize the effects of bias influencing the way we conduct our work. We want the differences in performance between toddlers and 10 years, for example, to be due to real differences between them, as indicated by our measures, not due to our own idiosyncratic, or biased, procedures. For example, we would want to make sure that all children were exposed to standardized and clearly documented procedures. Further, we would want to make sure that the researchers testing the children were not aware of our hypothesis. This knowledge could result in them treating children differently, albeit subconsciously. For example, if the researchers knew our hypothesis about age differences and perspective taking, they might assume that toddlers would do poorly. Consequently, they might treat them differently while testing them (e.g., they might hurry the younger children through the task while taking more time with the older children).

After observing children's performance on our measures of perspective taking, we compile them and score them. Again, objectivity is the order of the day. A standardized scoring protocol should be followed, so all participants are scored in the same way. Similarly, scorers should not be aware of the hypothesis or the age of the child so that they can score the protocols objectively, and without bias.

In this hypothetical study, the researcher would score the audiorecording of children's responses. We would also want to be sure that the scoring of the protocols is not idiosyncratic to a specific researcher, so we must assess intra- or inter-scorer reliability. In the first case we would compare how the same researcher scored the same protocol. In the second instance, we would compare how two researchers scored the same protocol.

In the next chapter I discuss the specific types of measures used in psychological research and go into much more depth on reliability and validity.

To summarize, scientific inquiry involves using inductive and deductive processes in the service of answering a questions. My view of scientific research stresses objectivity. By objectivity I do not mean that I propose that we are expressing our views in a value-free manner or that some ideal form of a phenomenon exists. Scientists are humans, and human have values. We must make these values and points of view clear.

Similarly, as humans, we perceive our world in many different ways and assume that there is some objective reality. From the earliest cognitive psychologists in the early- and mid-20th Century (e.g., Bartlett, 1932, and Bruner, Goodnow, & Austin, 1958) we have acknowledged that human's perception is constructed in light of their extant mental schema.

This view of objectivity means simply that we make explicit what it is we do; that is, we describe our procedures and measures in clear and measurable terms. This enables others to both understand clearly what we have done and attempt to replicate our work. After all, *science is a public enterprise*. Our questions, hypotheses, and methods are derived, in part, from the public domain: Research is often supported with tax payers' money and papers are written and published in scientific journals for public consumption. That our finding are public also puts them up for public scrutiny. They are scrutinized, first, by editors and reviewers before they appear in print. Then, they are scrutinized by the scientific community. The assumption here is that public scrutiny advances science. One view of science, as I discuss later, holds that science advances through the process of supporting hypotheses while ruling out alternative explanations. Findings and ideas are examined and debated, again publicly. The public record, as represented in our scientific journals, not only chronicles our past, but points the directions for future research.

That science is public and open to public scrutiny certainly does not guarantee a constant march forward. Indeed, science as a discipline is very conservative and very reluctant to challenge or overturn established views (Kuhn, 1962; Russell, 1959). There is a clear bias in science to accept or confirm current knowledge and be skeptical of new views. This conservative perspective is appropriate, for evidence should be substantial before conventionally accepted beliefs are overturned. Yet, there must be avenues for findings that are counter to the prevailing dogma, and modern science, by its very nature, provides those avenues. There is no quicker route to scientific fame than to provide evidence that overturns a popular theory. Progress is made particularly as we try to *disconfirm* (and not just to confirm) hypotheses (Popper, 1959). From this view, science advances by establishing that ideas are important through both confirmation and disconfirmation. In the latter case we identify the ideas that are not useful.

WHAT SCIENTIFIC PSYCHOLOGY IS NOT

To further clarify what it is I mean by scientific psychology, I examine some things that it is not. Science is but one way of knowing, and there are others that contrast with scientific knowing. These ways of knowing, or ways of fixing a belief, were specified by the Elizabethan jurist and scientist, Francis Bacon (Broad, 1959) and later and more commonly by the philosopher Charles Pierce (Buchler, 1955, as cited in Kerlinger, 1996). First according to Pierce, we know, or believe, based on the method of *tenacity*. Similar to Bacon's *Idols of the Market*, knowledge from this perspective is that which has always been known. New views that conflict with these traditional views are seen as false.

Sometimes the method of tenacity can infect the scientific process, however. Indeed, until the 17th Century, the dominant view of science was traditionally set in the views of Aristotle and his interpreter, St. Thomas Aquinas (Broad, 1959). Their views of physics, for example, were uncritically accepted, until Bacon's critique (although, see Thorndike, 1966, for a more critical view of Bacon). History is full of examples in which traditional theories or views can be treated as hallowed simply because they have always been held. Kuhn (1962), in his classic critique of science, points to this view inhibiting progress in science. Traditional beliefs are relinquished only very reluctantly.

An example of this in contemporary psychology was the dominant view that, since its inception as a science, knowledge was attainable only through laboratory experiments. Additionally, B. F. Skinner (1974) viewed any form of psychology other than his version of Behaviorism as unscientific. All other forms of knowledge were viewed with skepticism.

Related to the method of tenacity is the method of *authority*, which Bacon quaintly labeled this, *Idols of the Theatre* (Broad, 1959). From this view, knowing is derived from specified authority. If an authority said it, it must be true. The statements are not held up for independent verification or disconfirmation. Of course, this level of knowing is more consistent with religion than science, but it is not unknown to science. If it is said in the Bible or in the Koran, by Marx or Mao, or by Piaget or Chomsky it must be true because it represents the word of an unassailable authority.

There are certainly examples of this is the history of psychology and modern science. For starters, Bertrand Russell (1959) recollected that when he first began teaching at Cambridge, in the first part of the 20th century, he recommended that laboratories be established so that students could test out their ideas empirically. The initial response from the University, according to Russell, was that laboratories were not necessary to test ideas; the ideas were true because their masters told them they were!

More recently, of course, we have variants of creationism being used to explain human nature. According to this view, human kind originated in the Garden of

Eden, according to the views expressed in the Bible. Although creationism is incompatible with modern science, it has not always been that way. Today, for an explanation to be considered scientific, it must explain some phenomenon in terms of natural mechanisms. If a miracle is necessary to explain a phenomenon (e.g., the creation of Adam and Eve by a omnipotent God), it is not within the realm of science. This perspective, however, is relatively recent. Scientists of the 17th, 18th, and even into the 19th centuries viewed their job as discovering the phenomenon and laws created by God. Science was one way to understand the mind of God. Many people may still believe this today, but any account that posits a special creation, divine intervention, or any supernatural cause to explain a phenomenon is beyond the scope of modern science.

The third way of knowing is the *a priori method*. The a priori method states that knowledge is self-evident to the extent that it must agrees with reason, and not necessarily experience or other forms of evidence. It was a result of rational discussion between people. So an idea can be expressed, a priori, and supported (deductively) through discussion. A different set of people, however, with a different set of views on the same a priori statement, could reach very different conclusions.

Scientific knowing, by contrast, is not limited to the opinions of one set of individuals. The notions of objectivity and public scrutiny as specified above moves us beyond knowing being limited to different sets of people.

Most basically, scientific processes, including psychology, can be differentiated from nonscientific processes by the fact the in science our statements are objectified in that they can be measured and tested. Most importantly these ideas, as represented in evidence, can be confirmed or disconfirmed through empirical testing (Broad, 1959; Popper, 1959). What this means in practice is that we can all make assertions, but only those assertions that can be disconfirmed are considered scientific.

Having to meet the criterion of disconfirmation eliminated all ways of knowing except the scientific way. Let's use the example of the following proposition: Children learn language by reinforcement. Tenacity, authority, and a priori methods can all be disconfirmed through direct observations of children using forms for which they were never reinforced, such as "I go*ed* to the store yesterday."

Some questions do not qualify as scientific questions simply because, by their very nature, they cannot be held up for disconfirmation. The belief in Creationism is one such case. A belief is a way of knowing based on faith, not a confirmation or disconfirmation; thus it cannot be considered scientific.

To conclude, to qualify as scientific inquiry a theory-testing process must be evidence based and be held up for public scrutiny through the processes of confirmation and disconfirmation. Despite this rather strict qualification, scientific psychology has a number of different goals.

WHAT ARE THE GOALS OF PSYCHOLOGICAL RESEARCH?

There are generally four goals in psychological research, as displayed in Table 2.3, and corresponding questions that help in reaching those goals (Sternberg, 2001).

Closely related to the goal of explanation is the goal of prediction. Indeed, one indicator of being able to explain something is the ability to predict what will happen next. Simply, prediction involves a researcher forecasting what will happen in the future. He or she can either predict the result of an experiment or of an observation. To use these examples, a researcher would predict, in advance, that giving androgen to female monkeys would result in those monkeys, relative to nonadrogenized female monkeys, exhibiting more R&T. Similarly, the anthropologist going into the field to study sex differences in R&T among the Kung would predict, in advance, that they would observe males engaging in R&T more than females.

There are both positive and negative aspects to predictive science. At one level, it is a strict test of the degree to which you understand the way in which something works. You think you understand, for example, the mechanism responsible for sex differences in R&T. You demonstrate your understanding by proposing what will happen when you tinker with that mechanism.

Additionally, predictions are an integral part of deductive theory testing. Stating an hypothesis in advance, or a priori, in some ways objectifies the scientific venture (Kerlinger, 1996). By this I mean that by predicting the outcome of a research study before we collect the data reduces the possibly of coming up with explanation for a finding that are not consistent with this theory. Explanations generated after data have been collected are referred to as post hoc explanations. To paraphrase Kerlinger (1996), if one bets on the outcome of a game *after* the game is complete, one has violated the rules of betting. Deductive science stipulates that we state prediction in advance.

There is also a negative dimension to prediction (Sternberg, 2001). If we understand a phenomenon so well that we can predict the outcome before it occurs, we may also be biased in the way in which we design the study or collect the data for the study. Let's take the example that we can predict, in advance, that aggressive children will also be disliked by their peers. This belief may lead us to observe disliked children as aggressive.

The final goal of psychological research is to control or influence people. This goal of scientific psychology is often the domain of educational and clinical psychologists. The ability to control or influence people is closely related to the ability to predict a result. Based on a theory, we design experiments in which we have different conditions that should influence people differentially. For example, an educational psychologist might design a research to study find out an effective way for children to learn letter–sound correspondence. The clinical psychologist might development, experimentally, an effective methods for helping adolescents control their aggression.

Let's look more closely at one example: controlling aggression. There is a theory that states that aggression is the results of a number of factors, but two are especially important: negative attribution bias and the inadequate group entry skills (Dodge, Petit, McClaskey, & Brown, 1986). In the experiment children are trained to minimize attributional biases (e.g., having them pay attention to facial expressions), and they are trained in the use of different group entry strategies (e.g., asking to join in). We compare the aggression of treated aggressive children with a comparison group of nontreated aggressive kids. Results from these experiments could be exported through organized programs in school and in clinics.

To summarize this section, I show that there are different sorts of psychological research. All types of research involve using theory for guidance. The basic form of research is descriptive to the extent that we cannot explain, predict, or change a phenomenon until we can describe it. The experiment, however, represents, to many the quintessential scientific method.

Science as Experiment

The experiment, in many ways, enables psychologists to make the strongest claims about their theories and hypotheses. At the heart of these claims is the importance attached to making causal statements about the relations between two variables, *x* and *y*. In this section, the logic of experimentation and the way in which it leads to scientific advancement and the advancement of knowledge is discussed. Examined are the conditions that must be in order to make those deductive inferences that enable us as a field to move forward.

Experiments, most basically, involve a treatment (or condition), an outcome measure, and some comparison between conditions. When properly conducted, experiments allow us to approach cause–effect relations. This level of explanation allows us to make explanatory and predictive claims. We begin, however, with a brief discussion of what it is we mean by causality.

Causality

Experiments are designed, we are told, because they enable the researcher to make a causal inference. By this I mean that *x* effects *y*. Other forms of research do not allow us to make this sort of powerful statement.

As it turns out, the concept of causality, although seemingly simple on the surface, is quite complex. Philosophers have debated the meaning of causality for centuries, and this has implications about the nature of our conclusions as well as the ways in which we design experiments to approach causal explanations.

At one extreme, the British empiricist Hume (cited in Cook & Campbell, 1979), suggested that scientists cannot make causal statements about the relation between two variables, *x* and *y*. Although this level of proof can be provided in mathematics and logic, most scientists cannot observe directly the mechanism responsible for the change (Cook & Campbell, 1979). Consequently, Hume, and later Russell, suggested that perfect correlation, when paired with other conditions, could be used to approach a causal explanation. By perfect correlation they meant that variation in one factor would co-occur with variation an another on a 1:1 basis. This condition was referred to as constant conjunction. The other condition was that of temporal precedence, that is, *x* must precede *y* in time. When these conditions are met, causal statements could be made.

Co-occurrence cannot be considered causal as there are probably numerous possible antecedents to a specific consequence and although *x* may always lead to *y*, there may be other explanations. For example, that day leads to night does not mean that day causes night.

To address the problem of not being able to directly observe the way in which *x* affects *y* led some philosophers to the notion of operational definitions. In an *operational definition*, a concept is defined in terms of the operations that must be performed to define it. So weight would be defined in terms of the operations necessary to measure it.

One problem, of the many, with operational definitions in psychology is that we often do not have direct access to the phenomena we wish to measure. *Constructs*, such as intelligence and aggression, are by definition abstractions and cannot be operationally represented. This quandary led psychologists to define processes and outcomes in terms of specific constructs (Cronbach & Meehl, 1955). Constructs, by definition, are not observable and their measurement is only approached through the use of multiple measures, such as directly observable behaviors and explicitly specified procedures.

The later British Empiricist, John Stuart Mill (Cook & Campbell, 1979) did, however, extend Hume's work, in a way that is more workable for psychologists in identifying causality. He did this by suggesting three conditions that must be met to address causality. They are displayed in Table 2.4.

Like Hume, Mill suggested that *x* must precede *y*. Keeping with the R&T and hormone example in females presented above, the administration of the male hormones to females must precede the observation of R&T. Additionally, R&T and male hormones must covary to the extent that when the hormones are present we observe R&T, and when they are not present, we don't.

Mill's last criterion is his most important to the scientific method, according to Cook and Campbell (1979). The notion of being able to rule out alternative explanations for the observed relation between *x* and *y* is crucial. In this regard, we go beyond describing co-occurrence and begin to move toward causality.

Co-occurrence would show that R&T and hormones co-occur, and there may be numerous reasons for that. For example, it may be something about mothers who choose to use hormone therapy that results in them having daughters who

TABLE 2.4
Mill's Conditions for Causality

Condition	*Example*
x must precede *y*	Hormone enrichment in females precedes onset of R&T
x and *y* covary	When hormones present, so is R&T
	When hormones not present, no R&T
Eliminate alternative explanations	Compare females with and without hormonal treatment

are more androgynous, relative to mothers who do not choose to use hormones. To establish causality between the hormone and the behavior, we must eliminate the alternatives.

We could design an experiment using nonhuman primates, whereby we have two groups of pregnant females: One gets hormones and the other does not. We then compare the behavior of their female offsprings. Such as a comparison minimizes some alternative explanations, thus the importance of a control or comparison group in psychological experiments.

This discussion so far has been about confirming hypotheses, or establishing support. Equally important in the progress of science is that idea of disconfirmation, or the falsification of hypotheses. Karl Popper (1959) is the philosopher of science who stressed the role of both confirmation and disconfirmation for science to move forward. Popper's idea was that in order to establish causality we conducted experiments to confirm hypotheses. Experiments were designed such that they successively eliminated alternative hypotheses. The collective experimental knowledge in a community of scientists would work toward this end. Additionally, to move the venture forward, Popper suggested, theories should complete with each other in the scientific arena and try to disconfirm each other. An hypothesis is disconfirmed, or falsified, when is it not supported.

Continuing with the R&T and hormones example, an alternative hypothesis could be that it is the socialization of children, not hormones, that are important in girls' R&T. The critic might argue as follows: In cases of girls being androgenized *in utero*, they often have remnants of male genitalia and these genital remnants may cause parents to treat girls like boys, not the hormones per se.

To conduct such an experiment we would compare androgenized girls who have had any remnants of male genitalia removed with a comparison group of nonandrogenized girls. The hormonal hypothesis would be disconfirmed if there were no between-group differences in this experiment. According to Popper (1959), multiple confirmations and multiple disconfirmations are necessary given the idiosyncracies of experiments.

This combination of confirmation and falsification moves knowledge forward. The stress on multiple replications and falsifications is especially important to stress in the advancement of knowledge. When different groups of scholars work on a related problem they approach it, usually, from different perspectives. If a finding is real it should be found repeatedly. These stubborn facts (Cook & Campbell, 1979) will be observed, and not be falsified, across most situations and across most theoretical orientations.

Exactness of Causal Explanations

Experimental results can provide support for causal hypotheses, whereas nonexperimental research can provide support for associative hypotheses (Bronfenbrenner & Mahoney, 1975). *Associative hypotheses*, by definition, posit a statistical relation between two variables, a and b, without specifying which variable influences the other. For example, Physical exercise (x) is related to car-

sample has an equal opportunity of being assigned to an experimental condition. In this way, any individual differences, say in weak hearts, would be randomly distributed across conditions. Consequently we can make statements about the effects of an independent variable on dependent variable with no confounding influences.

That much of our research is conducted in the real world, such as schools, hospital, and the work place, means that we cannot always randomly assign individual to conditions. In such cases we use *quasi-experimental* research designs. Experimental designs, then, are differentiated from quasi-experimental designs in that the former employs random assignment and the latter does not (Cook & Campbell, 1979). An obvious challenge for quasi-experimental design lies in the ability of the researcher to make sure that the experimental groups, though non-equivalent, have minimal confounding influences.

CONCLUSION

This chapter has covered a wide and varied range of topics, including the history and philosophy of science. This discussion is important as it emphasizes the dynamic view of science. Science is dynamic to the extant that what is considered science and scientific changes. Indeed, this is an important "take-home message" of this chapter. Science in early 20th-century Cambridge, a paragon of science then, as it is now, was based on authority, not independent verification of observations. Indeed, the public interchange between scientists is surely an important cause of this dynamic aspect. Science, like other aspects of our lives, is influenced by and influences other values.

The current view of science is such that we stress the role of objective measurement, while recognizing that these measures are also human constructions. Our job is to specify a theory justifying a specific approach to designing a study and measuring relevant phenomena. With all these trappings of objectivity, we also recognize that human beings are value laden creatures and these values influence our work as scientists.

That we have these different views adds to the scientific enterprise to the extent that different researchers will approach the same problem in a variety of ways, using different theories and different measures. Further, the resultant competition between theories should lead to efforts to confirm and disconfirm hypotheses. Our confidence in a set of findings is maximized when similar findings are reported from these desperate camps. If there is one lesson that the history of science has taught us, it should be that we should be tentative about our claims.

SOME THINGS TO THINK ABOUT

1. Give three examples pf hypotheses related to applied scientific issues. Under each list a corresponding theory from which it could be derived.

A. Hypothesis

____

____

____

i. Theory

____

____

____

B. Hypothesis

____

____

____

i. Theory

____

____

____

C. Hypothesis

____

____

____

i. Theory

____

____

____

2. Is a novelist's description of life in a small town "scientific"?
Why or why not?

____

____

____

3. Were medieval alchemists scientists?
Why or why not?

____

____

____

4. List three psychological constructs and three indicators of that construct under each.

A. Construct

i. ____

ii. ____

iii. ____

B. Construct

i. ____

ii. ____

iii. ____

C. Construct

i. ____

ii. ____

iii. ____

5. Fill in the conditions that must be met to approach the idea that smoking (x) can cause cancer (y) in humans.

A. Antecedent-consequence relations

____

____

____

B. Covariation

____

____

____

C. Rule out alternative hypotheses

____

____

____

3

Ethics in Research

The Oxford Concise Dictionary (1982) defines ethics as "relating to morals; morally correct, honourable" (p. 331). What, you may ask, is the question of ethics and morality doing in a textbook on research methods in psychology and education? Scientific research is after all, an honorable enterprise, aspiring to the lofty heights in search of truth. However, what is deemed to be ethical to one person may not be so obviously to another, and, unfortunately, scientists sometimes take less than ethical routes to these heights.

Problems associated with ethics are present in many disciplines, and the fields of psychology and education are not immune. Most basically, scientific inquiry is based on the perception that observations are made by an objective community of scientists. When this objectivity is questioned the value of the information generated by science, more generally, too becomes tainted. So for example, the recommendations we make for a clinical treatment or for an educational program will be overshadowed by doubts concerning the integrity of the system making these recommendations. In short, the perceived worth of our information will be undermined.

At a more pragmatic level, ethical doubts will also jeopardize our ability to recruit students, participants into our research programs, and attract funding to support research. In short, the very structure of our discipline will collapse.

Newspapers in many American cities have all too frequent reports of ethical lapses of research psychologists and educators. For example, in recent weeks in the Twins Cities there have been allegations that a clinical psychologist was sexually abusing some of his clients. There are other cases of financial abuse on research funds. Again, using the Twin Cities as a case (and probably a representative one at that), the story of the misuse of funds from a National Science Foundation (NSF) research grant by a researcher in the University of Minnesota's Medical School has been in the news for the past several years. This has tainted the view of "The U" in the eyes of the public and of the Legislature that funds us.

When one scratches below the surface of these cases in the general public view, the problems become more numerous, it seems. For example, the American Psychological Associations (APA), one of the guardians of ethics in the field, routinely publishes lists of psychologists who have been sanctioned. A copy of the APA's Ethic Code can be accessed directly from their Web site.

Many academics have first- or second hand knowledge of these cases and can talk about cases of academic dishonesty, such as falsifying and "manufacturing data" that they know about. For example, when I was a graduate student at Ohio State University, there was a story circulating among the students in a class we were taking on the analysis of variance. A requirement in that course was for students to come up with a data set that resulted in one main effect and one interaction. The rumor was that a student had actually used the data he or she constructed for that course in his or her dissertation, and was discovered during the final orals.

There are also more famous examples of scientific misconduct. For example, it has been suggested that the father of modern genetics, Mendel, may have "cooked" his data on the genetic assortment of colored peas. That is, the assortment of the colored peas Mendel reported matched exactly his theory. That this level of precision is not seen in natural assortment lead to the conclusion that the data presented may have been less than truthful.

The seriousness of these problems has lead many institutions to require some form of safeguards against abuse. Probably the most common example involves the requirements associated with obtaining informed consent for individuals to participate in research. Informed consent requirements, or stipulations for exemption, are codified in most, if not all American colleges and universities. Schools and other institutions, like hospitals and prisons, also have procedures addressing scientific ethics. Indeed, the problems with ethics in scientific research has become such a volatile issue that some universities, such as the University of Minnesota requires scientists conducting any externally funded research to participate in a series of formal seminars addressing the many facets of ethics in scientific research. The topics covered in these seminars include: social responsibility and scientific fraud, authorship and plagiarism, research data management, and rights of human and animal subjects. The full curriculum for these seminars can be found at www.research.umn.edu/ethics/curriculum.

In this chapter I draw from the materials on ethics in scientific research developed by professional organizations, such as the APA (1999; www.apa.org/ethics/code), the Society for Research in Child Development (http://www.srcd.org about.html#standards) and the Animal Behaviour Society/Association for the Study of Animal Behavior (Dawkins & Gosling 1994), scientists working in the field (e.g., Fisher, 1993), and materials developed by the University of Minnesota (www.research.umn.edu/ethics/curriculum).

SOCIAL RESPONSIBILITY AND SCIENTIFIC FRAUD

Scientists, like other members of society, have responsibilities to the communities in which they live. To the immediate scientific community, honesty, integrity, and public skepticism and scrutiny are bases of objective inquiry. The advances of a scientific community are based on the theory and findings of its members. The values of a scientific community are also transmitted to new members of the profession through educational training and research fellowships. Concomitantly, members of the scientific community monitor these practices themselves to insure public confidence. Questions about the ethical integrity of either theory or research findings undermine the common goal of scientific inquiry as well as the individuals, professions, and institutions associated with the ethical problems.

Socializing members into a scientific community can be effectively accomplished through educational experiences and fellowships (Bebeau, 1999). Teachers and mentors should serve as role models in ethical practices in the day-to-day conduct of conducting, analyzing, and reporting research. Institutions should help to support this enterprise by providing guidelines for ethical practice as well as seminars where these practices are discussed.

As noted earlier, these sorts of seminars are required at the University of Minnesota, and they are valuable. I was a reluctant participant in a recent seminar because like everyone else I was "too busy." To my surprise, the seminars were very informative. There were many cases where scenarios with familiar rings were presented and for which there were no clear cut answers. That these seminars were lead by other very active and very well-known researchers added to their "real-ness" and credibility.

Social responsibility extends beyond the scientific community and into the larger community of consumer of researcher and taxpayers who support the research. Taxpayers often support research, either through the funding of public colleges, universities, and other educational institutions or through state and federal funding agencies such as state departments of education, the National Science Foundation, and the National Institutes of Health. Obviously, support would, and should, stop where ethical problems exist. Relatedly, the extent to which research is accepted and used, say in clinics, schools, and hospitals, will also depend on the credibility of the research. Treatments are not likely to be adopted if there is ethical concern with an investigator.

Scientific fraud is defined, at this point, generally, as fabrication or falsification of data, research procedures, or data analyses (University of Minnesota Board of Regents Policy on Academic Misconduct, 1997; see www.umn.edu/regents/policies/academic/conduct). The scientific enterprise, in its best form, involves the quest for knowledge, for its own sake. Unfortunately, and as noted earlier, the paths to these lofty heights can pose some serious problems. The researcher, like Ulysses on his quest for Truth, is presented with temptations. The scientist, in his or her journey to promotion, funded research projects, or fame, may be tempted to tailor data to meet his or her proffered theory.

It is important that we differentiate different levels of error in scientific judgment. At the less felonious, but still serious, end of the spectrum are *honest* errors, such as misinterpreting ambiguous results. For example, there are often cases where the results are equivocal and subject to a number of interpretations. An honest mistake may be when a scientist over interprets the results in terms of his or her own theory. This sort of problem can be dealt with through the regular scientific enterprise. That is, in scientific research results and explanations of results are made in the scientific community in published papers and at conferences. Results, if presented in an objective and truthful manner, should stand the test of scrutiny. Overly sympathetic interpretations should be detected and challenged in the review process or after the data have been publicly presented.

Most scientists know that data are open to multiple interpretations. Part of the process of writing up a research report involves presenting and addressing those alternative interpretations. Editors and reviewers should also check that these alternative interpretations or limitations of the study are presented in print. Alternative interpretations can be discussed at the level of theory or by other data in the study or by other studies. Where there is still ambiguity, the researcher should present ways in which these alternative interpretations can be tested in future research.

Another form of an honest mistake could involve an unintentional misrepresentation of data or procedures. For example, in writing the results section of a research report and accompanying tables, a scholar may have mistakenly miscopied data from one category into another. Such cases do not question the scientists' honesty, but they certainly call his or her competence into question. When and if the scientist discovers the error, it is incumbent on him or her to publically correct the mistake. Many research journals publish Erratum to address such problems.

The misrepresentation of data in these cases could be considered "sins of omissions" as mistakes were not made deliberately or with the intent to defraud. They were made by failing to be thorough or careful. Although these mistakes are indicative of professional competence, they do not usually call into questions the integrity and honesty of the scientist.

More problematic are errors by commissions, where data or procedures are systematically and purposefully misrepresented. This sort of case might involve deliberate falsification of data or of a research protocol. Examples of this sort of abuse include the allegations made about Mendel's data previously discussed.

What might be the most visible accusation of scientific fraud involved Cyril Burt, the famous British psychologist (Dooley, 2001). Burt studied the environmental and genetic bases of intelligence. As part of his work he documented the heritability of intelligence by studying identical twins (who are genetically identical) reared apart and reared together. He then calculated correlation coefficients between the IQs of twins reared either together or apart. High correlations between the twins, whether they were reared apart or together, were taken as evidence supporting role of genes in intelligence. An environmental argument would posit high correlations when they were reared in the same environment, not in different ones.

Of course, the role of genetics in intelligence is a politically volatile topics, being subject to political and scientific attack and counter attack. Against this political backdrop, allegations of fraud first arose when Burt reported the same correlation coefficient ($r = 0.77$) for the intelligence of twins reared apart in different scientific papers. The concern here was the low likelihood of arriving at the same coefficient with separate samples. This perceived problem was magnified when co-authors on some of Burt's papers could not be found. Consequently, charges were publically leveled that Burt had falsified the data and assigned authorship to fictional people.

Subsequently, Burt has been exonerated, to some degree (Dooley, 2001). Research by scholars (Joynson, 1989), not invested in the nature–nurture debate in intelligence, found that the "fictional" authors did work on Burt's project, but that they did not co-author the papers, as stated by Burt. Thus, as discussed later in this chapter, Burt's behavior was not ethical in assigning co-authorship on a paper. As for the identical correlations, it was suggested that he used the same data from different research reports. That is, the .77 correlation was not found in separate studies, but was found in one study, and reported multiple times, thus creating the false impression of replicated findings. The ultimate test of the fidelity of Burt's data, however, is through replication, or the degree to which other members of the scientific community come up the same results. In subsequent studies, Jensen (1992) found correlations of .77 between the intelligence of twins reared apart! From this view, the openness and public dialogue in the scientific community was responsible for policing their own profession.

AUTHORSHIP, PLAGIARISM, AND DUPLICATE PUBLICATION

As noted previously regarding the Burt case, there are rules governing authorship on scientific papers. The spirit of the rules governing authorship relate to the guiding principles of the scientific enterprise that we have been discussing: searching for truth and putting up those claims for public scrutiny. Authorship, then has benefits (part of the claims associated with the ideas put forth in the paper) as well as responsibilities (having participated in the enterprise at a meaningful level, sharing responsibility for the accuracy of the work presented); thus authorship is something that should be claimed after careful thought.

Authorship

Issues of authorship include properly crediting individuals with the work done, and this can have two possibly problematic dimensions: omitting and adding authors inappropriately. Generally, the Minnesota code suggests that authorship should go to parties who have contributed "substantially intellectually to the work." There is obvious ambiguity in what exactly constitutes substantial contribution. The APA Publication Manual (1999) and the Code of Conduct reproduced in Appendix I (Section 8.12 Publication Credit) clarify this ambiguity somewhat. Authorship should be credited only for those who actually worked on the project and made intellectual or scientific contributions to the work. Examples of substantive contributions include: formulating the research questions or hypotheses; conceptualizing the experimental design and statistical analyses; interpreting the results; writing a major portion of the paper.

The order of authorship list should reflect the relative importance of each contribution, with the name of the principle contributor appearing first. In cases of equal principle contributions, names should appear in alphabetical order, with a footnote indicating how order of authorship was determined. All listed authors should have consented to be listed as authors and reviewed the manuscript before it was submitted. Indeed, for papers accepted for publication in APA journals, each listed author must verify in writing that he or she served as an author and accepts responsibility for authorship. All authors listed also assume responsibility for the accuracy and content of the report.

Credit is NOT given for being in a supervisory position (e.g., department head), designing or building research apparatus, statistical consulting, modifying a computer program, collecting or entering data, or helping with recruiting research participants.

An especially interesting problem surrounding authorship relates to entry-level scientists, such as students, postdoctoral fellows, and trainees. As noted in the University of Minnesota Code of Conduct, it is best to address issues of authorship before the project begins. For example, the lead researcher should specify what opportunities for authorship exist on the project and the responsibilities that authorship entails. It also may be the case that an original agreement changes as the project progresses. It is typically the case that a research report of a student's thesis or dissertation will list the student as first author as a condition for this work is that it should be original work. In cases where additional data collection, analyses, and conceptualization are needed, the order of authorship should reflect the actual work done.

Plagiarism

Plagiarism is an authorship related issue. *Plagiarism* is defined by the APA Code of ethics (2001, 8.11) as presenting substantial portions or elements of another's work or data as their own, even if the other work or data source is cited occasionally. From this perspective a person is falsely claiming credit for someone else's work.

To anyone who has either written a paper for public consumption (e.g., in a class or for publication) or who has read those papers (as a teacher or reviewer), the lines can be very fuzzy between plagiarism and appropriately using and citing others' ideas. This ambiguity is reflected in the following more, in-depth definition of plagiarism, provided by Mary Dworkin (1999) in the University of Minnesota's Curriculum for Education in the Responsible Conduct of Research (www.umn.edu/regents/policies/academic/conduct):

> The spectrum is a wide one. At one end is the word-for-word copying of another's writing without enclosing the copied passage in quotation

> marks and identifying it in a footnote, both of which are necessary. It hardly seems possible that anyone of college age or more could do that without clear intent to deceive. At the other end there is the almost casual slipping in of a particularly apt term which one has come across in reading and which so admirably expresses one's opinion that one is tempted to make it personal property. Between these two poles there are degrees and degrees, but they may be roughly placed into two groups. Close to outright and blatant deceit—but more the result, perhaps of laziness than of bad intent—is the piecing together of random jottings made in the course of reading, generally without careful identification of their source, and then woven into the text, so that the result is a mosaic of other peoples' ideas and words, the writer's sole contribution being the cement which holds the pieces together. Indicative of more effort and, for that reason, somewhat closer to honesty, though still dishonest, is the paraphrase, an abbreviated (and often skillfully prepared) restatement of someone else's analysis or conclusions without acknowledgment that another person's text has been the basis for the recapitulation. (Martin, Ohmann, & Wheatley, 1969, cited in Dworkin, 1999)

This quote presents the shades of gray between the blatant cases of dishonest and the more subtle cases of unacknowledged borrowing. It seems pretty easy, however, to be guided by the following rule: When you take language verbatim, put it in direct quotes. When you use another person's ideas, cite him or her. When I have used this rule in my teaching, some students say, well, most of the sentences in the paper will have citations. The response is: That may be true, and there is nothing wrong with that. In terms of erring, it makes much more sense to err on the side of overcitation than undercitation, despite the fact that principles, such as those previously noted, are presented.

It is important to note, based on personal experience, that plagiarism at the varying degrees alluded to in the aforementioned quote, is relatively common. Certainly at the level of undergraduate and, less frequently, graduate papers submitted for course work, there are instances of plagiarism. For example, when I was teaching an undergraduate child study course at the University of Georgia a student submitted a course paper where she had taken text verbatim, without quoting or citing, from a paper written by the course instructor! Mind you, this is an extreme case, but it does indicate, at some level, what students think about what counts as their ideas. This level of infraction may also indicate lack of student writing skills.

Plagiarism is not the purview of the naive undergraduate alone. There are certainly cases of established professors plagiarizing. Sometimes this happens when a professor plagiarizes a student's work. I had the experience of being at a conference, right after graduate school, and walking through the publishers' exhibits with a colleague. The colleague picked-up an edited book of interest and found a chapter by his former major professor. The chapter was the "reworking" of a paper my colleague had written based on his doctoral dissertation and sole authored by his professor! Although my colleague was acknowledged in a footnote to the chapter, the work was his, and the professor was taking credit for that work.

Similar abuses have been known to occur when academics review research proposals or manuscripts for publication. Plagiarism occurs when the reviewer reads about an interesting problem in these confidential documents, and then takes these ideas and presents them as his or her own.

Professional vigilance in courses, professional organizations, and journals, as well as funding agencies, is needed to both educate and monitor abuses associated with plagiarism. Certainly educational programs are necessary. For students, virtually all courses and texts in research methods have sections on ethics and plagiarism. At the professional level, too, inservice education on research ethics, of the sorts required by the University of Minnesota, can be preventative. In cases of abuses, professionals must be willing to take the often substantial amounts of time required to address these abuses. In cases of student plagiarism, a substantial time investment is necessary for teachers (e.g., they must write reports, attend meetings, and hearings, and often meet with students and parents). Longer time investment is often required with professional abuses. In the case of the plagiarizing professor previously described, his former student reported the problem to the professor's dean, and the professor was prohibited from interacting with students on research projects for a specified period, while he attended a professional counseling program.

Duplicate Publications

An associated problem of authorship relates to duplication of publications. Recall from the discussion of the Burt case, there were allegations that he used data from one data set in multiple publications; thus the ubiquity of the .77 correlation coefficient. Duplicate publication involves, then, the publication of the same or virtually the same manuscript in different places. Duplication of publication takes many forms. In the most blatant cases, we have the exact same manuscript being published in different places. For example, a manuscript could be published in two scientific journals or one could be published in a journal and the other could be published in a book chapter. Most academic journals explicitly prohibit simultaneous submission of a manuscript. In the case of APA journals, the author must state, in writing, that the manuscript is not being considered by another journal.

Scholars may be motivated to use the exact same piece of work or a variant of it in a number of different publications, rather than one, for reasons associated with promotion or tenure, salary reviews, or grant applications. The perception is that more publications are better than few publications.

That this practice is unethical (see Principle 6.24 of the APA Code of Ethics) relates to the false perception created by multiple publications using the same data or the same manuscript. Again, recall the Burt case. By presenting the same correlation coefficient in a variety of places, the perception was that the reported results were replications of earlier work, rather than duplications. Consequently, the archival foundations of science are weakened to the extent that they are being built with inflated values.

At a more direct level, duplicate publication could result in copyright violations. In cases in which portions of a journal article are used in a book chapter, the author should noted that the chapter is based on previously published work, and cite that work.

The term *salami science* is often used to refer to a related practice, that of taking many thin slices from the same data set and publishing it in many rather than fewer places. For example, an investigator may have a large project on school effectiveness with a number of measures. Salami science would be exemplified in taking small portions of that data set, for example, one paper addressing the role of teacher expertise and another paper on teachers' job satisfaction. Clearly, in this case, the topics are closely enough related that a single publication would be more parsimonious.

Again, the motivation for this sort of practice relates to the scientist being concerned with judgments made about his or her work based on the quantity of publications produced. All of this is not to say that the scientist can not use the same data set for reanalyses. Indeed, in most large data sets, most of the data do not get analyzed, let alone published. Indeed, the APA and many other organizations recommend that extant data sets be utilized for a multitude of analyses. Reanalyzing extant data sets is not only economical (collecting data is very expensive) but it also spares subjects from the rigors of participation.

In cases in which the author is in doubt about the appropriateness of his or her use of data from earlier work, he or she should present the issues involved in the letter to the editor of the journal to which the paper is being submitted.

RESEARCH DATA MANAGEMENT

The way in which scientists manage the data from their research projects also has ethical implications. Specifically, research data are the materials on which we base the judgements we make and constitute the archives and collective wisdom of our field. Thus, one important ethical dimension of data management relates to the integrity of the data. Additionally, data could and often should be shared with colleagues so as to promote further development of the field.

Research data are defined as the "quantitative information generated through research or, more generally, recorded information generated through systematic inquiry" (Heberlein, 1999, p. 2). More specifically, data can be classified as raw data (or quantified information contained in lab notebook, manuals, computer files, etc., pertaining to a research project); processed data (graphs and equations displaying analyses, descriptions, or conclusions contained in reports), and published data (information distributed to people beyond those involved in data acquisition and administration). Management of these sorts of data has ethical implications in terms of the accuracy and validity of the data presented. There are also implications in terms of data ownership, and the corresponding benefits and liabilities associated with the data and their uses. Consequently, an important aspect of data management involves keeping thorough and accurate records. In this chapter I, first, outline procedures for researchers for keeping an accurate and on going record of their research procedure, either in the form of a project manual or a laboratory notebook.

Project Manuals and Laboratory Notebooks

Keeping a record of what is to be done and what actually gets done is an important aspect of managing research data. This information is useful on a number of fronts. First, these records serve as plans of research to be carried out. They also record any changes in those plans. Record of changes are necessary as researchers may forget these details and need this record as they are writing up reports. The written record is also a way of documenting that what the researcher said happened, in the research report, actually happened. These records can be used as evidence in claims of unethical behavior.

Project manuals are typically works in progress. Project manuals contain a record of the plan of the research, instruments used, procedures to be followed, and schedule of administration. They begin well before the research project begins. Most typically, manuals contain copies of the actual instruments used with accompanying instructions used in the administration, procedures and protocols for other procedures, such as plans for direct observational sampling and recording rules, as well as definitions of behaviors to be observed and coding forms. In one of my research manuals I also included protocols for data management and data entry. Importantly, an explicit schedule of data collection is also presented in the manual.

In the course of conducting research, "stuff happens" and procedures outlined in the manual may have to be changed. For example, you may have been scheduled to interview a class of students on Thursday, February 22, at 9:00 a.m. When you show up, you find that most of the kids are out of school with the flu. Consequently, you must reschedule. All changes in protocol should be explicitly recorded, dated, and signed by the supervisor of the project.

A number of specific guidelines for managing data, as suggested by Stouthamer-Loeber and van Kammen (1995), can be incorporated into project manuals. Identification of participants should also be addressed in the manual. If code numbers are used instead of names, there should be some way in which the two could be tied. It may be that only the Principal Investigator (PI) has a list of the names and the corresponding codes.

Procedures for tracking the data should also be specified, and where possible, assigned to identifiable people. Specifically, preparation, copying, and filing of instruments should be specified. Then the specific dates of administration as well as administrators should be specified. This should be followed by the filing of completed data and listing of missing cases. Procedures for scheduling make-up exams should be specified as well.

Procedures for coding and scoring of research protocols should be specified, as should the personnel responsible for these tasks. It makes sense to specify and schedule routinely a mechanism to check on the accuracy of scoring and completeness. An additional checking stage should also be specified for data entry onto computer disks.

Laboratory notebooks provide a similar record to the project manual, but they are more of a day-to-day record of procedures. As the name implies, laboratory notebooks have been used and developed in the "hard" sciences where laboratory research is the norm. Like project manuals, lab notebooks can be used to support the validity of results and used as evidence in cases involving copyrights or patients. The University of Minnesota, as part of their efforts to maximize the ethics in research has published a Guidelines for Maintaining Laboratory Notebooks (http://ptm.umn.edu). They suggest that records in notebooks should be permanent, complete, and continuous. A bound notebook with numbered pages is suggested. This recommendation minimizes perceived problems associated with additions or deletions of the experimental record. For related reasons, they also recommend that entrees be made in ink, not pencil. All entries, including changes, should be dated and signed.

In terms of what gets recorded, the researcher should err on the side of thoroughness. A rule of thumb in this venture should be that a notebook, like the Method section of a research report, should be explicit enough so that an outsider, who is not familiar with the specifics of a particular project, can understand what was done without the help of the person making the entrees. More specifically, what was done, why it was done, who suggested it, who did it, when it was done, the results, and the conclusions should be recorded.

Besides the details of the actual experimental sessions, notebooks should record the results of meetings where ideas were generated and discussed, as well as plans for future experiments. These sorts of records are important regarding any contested claims about authorship or intellectual property rights.

RESEARCH PARTICIPANTS

The ethics governing research participants is a major concern in psychology and education. These concerns and subsequent principles guiding the ways in which we interact with research participants have their roots in a series of serious abuses. Probably the two most commonly cited examples of abuses associated with the use of human participants in research come from abuse of inmates in Nazi concentration camps, research on syphilis in Tuskegee, Alabama, and, more recently, the U.S. Army's use of the drug LSD on recruits.

In order to minimize the possibility that these types of abuses would not be repeated, the National Commission for the Protection of Human Subjects of Biomedical and Behavioral Research established ethical standards for interacting with human subjects (Fisher, 1993; Klinger, 1999a). These practices were guided by the following moral principles: Respect for persons, beneficence, and justice. Generally, these principles obligate the researcher to protect the welfare of their subjects, respect their autonomy and privacy, and to ensure that the costs and benefits associated with the research procedure are equitably distributed (Fisher, 1993).

Beneficence is defined in the realm of ethics and human subjects in terms of maximizing possible benefits for and minimizing possible harm to the subjects (Fisher, 1993). Benefits can be either direct, as when a participant gets a gift, a treatment that helps a medical condition, or book that accompanies a training project. Benefits can also be indirect, such as increasing the body of knowledge or knowing that knowledge will be applied beneficially later. Risks can be incurred through being assigned to a control group where subjects are not given a beneficial treatment.

The principle of beneficence is directly applied by Institutional Review Boards (IRB) when they ask applicants to specify costs and benefits of their research. This ratio must be specified to both the board and to the subject.

The estimate of costs and benefits is far from clear cut. A precondition for established benefits, of course, involves using valid procedures (Fisher, 1993). If the experimental or assessment procedure has questionable validity, so to, then, do the results. This obviously compromises any proposed benefits. Indeed, it is not unreasonable to propose that procedures with questionable validity do not merit study at all.

Even in cases of valid procedures and measurement, researcher must be careful to not inflate possible benefits from their research (Fisher, 1993). Descriptive research can be especially vulnerable to over estimation of possible benefits by stating that the research could be useful in designing interventions. There is a great distance between results from descriptive research being implemented into an effective intervention program.

Respect as applied to the ethics of research translates into treating individuals as autonomous beings (Fisher, 1993). It is especially important that vulnerable groups (e.g., children, prisoners, handicapped individuals) be respected. For this reason, minors are given special consideration in research. Most basically, minors cannot, legally, give consent. Additionally, before a ceratin age, they may not have the cognitive capacity to understand the implications of participation or refusal. Consequently, parents or guardians must do so.

A sample consent form used with adolescents is displayed in Fig. 3.1. As can be seen in the sample consent form, participants are being offered incentives to participate in the research, in the form of $20 per year. Incentives should be used as a reasonable compensation for participation in the research. An obvious tension exists between compensation and coercion or bribery to participate (Fisher, 1993). Possible solutions to the problem include treating incentives as you would compensation for work done. Compensation should go directly to the participant. In cases involving children and adolescence, payment should be made directly to them, not to their parents or guardians. The degree to which incentives are coercive is related to the social economic status of the participants. Some people may participate simply because of the financial incentive. This, in turn, unfairly exposes them to the possible risks and benefits of the research.

Bullying, Dominance, and Heterosexual Relationships in Adolescence

Your child has been invited to be in a research study of the relations between bullying and relationships with other boys and girls as students make the transition to high school. He/she was selected as a possible participant because your child participated in an earlier and related study of bullying during middle school. We ask that you read this form and ask any questions you may have before agreeing to be in the study.

This study is being conducted by: Dr. Anthony D. Pellegrini of the University of Minnesota.

Background Information:

The purpose of this study is: Examine the continuity in bullying and victimization from middle to high school and to see how aspects of the school environment relate to it. Additionally we are interested in the ways in which bullying relates to later dating behavior.

Procedures:

If you agree to have your child be in this study, we would ask the child to do the following things during each of your high school years: Two times yearly, complete a battery of questionnaires asking about aggression and the ways in which he/she interacts with other boys and girls. We will also ask about the frequency of your dating behavior and what other boys and girls you socialize with. Each session should last about 30-mins and will be conducted at a time when students are not missing important class work. We will also observe them at various times during the school day and ask them to keep a diary each month.

Risks and Benefits of Being in the Study:

The study has several risks: First, the student may not want to complete all the questionnaires. If this is the case, he/she can stop at any time and may withdraw from that activity or the whole study.

The benefits to participation are: In the past these students have actually enjoyed participation. Also the student will be given $20 each of the years of the study for full participation.

The student will receive payment: $20/year for each of two years. Payment will be made to the student in the form of a check at the end of each year for full participation.

Confidentiality:

The records of this study will be kept private. In any sort of report we might publish, we will not include any information that will make it possible to identify a subject. Research records will be kept in a locked file; only researchers will have access to the records.

Voluntary Nature of the Study:

The decision whether or not to participate will not affect the student's current or future relations with the University. If the student decides to participate, he/she is free to withdraw at any time without affecting those relationships. If he/she does withdraw, however, he/she will not be paid for participating during that year.

Contacts and Questions:

The researcher conducting this study is Dr. Anthony D. Pellegrini. You may ask any questions you have now. If you have questions later, you may contact them at the Department of Educational Psychology at the University of Minnesota; Phone: (612) 625 4353.

If you have any questions or concerns regarding this study and would like to talk to someone other than the researcher(s), contact Research Subjects' Advocate line, D528 Mayo, 420 Delaware Street Southeast, Minneapolis, Minnesota 55455; telephone (612) 625-1650.

You will be given a copy of this form to keep for your records.

Statement of Consent:

I have read the above information. I have asked questions and have received answers. I consent to participate in the study.

Signature ____ Date __________

Signature of parent ________________________________ Date __________

Signature of Investigator ___________________________ Date __________

FIG. 3.1. Consent form: students under 18 years old.

A related recruitment issue involves the use of deception. Deception may be called for in some research in which the participants should not know directly the purpose of the research for it would threaten the validity of the results. For example, in the famous Milgram studies of conformity, subjects were not aware that the purpose of the study was to examine the effect of authority on subjects' use of (contrived) cruel treatment of other subjects. If they knew that their conformity to authority was the subject of the study and if they knew that the confederates were not getting actual shocks, the results would probably have been very different.

The cost-benefit standard is applied to uses of deception. Do the benefits associated with the use of deception outweigh problems? Some argue (Baumrind, 1985) that the uses of deception are so insidious (e.g., the public would loose respect of results derived from psychological research; participants would assume they are being deceives and act unnaturally) that they should rarely if ever be used. This is not an easy issue to address, and the real cost and benefits should be carefully weighed in making a decision on the use of deception.

In addition, children must give assent to participation. "Assent means that a child shows some form of agreement to participate without necessarily comprehending the full significance of the research necessary to give informed con-

SOME THINGS TO THINK ABOUT

1. Is being "ethical" the same as "doing the right thing"?

How?

2. You are a student working on a project and you suspect that one of your fellow students is not following the observational protocol as he says he is.

What should you do?

How do you protect the integrity of the person you suspect? (They're innocent until proven guilty and lodging an accusation, even if they are vindicated, could damage their career.)

How do you protect yourself?

3. What would you do if the person in Question #2 was the professor supervising your thesis?

____

____

____

4. Can a 10-year-old child really give informed assent to participate in research?

List three indicators that the child might exhibit that would help.

A. ____

B. ____

C. ____

4. List five symptoms that might indicate that a researcher is falsifying or making up data.

A. ____

B. ____

C. ____

D. ____

E. ____

5. List three criteria that you would use to draw the line between student plagiarism and an honest mistake?

A. ____

B. ____

C. ____

6. List three university practices that might minimize the proliferation of "salami science."

A. ____

B. ____

C. ____

4

Choosing a Perspective: Qualitative-Insider and Quantitative-Outsider Distinctions

Observational methods, of course can be used in both laboratory and "naturalistic" settings. Chapter 2 discusses the ways in which experimentation helps the researcher to determine causality. One of the real advantages to the use of direct observations, however, is the ability to document behavior in situ. However, whenever we observe or study someone or something in the real world we can take a variety of perspectives on the phenomenon under examination.

At a global level, we can distinguish between two perspectives in the educational and psychological research: qualitative and quantitative. As discussed in more detail later, these labels are inadequate as they imply that one uses numbers and the other does not (Erickson, 1986; Shwreder et al., 1998). In this chapter I make a distinction in terms of an insider and outsider perspective, respectively.

In terms of global differences, the insider perspective tries to understand phenomenon under study from the point of view of the participants. Methodologically, this is often achieved by the researcher participating in and observing the events under study. Inferences are made about participants' cognitions and the symbol systems they use, such as language. An outsider perspective, in contrast, is usually more concerned with detached descriptions of behavior. Although inferences about participants' cognition can be made from observed behaviors, the extent to which this is done varies with one's theoretical orientation.

Strict behaviorists, for example, deny the existence of cognition because it cannot be directly observed. Cognitively oriented ethologists, on the other hand, make inferences about actors' intention based on behavior. Marc Bekoff (1995, 1997), for example, is an ethologist who studies the play fighting of wolves and coyotes. He attributes psychological intention to certain behaviors of these animals, much as a cognitive psychologist would for the behaviors of infants or children. For example, Bekoff suggested that wolves use play bows (i.e., crouching down on front legs while raising their rears) and exaggerated movements (e.g., shaking their heads) to announce to conspecifics that their behaviors are playful fighting, not serious.

Central to the developmental systems approach is the concept of *epigenesis*, which Gottlieb (1991) defined as "the emergence of new structures and functions during the course of development" (p. 7). New structures do not arise fully formed, but are the result of the bidirectional relation between all levels of biological and experiential factors, from the genetic through the cultural. *Experience*, from this perspective, involves not only events exogenous to the individual but also self-produced activity, such as the firing of a nerve cell. Functioning at one level influences functioning at adjacent levels, with constant feedback between levels. This relation can be expressed as follows:

genetic activity (DNA ↔ RNA ↔ proteins) ↔ structural maturation ↔ function, activity.

According to Gottlieb (1991):

> Individual development is characterized by an increase of complexity of organization (i.e., the emergence of new structural and functional properties and competencies) at all levels of analysis (molecular, subcellular, cellular, organismic) as a consequence of horizontal and vertical coactions among the organism's parts, including organism-environment coactions. (p. 7)

From this viewpoint, there are no simple genetic or experiential causes of behavior; all development is the product of epigenesis, with complex interactions occurring among multiple levels.

Evolved psychological mechanisms can be thought of as genetically coded messages that, following epigenetic rules, interact with the environment over time to produce behavior. Because the experiences of each individual are unique, this suggests that there should be substantial plasticity in development. Yet, there is much that is universal about the form and function of members of a species, despite this plasticity. The reason for this is that individuals inherit not only a species-typical genome, but also a species-typical environment, beginning with the prenatal environment. To the extent that individuals grow up in environments similar to those of their ancestors, development should follow a species-typical pattern. Animals (including humans) have evolved to "expect" a certain type of environment. For humans this would include 9 months in a sheltered womb, a lactating, warm, and affectionate mother, kin to provide additional support, and, later in childhood, peers.

Many behaviors that traditionally have been described as *instinctive*, can be better described as developing from the early interaction of the organism and aspects of its environment, broadly defined. For example, it is well-established that ducklings and other precocial birds, shortly after hatching, will follow the first moving, quacking thing they encounter (imprinting). This phenomenon was touted by Lorenz (1965) as an example of a complex behavior that requires no experience for its expression (i.e., an instinct). But that interpretation has since been challenged. For example, when ducklings are raised in isolation and cannot hear the vocalizations of their mother, their brood mates, and are even prevented from vocalizing themselves, this instinctive behavior disappears. When given the choice, after hatching, of approaching the maternal call of their own species or that of another (e.g., a chicken) the ducklings lacking auditory experience choose randomly (see Gottlieb, 1997). What was once thought to be instinctive and encoded directly into the genes (i.e., "genes for behavior") is now known to require the subtle interaction of an animals' auditory experience (even if just its own vocalizations) with "normal" maturation for its expression (see Bjorklund & Pellegrini, 2002).

From the developmental systems perspective, there are no simple cases of either genetic or environmental determinism. Infants are not born as blank slates; evolution has prepared them to "expect" certain types of environments and to process some information more readily than others. Yet, it is the constant and bidirectional interaction between various levels of organization, which changes over the course of development, that produces behavior.

This biological view of the individual embedded in the environment is an important underpinning to ethology. However, the exposition of the ways in which environments and individuals, even at the level of DNA, influence each other makes very explicit the interdependence of each and the problems with trying to dichotomize them. Although both etic and emic approaches share this view of individuals and the environment, they also differ.

BASIC DIFFERENCES: THE ETIC–EMIC CONTRAST

Given the similarity in views toward studying individuals in context, I now examine two ways in which researchers can proceed in their quest of organizing phenomena into meaningful categories. In short, how can researchers pose an initial order to the myriad of goings on in a research site? Dell Hymes (1980a, 1980b), an anthropological linguistic and one of the founding fathers of educational anthropology, suggests that researchers can take an *etic* or an *emic* approach, following the distinction first made by the linguistic Kenneth Pike (1965).

Pike took these labels from Sapir's (1925) distinction between phonetics, or the description and measurement of the physical properties of the sounds of a language. The term *emic* was derived from Sapir's notion of the phoneme. A *phoneme* is group of sound (individual phones) that co-occur is such a way that they are distinctive in terms of meaning from other phonemes. For example, the phoneme /l/ in English is comprised of a number of different sounds. This phoneme /l/ is meaningfully different from the phoneme /r/ in English: lice/rice. In some language these individual phones from different phonemes and are not usually perceived as being different by native speakers.

An *etic perspective* is concerned with the measurement of physical properties of phenomena, such as sounds. So, a phonetic analysis describes the sounds in an *objective* way. It is concerned with differences in degree. A phonemic analysis, on the other hand, is concerned with the function, or meaning, of these sounds for the community of speakers in which they are observed. An emic orientation is concerned with behaviors as social signals that are embedded in a system of other social signals. Further, functional contrast, not measurement of individual/isolated phenomena, is the way in which behavior is rendered meaningful. Thus, researchers with an emic orientation are concerned with distinctions in function, or meaning, not differences in degree. From this view, the emic orientation of qualitative research makes it concerned with meaning. Validity, or the truthfulness of the inference one makes about meaning, is a central concern in emic research.

Next, consider a nonlinguistic example of a specific social behavior: An etic approach would index all of the behaviors observed by children on the play ground, such as run, walk, swing. Moving to the level of assigning meaning, the emic, we would assign these individual behaviors to categories. For example, for some children, hit at, chase, and smile is an aggressive category. For other children these very same behaviors co-occur with other playful behaviors, such as turn taking and are assigned to a category considered playful, rather than aggressive.

This distinction is represented in Fig. 4.1.

To conclude this section, we see how the etic and emic perspectives can to complement each other, or more simply the etic can be used alone. To reach the emic stage, however, presumes understanding at the etic level first (Hymes, 1980a). In the following sections I discuss exemplars of each approach: Ethology and ecological psychology representing the etic approach and ethnography representing the emic approach.

The Outsider Perspective: Ethology and Ecological Psychology

The outsider perspective, in one extreme version, assumes that observers should divorce themselves entirely from any interpretation of insiders' meaning because such introspection and self-report data are too subjective and unreliable (see Blurton Jones, 1972, for a version of this position). Indeed, such assumptions are not unlike those made by behavioral psychologists, particularly in relation to their more cognitive counterparts. For example, behavioral psychologists, such as B. F. Skinner (1974), were insistent that the only scientific way to describe people and other animals was behaviorally; other means were bound to fail because they were too subjective. Thus, the observer, according to this position, should maintain the outsider perspective so as to maximize the objective and minimize the subjective. The limitations of this strict behavioral position have been repeatedly and convincingly pointed out (e.g., see Cheyne

OUTSIDER/ETIC	QUANTITATIVE	MEASURE DISCRETE BEHAVIOR
INSIDER/EMIC	QUALITATIVE	FUNCTIONAL CONTRAST

FIG. 4.1. Perspectives on observational methods.

& Seyfarth, 1990, for an interesting discussion of making cognitive inferences about social behaviors).

Methods derived from the outsider perspective were, however, particularly useful in early studies of animal behavior and human infants, both in the field and in the laboratory. After all, when working with animals and infants it is rather difficult to interview them to gain their perspectives on events! Yet, inferences about cognitive processes, such as motives and cognitions, can be made from observations of social behavior. In this regard, researchers using ethological methods have added considerably to our understanding of observational methods and human development.

Ethology. *Ethology* has been described as the biological study of behavior (Cairns, 1986; Pellegrini, 1992). Ethology is concerned with describing organisms in their natural environments. Only by rich descriptions of behaviors in their naturally occurring context can we begin to understand them. The theoretical underpinnings for this proposition relate specifically to the Darwinian origins of ethology. Following this general orientation, behavior develops and is learned by an individual in an interactive relationship with his or her environment; adaptation is a product of this relationship. Thus, we should try to understand the ways in which the behaviors of a specific group are interrelated with the specific characteristics of their environment. Individuals choose, adapt to, and shape their environments in ways that maximize their success in those niches. Success, from a Darwinian perspective, refers to reproductive success.

Ethologists typically work from the assumption that the categories into which behaviors are placed should emerge from the data. Categories take on specific meaning depending upon the contexts in which they are observed. A primary job of the ethologist is to describe behavior in context; so it follows that they should impose minimal structure on those behaviors in advance. Descriptive categories are induced by ethologists during the observational period. The generation of categories is very important to the hypothesis generation phase of the research enterprise. After the categories are defined and hypotheses generated, they can then be tested.

As in all observational and categorization enterprises, however, a question, or theory, guides the categorization and observational process. The steps in the ethologically oriented observational process are displayed in Fig. 4.2.

STEP 1	EXPLORATORY OBSERVATION
STEP 2	ETHOGRAM
STEP 3	SYSTEMATIC OBSERVATION

FIG. 4.2. Steps in ethological observation process.

QUESTION 1	HOW DOES IT WORK? (PROXIMAL CAUSES)
QUESTION 2	HOW DID IT DEVELOP? (ONTOGENY)
QUESTION 3	WHAT IS THE FUNCTION? (FITNESS/CONSEQUENCE)
QUESTION 4	HOW DID IT EVOLVE? (PHYLOGENY)

FIG. 4.4. Ethologists' four questions.

with children's conflicts, we should try to describe the behaviors preceding conflicts and those following conflicts. The antecedents suggest possible causes of conflict while the consequences tell us something about possible functions of the behavior. For example, if children's conflicts are preceded by disagreement about possession of toys we can assume that object disputes lead to aggression (see Smith & Connolly, 1980). Further, if possession of the prized toys follows the aggressive acts, we can assume that the aggression was motivated by the desire to possess the toy.

Tinbergen's (1963) second question is: How did the behavior of the individual develop during its life time? This developmental, or ontogenetic, question is particularly important to those of us interested in observing young children and adolescents. Childhood and adolescence are periods during which the organism undergoes rapid and dramatic change. The second question explicitly tells us to focus on comparing these change processes. We try to examine, through the second question, the way in which specific behaviors change across time. A clear example of such developmental change involves children's attachment relationships with their primary caregiver. We may, at time 1 (say during the toddler period) observe two children's attachment status. One may be secure and the other may be insecure. We track these relationships across time by observing the extent to which these relationships with their primary caregivers predict their relationships with their peers during the preschool period. It may be that the secure attachment relationship results in a child being friendly and popular with peers whereas the insecure relationship may predict more troubled peer relations, with this child being aggressive and unpopular (Sroufe, 1979).

The importance of such documentation can be illustrated most clearly when I address the third question: What is the function of the behavior? Although function in the strict biological sense refers to the reproductive success of the target organism or his or her kin, we can also consider function in terms of beneficial consequence (Hinde, 1980). Thus, the third question can be answered by examining consequences of behavior. This issue is relevant to the second question to the extent that the same behavior may have very different functions at different developmental periods. For example, crying for infants may be used to keep an adult in close proximity. With adolescents, on the other hand, crying may be a more private act.

An important concern in answering this question is to document the functions of behaviors within specific developmental periods. This translates into our being concerned with the meaning, or function, of the behavior for the child in question; we should not assume that the meaning of a behavior for a child is the same as for an adult. Considering the consequences of target behaviors for children within a specific developmental phase as well as future consequences help to sort these things out.

The fourth, and final, question is the phylogenetic question and is concerned with the evolutionary history of the behavior: How did the behavior evolve across the history of the species? Although this may be of limited concern to most of us studying children it is important to keep in mind that behaviors have a place in evolutionary history.

By way of illustration, I apply these four questions to the case of rough-and-tumble play in a hypothetical kindergarten child. Adam likes to playfight with his buddies on the playground at recess. They chase each other, stop, and wrestle each other to the ground. Adam starts off on top in the wrestling bout and then his friend and playmate, Danny, is on top, and Adam is on the bottom.

Applying the four questions to boys' R&T we can say that the first, proximal question, may be related to the presence of male hormones in both Danny and Adam. These hormones organize the nervous system of the developing male fetus in such as way as to predispose them to rough and vigorous play. Further, these biases are supported when these boys are placed in a spacious and permissive setting like the play ground.

The second, developmental question, allows us to situate R&T in the lifespan of Adam and Danny. R&T peaks in terms of frequency of occurrence during the preschool and early elementary school years (Pellegrini & Smith, 1998). It is preceded developmentally, by males engaging in varying forms physically vigorous movements. During infancy, rhythmic stereotypes are exhibited. These behaviors include foot kicking and body rocking and tend to peak at around 6 months of age (Thelen, 1979, 1980). Exercise play and R&T begin to be observed at this point. Exercise play is the more general category of vigorous play behavior and R&T is this sort of play in a social context.

The third question, that of function, points us toward examining the consequence of behaviors. During childhood, R&T is used by boys for a number of different reasons (Pellegrini & Smith, 1998). First, vigorous movements, generally, build and develop the skeletal and muscular systems. Additionally, boys seem to use R&T, specifically, as a way in which to bond socially with other male peers. R&T is a common activity during which boys learn and test social skills and build friendships. During adolescence, however, R&T is used by boys to exhibit dominance over their male peers. That is, they use their strength and social cunning to lead their male peer groups. Ultimately, dominance may be related to status with female peers and dating behavior (Pellegrini & Bartini, 2001).

is attained through observation and participation, with an eye toward understanding the ways in which participants make and comprehend meaning.

Observation and Participation. As a basic starting point, observation and participation should be systematic. By systematic, Hymes (1980) meant comprehensive. A comprehensive ethnography, then, would involve documenting all aspects of the culture under study: its geography, economic base, religious practices, kinship systems, etcetera. The reader might rightfully gasp at the magnitude of this goal. Clearly, such a venture takes many years to complete. Excellent examples of comprehensive ethnographies include Shirley B. Heath's (1983) study of language and literacy in the Carolina Piedmont and Susan Philips' (1972) study of Warm Springs Indian children in their community and school. In each of these studies, the researchers lived within the communities under study, spending considerable time there. Such a comprehensive approach is necessary, they argued to understand the children they were studying. For example, in order to understand how children from the communities under study approached schooling, a wider knowledge of language and values in the communities and families was necessary.

This level of comprehensiveness is similar to that required in ethology, to generate an ethogram. Just as I recommended that the ethological researcher might make his or her job more possible by narrowing the focus, for example, developing an ethogram for children in one specific location rather than across all locations, so to with ethnography. Ethnographers can narrow the systematic nature of their study by considering a specific topic. For example, ethnographic researchers may be especially interested in sleeping habits of children and adults within nuclear families. Observations of and interviews with participants could lead the researcher to narrow his or her focus to answer this more specific question.

The question still remains as to what comprehensive really means in terms of time investment by the researcher. As noted in trying to answer a related question for direct observational research: the more data the better. Obviously, this provides very little practical help, yet the research should aim to collect enough unobtrusive information across the targeted time frame to satisfy himself or herself that the information is valid. By unobtrusive I mean that the participants should habituate to the observer's presence to the extent that they are behavior "normally." Observers can document this by providing examples of participants exhibiting behaviors they might not ordinarily exhibit in the presence of strangers. For example, I illustrated how children habituated to observers' presence when they started using "nasty language" to their peers while the observers watched. Additionally, children and adolescents in schools do not usually fight in the presence of an adult observer; when this happens the observer is becoming obtrusive. A similar case can be made for researchers studying families: Instances of family discord are evidence that observers are relative unobtrusive.

A related time-frame issue concerns the time interval that is to be observed. Starting with a rather simple example, if we are doing an ethnography of a classroom, it seems that the frame, minimally should be the school year, from beginning to end. If we are studying transitions, we would want to study the end of one point, say kindergarten, the transition to the next point, say the start of first grade, and then subsequent adjustment after the initial transition, say until the end of the first-grade year.

A more complicated example is illustrated with studying children sleeping with adults. Clearly, observations from the onset of the bedtime routine through the morning wake-up routine are necessary. This can be done continuously or at different intervals across a number of days. Ratcheting-up the level of complexity, we must decide when to begin and when to end observations. When to begin, at least in this case, might be simpler: when the baby is born. When to stop observing is more complicated and should be based on theory and the pragmatics of gaining and maintaining access to the participants. It might be that the culture has a specified time when this is done.

In terms of the data collection being guided by validity concerns, observers should relate the interpretations derived from observation data with data from other sources, such as archives or interviews. If the data converge on the same interpretation, the observational data are probably valid.

Lastly, Hymes (1980) suggested that ethnography should be comparative. For example, comparisons between working-class White and working-class Black children and families studied by Heath (1983) illustrate the different ways in which children from each groups are socialized and the implications of each styles for children's literacy. Comparisons are important because they provide bases for the contrasting of meaning.

These three levels of analysis should be united in ethnographic study to generate typologies of different systems within and across groups. These typologies, or category systems, are central to ethnographers' quest for meaning. For instance, within one group, schools or families might be categorized along certain dimensions. For example, schools in one part of a city might decide to develop a program to prevent teen violence and pregnancy by using expert knowledge to design and implement programs. Other schools in the same district might try to solve the same problems by looking toward those resilient families and students in the community who are successful in these areas.

Relatedly, each of the hypothetical schools discussed in this example may arrive at a seemingly similar program (in terms of components) but through different means (expert vs. local knowledge). By attending to only the program components and not the meaning of those components for each of the schools, researchers might miss the closer understanding of the programs and reasons for their differential success or failure. Thus, the validity of the ethnographer's conclusions is dependent on the degree to which their interpretation of events corresponds with those of participants in those events. The possibility of different interpretations of similar categories make ethnographers distrust a priori constructed questionnaires or category systems.

This view of ethnography is not inconsistent with tradition views of science as expressed by ethologist. This "generous view of scientific method" (Hymes,

1980a, p. 95) imposes rules and conditions for satisfying concerns of validity and appropriate research designs to address these needs. More exactly, ethnography, like other modes of scientific inquiry, is concerned with valid descriptions and testing of hypotheses. Valid descriptions are derived from the systematic phase of ethnographies. Based on these descriptions, hypotheses can be generated and tested. The example of hypothesis testing in ethnography given by Hymes is Whiting and Whiting's (1975) six culture study. In this case, hypotheses are generated on the relations between different socialization patterns and children's behavior.

Perhaps what differentiates ethnography from more psychological approaches to science is its dialectic nature. By this I mean that the research question and the methods are dynamic in the sense that they can change in the course of the fieldwork. This is not to say, again from Hymes (1980), that ethnography is "empty minded" or naive (p. 92). Research questions should be grounded in the through training in the content area as well as in the methods to be used. The more adequate each is, the more adequate the question and methods. Hymes recommended that the ethnographic researcher begin his or her fieldwork with an etic description of behaviors under study. This should be followed by an emic analysis, illustrating the ways in which these behaviors are functional. In the end, individual behaviors are related to the larger system of meaning making.

Specific Methods Used in Ethnography. In this section I consider various aspects of ethnographic collection (Fetterman, 1998), as displayed in Fig. 4.6.

Fieldwork is a generic label given to the time an ethnographer spends at the research site, using a variety of methods to understand the culture under study.

Fieldwork

Selection and sampling

Site entry

Participant observation

Interviewing

Lists and forms

Questionnaires

Projective techniques

Unobtrusive measures

FIG. 4.6. Aspects of ethnographic data collection.

The specific field location studied and the length of time spent there will vary, as previously noted, according to both theoretical and pragmatic concerns.

Consequently, the *selection* of a field site requires a fair amount of work, of the sort described earlier. The researcher begins with a thorough grounding in the research literature in the relevant field. For example, if we are interested in studying children's transition from preschool to primary school, we should explore the relevant theoretical questions that have been asked. For example, Ladd and Price (1983) showed that having friends from preschool in your kindergarten class made the transitions easier. Specifically, children who were friends in preschool and moved to the same kindergarten classroom had fewer adjustment problems, relative to children without "old" friends. This information should guide the research to select sites where they knew some children would move from the same preschool to the same elementary school.

This level of choice is also relevant to the sample selection and the specific question to be asked. Ethnographers usually start at a general level, after they have identified the research site. Staying with the school transition example, the ethnographer can spend time in a school identified in the selection phase. Spending time means spending time as a participant, so the researcher can act as a classroom volunteer, playground supervisor, teacher, etcetera. During this time the researcher informally observes youngsters in a variety of settings; listening to their conversations; and talking with the kids, their peers, and a variety of adults in the school.

In this phase, the ethnographer is casting a very wide net, continually refining his or her methods and research question. This is an illustration of the dialectical nature of ethnography: Questions and methods get refined with experience in the field. As noted previously, one's choices should be ground in the relevant research literature. This knowledge and subsequent experience will lead the ethnographer to seek out those participants and events that are most pertinent to the question at hand.

Entry into the field is the next aspect of ethnography. Entering a research site, for any research is a very delicate and time-consuming process. A detailed description of this process can be found in another chapter. In this section I discuss some of these same concerns, while adding some that may be unique to ethnography.

Most generally, a researcher can gain access to the field either directly or indirectly. Direct access to the field is typically provided by a member of the community to which the researcher is trying to gain access. For example, we may want to conduct an ethnography of college hockey fans, and we may have a student in one of our classes who is a fan and goes to games with a regular group of fellow students. We can gain direct access to that group through the student.

Access to college hockey fans can also be indirect, such that the ethnographer attends games on his or her own, observes a number of different fan groups, and then tries to gain access to a specific group or groups. This could be accomplished by moving around the arena and observing different groups. For example, there may be groups that "hang out to be seen" at the top of their seating section during the breaks between each period. There may be others in the "home" student section, other in the visitors' sections, and yet others near the band. The ethnographer would look to see which group is most interesting and try to gain entry into that specific group.

The benefits and costs associated with each approach should be readily apparent. First, in the direct case, we gain immediate access to a group without having to spend time searching for a group and then trying to gain insider status in that group. A direct approach may be especially useful to gain access to relatively restricted sites, such as schools and hospitals. In these cases, unlike the hockey example, outsiders are not routinely given access. Consequently, an indirect approach would not work in these cases. Having a friend who is a teacher, principal, doctor, nurse, or hospital administrator would be very helpful in getting in the door.

There are, however, costs, associated with direct access. For example, the group to which you have direct access may not be ideal for your purposes, as you might find out. Further, members of the group may associate you with the person who gave you access, and this may have certain repercussions. For example, you may not have access to certain subgroups who do not like this person. In such cases it is imperative that the researcher establish their independence once they have gained access.

Another example, from personal experience, is also illustrative. I once gained access to conduct research in school through a student in one of my classes. I was speaking about my upcoming research project in class and also mentioned that I was in need of a research site. This student was a teacher in a local elementary school and said he thought I could conduct the research at his school. He set up a meeting with the principal and me. In that meeting, I presented my "best case scenario" for conducting the research project, and the principal gave me immediate access to study children at one grade level the next year. We agreed that the project would begin at the start of the school year and run until the end of the year. Too good to be true?

When the next year came, however, the principal was gone. She moved to another school district (without telling me). So, when I called in August to plan the introduction of my research associates to the school, I was greeted by a new principal. I had to renegotiate with the new principal, who also granted me access. In the course of the data collection, my research associates and I sensed some reluctance to participate on the part of the teachers; for example, they were tardy in sending out parental consent forms; there were low-return rates in three of the four classrooms; teachers in the same three classrooms were reluctant to give us time to interview children. In the course of the school year we found out that these three teachers were indeed less than enthusiastic to participate and this was a result of the former principal "volunteering" them and their classrooms for the project without consulting them. Their recalcitrance resulted in our withdrawing from the school after 4 months. The costs of this direct access were very high and, yes, it was too good to be true.

Consequently, I recommend that as researchers try to gain access to a field site, they approach "gate keepers" with a variety of research plans. Further, as illustrated by the example, researchers should try to engage as many of the relevant gatekeepers as possible. The plans should vary from the "best case" scenario in which the research gains access to all relevant data sources, to those that are minimally acceptable, or a bare-bones plan in which only the minimum of acceptable access is granted.

It often helps if the researcher enlists a member or members of the field site as participants in the research team. There are obvious pragmatic benefits to this, such as increased access and cooperation. The quality of the data collected may also be improved. For example, teachers may know the best places to observe certain phenomena and who might be central figures to interview.

At another level, involving participants in the research enterprise "democratizes" the process (Hymes, 1980b). By this I mean that the research enterprise no longer dichotomizes experts from nonexperts. Treating participants as coequals with researchers also minimizes the extent to which researchers come into a setting and exploit it for their own ends.

There are interesting, and to my mind, unresolved ethical issues associated with participant observation. For example, should participant observers inform those with whom they are working of their status as researchers? It is my view that they should, as to not do so would be deceptive. Deception is psychological and educational is a dangerous and slippery slope as it endangers the integrity of the individual project as well as research more generally. An extended discussion of deception is presented in the chapter on Ethics (chap. 3).

Participant observation, according to Hymes (1980a) and others, is one of the very central components of ethnography. It requires a difficult balancing of participating in the lives of the people under study necessary to gain access and understand participants' views with the objective and professional distance necessary to gather and weigh evidence objectively. Participation requires emersion in the culture under study. Common examples include participant observers acting as teachers in classrooms to conduct educational ethnographies (as done by Courtney Cazden (1975) in a San Diego first-grade classroom for an entire school year), an ethnography of medical education (where the ethnographer enrolled as a student and progressed through the program with his cohort), and an ethnography of undergraduate student dormitory life (where the researcher enrolled as a nontraditional student and lived in a freshman dorm!).

In less ideal situations, the participation may be less sustained, as the researcher enters and re-enters the field at various times across the study. Of course, the issues associated with when to observe and how much to observe are in the forefront of issues confronting the researcher. As noted, it makes sense to sample all relevant time segments, such as time of the day, day of the week, month of the year, and so forth, so, instead of spending a whole year in a school, an ethnographer might act as a teacher's aid and participate at predetermined intervals.

In either case, participant observers begin by generally surveying the site and gradually sharpening their focus. The job here is to identify people, places, and things that are relevant to the general research questions. Exploring these aspects of the field site should, in turn, result in the researcher, sharpening the research question.

Interviewing is another aspect of ethnographic research. Interviews are among the most important ethnographic tools as they provide direct access to the points of view of participants. Interviews can be structured, semi-structured, informal, or retrospective (Fetterman, 1998). Structured and semi-structured interviews are a version of self-report questionnaires used in traditional psychological research. The ethnographic approach often departs from psychological studies, however. Ethnographers should take great care that their meaning of the questions being asked correspond to the meaning from the participant's point of view. For example, Hymes (1980a, 1980b) reported that the same word has different meaning in different parts of the same factory in the city of Philadelphia.

Many of us have experienced a similar phenomenon. For example, one summer I taught a research methods course at the University of British Columbia and used the term *shagging about* to describe the initial phases of field entry. *Shagging about* had a very different and very unsavory meaning in Vancouver. Consequently, questions for interviews should be generated only after considerable participant and piloting.

Informal interviews are a mixture of interviews and conversations. Although they can be very productive they are also very difficult to conduct. The interviewer should have a list of questions he or she wants to ask and must wait until an opportune time in conversations to ask them. As with formal interviewing, it generally, makes sense to pose the most probing, or personal, questions after rapport has been established. The lack of uniformity, of course, may bias results (e.g., some participants may hear all the questions whereas others hear a different subset or questions in a different order).

Informal interviews also may pose ethical problems for the research. In the course of informal conversations, especially when the interlocutors are familiar with each other, a participant may disclosure of information that is very personal or indicative of illegal activities. In such cases, the researcher might do his or her best to change the topic. Certainly, this information should be treated as confidential. A real dilemma is presented when the researcher is put into a position in which he or she is legally required to disclose certain types of information, such as case of suspected child abuse.

Retrospective interviews can be either structured or informal. As the label implies, this sort of interview asks participants about events in the past. Consequently, problems associated with selective memory exacerbate the other problems. However, when this is the only source of data, we should use it but with caution.

Each interview form can ask specific types of questions: Survey, specific open-ended or closed-ended questions (Fetterman, 1998). Survey questions are general questions that help to define the boundaries of the study. Information on the physical setting, universe of activities, and thoughts of the participants can be gained through survey questions.

Researchers move between survey and specific questions as they focus their research question and methods. Specific questions are used to probe the meaning of the more general information gained in the survey questions. For example, we might have a general question on where students spend their time in the dormitory, so we get a list of different places within a dormitory. Some places might include the television lounge, the study room, and the rooms of specific students. Specific questions would probe the specifics of where in the dorm these places are located, who goes there, when, and why. Answers to these questions provide meaning to the categories.

Open- or close-ended questions can be used. Open-ended interview questions cannot be answered from a specified set of responses, such as yes or no or multiple choice. The respondent must use his or her own words to respond; consequently they allow for individual interpretation and response.

Closed-ended questions are the converse. The range of respondents' answers are determined, in advance, by the researcher. Consequently, they are easier to quantify than open-ended questions, but they are also less likely to yield novel insights. For these reasons, open-ended questions are more frequently used by ethnographers. However, closed-ended questions might yield valid information if the ethnographer has an in-depth knowledge of the culture already.

The question of who gets interviewed is, at the root, a sampling question, so the choice should be a systematic one. Ethnographers chose "key informants" to provide information on a culture and as checks of ethnographers' interpretations. Most basically, a key informant is a member of the culture under study who has a detailed knowledge of that culture. Choosing a key informant should be based on a number of other factors as well. The key informant should also be willing and able to share these insights with the ethnographer, usually through interviews. For example, if one is studying the socialization practices in youth gangs, a present (or, less optimally, past) member of a gang should be an informant.

Ethnographers may choose to use one or two key informants, depending on time constraints, as well as varied levels of expertise of the informants. Although time constraints often limit the number of key informants used, we should beware of the fact that the data provided by key informants should not be accepted without reservation. Perhaps the most famous example of accusations that a key informant "duped" an anthropologist comes from Margaret Mead's (1954) studies of adolescent sexuality in Samoa. A key informant in the original Mead was re-interviewed by another anthropologist many years after the fact and she stated that much of the information given to Mead was false. Although this "revisionist" view of Mead's work is controversial, we should be careful to check the validity of the key informants' information, and these procedures are discussed later. Information from key informants can also provide very useful and insightful information for case studies. The remainder of this section discusses other means by which ethnographers collect data in the field (Fetterman, 1998).

Lists, Forms, and Questionnaires. Lists, forms, and questions can guide the ethnographer to the relevant questions to be asked during interviews or while observing. In the interviewing processes, lists, forms, and questionnaires can provide the general sorts of information guiding informal interviewing.

Lists and forms, specifically, can provide general or specific guidance for a field observer. For example, researchers studying children and their families can use this format to direct their attention to relevant aspects of the home environment. It may be the case that they should look for the presence of books in the home and the amount and types of children's toys present. Of course, as in case of questionnaires, the ethnographer should take care that the lists and forms are meaningful to the participants. In Fig. 4.7, an example of one such form is displayed for use in home visits.

Projective Techniques. Projective techniques involve ethnographers presenting a stimulus to an informant an asking him or her want it is and what it means. From the answer, the ethnographers makers inferences about the meaning of the stimuli for the focal participant. Stimuli presented can be an everyday object from the field, such as a jacket from a gang member. Fetterman (1998) suggest that photographs or videoclips be used as stimuli, as well. More formally, participants can be interviewed with standardized psychological projective tests, such as they Rorschach inkblot test.

Whatever the projective technique used, the ethnographer should maximize the likelihood that the procedure is meaningful to the respondent and that his or her responses are interpreted in a culturally sensitive way.

Unobtrusive Measures: Artifacts Outcroppings. As a complement to projective techniques, ethnographers can also examine naturally present artifacts produced by a group. For example, an ethnographer of schooling might examine the following artifacts: children's homework, seatwork, and teachers' lesson plans, whereas social ethnographers may collect Cub Scout projects. Outcroppings are things in the field that "stick out" (Fetterman, 1998), such as graffiti on the wall of a school in the Catholic neighborhood in Belfast. These pieces of data allow the researcher to make a projection about meaning without asking a participant. Of course, the researcher could take a photograph of these things, present to a participant as a projective stimuli, and examine the degree to which the two interpretations converge.

Making Sense of Ethnographic Data. For the ethnographer, the specific goal of research is to understand the phenomenon as the participants in that culture understand it. The validity of an ethnographer's interpretation of events is determined by the triangulation, or convergence, of data sources. That is, different data sources, such as observations and interviews, provide different sources of information about the same events. Validity exists when multiple data sources give the same interpretation. For example, triangulation was provided when both interview and observation data suggested that mothers weaned their babies so that they could return to work.

Focal Child ________________________________ Date ___________

Observer's Name ____

The social environment:

Who's present? Parent(s); Other adult kin; sibling(s); peers; ages; sex

How many?

Who's interacting with the focal child?

If so, is it directive/didactic?

Directive but child sensitive?

Laissez faire?

Are they using mathematics language?

Talking about numbers?

Arithmetic operations?

Time?

Measurement?

Counting?

Prices?

The physical environment

Are there props present that support mathematical thinking?

Counting books?

Number lines

Movable and displayed numbers

Ruler

Calculator

Thermometer

Timer

FIG. 4.7. Home visit list for observing children's mathematics-related behavior.

Reliability, like validity, is important for ethnographers. Reliability for ethnographers, however, involves identifying recurrent patterns in data. For example, an ethnographer may identify the following behavior in mother–child book reading: (a) mother presents child with a cognitive demanding question (e.g., "Why do you think she did that?"); (b) if the child provides an adequate response (e.g., "She might'd been scared!"); (c) the mother continues with using high-demand strategies; (d) if the child does not respond adequately (e.g., "I don't know."); (e) the mother's next move is low-cognitive demand.

The reliability of these patterns can been tested using statistical analyses. We can determine the probability of this sequence occurring, using sequential lag analyses. Basically, the technique tells us the probability of Event *A* leading to *B*; *B* leading to *C*, and *C* to *D*. By converting these conditional probabilities to z-scores, we can also determine the extent to which these sequences occur at a beyond chance level.

Patterns can also be derived from participants' use of certain words or phrases. It might be the case that members of a certain group use a distinctive set of words to mark certain events. For example, in Labov's (1972) classic sociolinguistic study of inner city youth, he found that Black and Puerto Rican teenagers not only used different words to describe the same event, but within each group there were different idiomatic patterns used by gang members compared to nongang members.

Although there a number of computer programs to help ethnographers conduct this sort of language analysis, the researcher must take extreme care that there is correspondence between the word used, what the speaker means, and what the researcher means.

Case Study. Case study can be part of ethnography or a separate mode of inquiry. Case study involves the examination of a single case. Data from all of the aforementioned discussed techniques can be used to gather the information that goes into a case study. Cases can be individual children, parents, a school, an event or any other single entity. Most importantly, cases studies should be used when we want to gain very specific information about specific cases. For example, physicians might construct a case study of a child's experience with a therapeutic regimen (Spitz, 1965). Similarly, economists sometimes use cases studies to examine successful corporation.

Case studies then offer information about the particular. To accentuate the particular, case studies often take the form of narratives, or stories. Good narratives, or narratives that grip the reader, typically provide a detailed and varied account about the case and the general context in which it is embedded. Specifically, historical background, information on the physical setting, other relevant cases, and information about other informants add life to case studies.

According to Stake (1994), there are three types of case studies. An intrinsic case study is undertaken because the researcher has intrinsic, or self-motivated, reasons for conducting the research. The particular case is not chosen for any specific reason; for example it may not be representative or successful, but the researcher finds the case interesting. For instance, someone may choose to write about the lives of the children and teachers in a specific classroom in a school, simply because he or she finds it interesting. Additionally, family histories are often intrinsic cases.

Instrumental case studies, in contrast, are used to inform practice or theory. For example, my son's first-grade classroom and teacher were an interesting example of a cooperative social unit. It would be interesting to conduct case studies with those same teachers in subsequent years. Following up on family history, histories of families from specific groups might be used to gain information about the ways in which specific groups lived at different times in history (Stone, 1977).

Collective cases involve the aggregation of numerous cases that shed light on a common problem. The result is a more general picture than a single case could provide. For example, in separate case studies it may be interesting to examine the ways in which cooperation does and does not develop between those same first-grade teachers and different groups of children. Separate family histories from a specific county during a specific period would also provide a more general picture.

Adequacy and Inadequacy in Evidence. With all of this said, when do we know if the data we have collected are adequate, or valid? Fred Erickson (1986) provided some suggestions for answering that very difficult question. First, we need an adequate amount of data. As noted previously, amount of data is a sampling issue, and we should have enough to satisfy those requirements. Relevant issues to address include the adequacy of the time frame sampled (e.g., within and across days), number of individuals sampled, and the number of times individuals are sampled.

Second, we should have a variety of evidence and examine the extent to which these different sources triangulate our interpretation. As with standard psychological research, the validity of a construct is related to the degree to which we have multimeasures of that construct, from a variety of participants. For example, in our studies of adolescent aggression (Pellegrini, Bartini, & Brooks, 1999), we defined aggression using different methods (direct observations, nominations, self-reports) and different informants (objective observer, peers, teachers, and self).

Using multiple measures from different informants should also maximize the possibility of gathering evidence that might not confirm one's view. A basic view of science, as advanced by Karl Popper (1957), is that evidence and hypotheses should be *falsifiable*. By this he meant that scientific evidence and ideas were good if they were subjected to a process in which they were tested for confirmation or disconfirmation (e.g., in the form of testing the null hypothesis). For the ethnographer specifically, the opportunity to disconfirm, again, relates to the amount of time spent in the field and the different types of data collected from different sources.

Third, involves a "faulty" interpretation. This a tough one as it relates to the degree to which the researcher has captured the complexity of the actions and meaning of the participants. This is tough because only the researcher and participants would see the interpretation as faulty. Erickson suggested that this problem is often a result of the researcher not spending an adequate amount of time in the field.

CONCLUSIONS

In this chapter I have described two general orientations toward research: The outsider and the insider perspectives. Both of these orientations recognize the importance of systematically and thoroughly observing participants in their everyday habitats. They both also recognize the importance of using a variety of measures and a variety of informants. The outsider perspective was represented by ethology and ecological psychology. Whereas ecological psychologists stress the role of the environment, independent of the participants, the ethological approach stresses the transaction between the environment and the participants. That is, participants and environments do not exist independent of one another; they affect each other.

The insider approach was represent by ethnography. In ethnography researchers try to gloss the meaning of phenomena under study from the perspective of the participant. From this view, the stress is on meaning. Meaning is typically viewed as being constructed by participants in specific locations. Consequently, ethnographers use participant observation procedures. In the end, they use both behavioral analyses and analyses of symbol systems to make their inferences.

SOME THINGS TO THINK ABOUT

1. Think of a naturalistic observational study, such as studying social interactions around "violent" videogames.

Next, think of a way in which this same issue can be studied using a field experimental design.

How could this be studied in a laboratory?

____

____

____

____

____

____

2. Give three examples of how individuals and context influence each other.

A. ______________________________________

B. ______________________________________

C. ______________________________________

3. Pick a behavior, such as aggression, or a system of behaviors, such as attachment, and scrutinize it according to Tinbergen's Four Questions.

A. What is its proximal cause?

____

____

____

B. How does it develop?

C. What is/are the function(s)?

D. What is its phylogenetic history?

4. What are three strengths and three weaknesses of participant observations?
Strengths

A.

B.

C.

Weaknesses

A. ____

____

____

B. ____

____

____

C. ____

____

____

5

Design and Specification in Observational Research: Some Important Issues to Consider

As we begin to consider conducting an observational project, a plan is crucial. Consequently, a fair amount of preplanning and thought are necessary in order to avoid some common problems that often afflict observational methods and research: An ounce of prevention .... In this chapter I discuss some "basics" to be considered when planning and designing an observational project. Although some of these are general and applicable to most observational work, such as observer bias, some are very specific to conducting observations with young children, such as specific concerns with studying the development of the child (see Martin & Bateson, 1993, for additional discussion).

Probably the most basic choice to be made is that between conducting observations in a naturalistic, field setting, and conducting observations in an experimental, laboratory, setting. This choice point is addressed first. Next, I discuss observer bias. Third, I discuss replication as a means to check against unusual, or aberrational, findings.

THE LABORATORY OR THE FIELD?

Although many of the issues associated with choosing between laboratory or field work are generally addressed in Chapter 4, aspects of those choices bear restating to the extent that is a probably the most basic choice in the design of observational work.

By way of further clarification, field work can be either naturalistic or experimental. Naturalistic field work involves the observer studying the natural occurrence of behavior at a particular site (e.g., Pellegrini's, 1988, study of children's school recess behavior). Field studies can also be experimental, as in the case of field experiments, where natural settings are experimentally manipulated. Examples of this include Smith and Connolly's (1980) manipulation of preschool classroom variables, Hart and Shennan's (1986) manipulation of children's access to specific type of playground equipment during recess, and Pellegrini and Davis' (1993) manipulation of recess timing.

Typically, the choice between the field and the laboratory is determined by the investigators predilection toward causal or descriptive work. Such a choice should be rooted in the nature of the question asked. The reader is referred to a number of useful sources, which further explicate these differences: Kerlinger (1996) and Shadish, Cook, and Campbell (2002).

Following Cronbach's (1957) characterization of the two disciplines of psychology (descriptive and explanatory), naturalistic observation typically belongs to the descriptive group whereas experimental or laboratory studies belong to the causal or explanatory group. Thus, if one's question is primarily descriptive, the choice of a naturalistic setting may be more appropriate. The implication of conducting observations according to each of these traditions is presented in Table 5.1.

One typically chooses to conduct experiments, either in the lab or in the field, because of the lure of causal explanations between independent and dependent measures. Causality is established by the manipulation of relevant (independent) variables and the control (or holding constant) of others in order to explain some outcome (or dependent) variable. Thus, children may be observed in a laboratory playroom in order to examine the effects of a specific set of toys (the manipulated, independent measures) on social behavior or language (the dependent measures). In laboratory procedures, a number of important variables are controlled, such as the composition of the play group in terms of age, gender, and familiarity, and the length of the play period. These variables are controlled so that they do not have an influence on the dependent variable. Any variation between groups, or between toys sets, is assumed to be due to the effects of the manipulated independent variables.

An experiment is said to be internally valid if the only factors affecting the dependent variable are those manipulated by the experimenter. The student interested in possible threats to the internal validity of experiments, or one's ability to make unfettered statements about the effects of independent variables on dependent variables, is referred to the classic work on the validity of experiments by Campbell and Stanley (1963) as well as the counterpart for field experiments (Shadish et al., 2002).

Observational methods applied to the laboratory would, obviously, be very useful in helping to answer the hypothetical questions just posed. The often noted limitation of the experimental approach, however, is that it informs re-

TABLE 5.1
Types of Research With Setting and Inference Implications

Type of Research	*Venue*	*Nature of Inferences*
Experimental	Lab or Field	Causal & Descriptive
Naturalistic	Field	Age Specific: Descriptive Longitudinal: Developmental Causal

searchers about what children, and other research participants, can do rather than what they *actually* do (McCall, 1977). In short, experiments may give us insight into the effect of an independent variable on a dependent variable in a very specific setting; that, however, may not represent the world actually inhabited by the research participants.

This level of explanation may be a very different one from the ways in which this dependent variable develops in children in real life, outside of the laboratory. Thus, if we are interested in understanding the ways in which children develop in their everyday world, it seems imperative that, initially at least, we spend considerable time observing them in those situations that they ordinarily inhabit. As noted in the previous chapter in the discussion of ethological methods, studying children in their natural worlds is important to our understanding of development to the extent that development is considered a transactional process between children and their environments. It follows, that in order to fully understand development children should be observed in those environments in which behaviors develop.

A promising compromise solution to a forced choice between the experimental/laboratory approach and the descriptive/field approach is the field experiment. Field experiments attempt to manipulate and control variables in real world settings. For example, Smith and Connolly (1980) constructed preschool environments with different social densities to measure the effect of this variable on children's social behavior. Also, the recess periods of children in preschool (Smith & Hagan, 1980) and elementary school (Pellegrini & Davis, 1993; Pellegrini, Huberty, & Jones, 1995) have been experimentally manipulated to determine the effect of confinement on recess behavior. In all cases, experimental control and manipulation was applied to children in real classrooms; thus, making causal inferences about children in real-world settings possible.

A very important aspect of field studies is the descriptive data that they generate. Observational methods are an important, and probably crucial, part of this descriptive process. The descriptions that we render can be focused, in turn, on one specific age period of children or adults. More broadly, we can focus on the developmental processes typifying a specific period or periods. Although observational methods are very closely associated with both age specific and developmental research, it is most closely associated with the naturalistic study of child development, rather than age-specific behavior (Applebaum & McCall, 1983).

Developmental research involves charting the *change processes across time*. Although the developmental approach involves studying the same children, or adults, across time, it is not concerned primarily with cross-age comparisons of different groups. While cross-age comparisons are often included in developmental research, the prime concern of developmental research is to describe the change processes and mechanisms associated with change across time. Longitudinal research designs are necessary to accomplish this goal.

In longitudinal designs the same individuals are studied across time. In this way we can chart the change processes in the same individuals as they develop, as well as make cross-age comparisons. Study of different individuals at different ages utilizes cross-sectional designs. An example of a cross-sectional design might involve 3-, 4-, and 5-year-olds and study the age-related change of their aggressive behavior. In longitudinal research, researchers study the ways in which a specific phenomenon, such as aggression, changes in a specific group across time. We might start off with a group of 3-year-olds and follow them, describing aggressive behavior, until they are 5 years old.

As noted previously, longitudinal designs are necessary in order to study development. Indeed, McCall (1977) called longitudinal research the "life blood" of developmental psychology. The reasoning is straight forward enough: If one is interested in studying the change processes across time, rather than difference between age groups, one must study the way in which a group of individuals changes across that time span. Like the marriage between naturalistic researchers and observational methods, so too, a marriage exists between longitudinal research and observational methods.

Although longitudinal designs are a necessary component of doing developmental research, they have the added benefit of allowing us to begin to make directional inferences about relations between sets of variables. Specifically, in longitudinal designs we have, by definition, variables in antecedent-consequence relations; for example, parent–child interaction patterns at Time 1 and sociometric status at Time 2. Such antecedent-consequence relations are necessary, but not sufficient, for making causal inferences. Further, with the advent of various path analytic and structural equation data analyses procedures we can begin to make causal inferences about longitudinal date.

I flesh-out this example a bit more so that we can understand this important point of how longitudinal designs can be used to proffer causal explanations. In order to make causal explanations, antecedent-consequence relations are necessary, but not sufficient. So if we want to make an inference about the effects of parenting styles on children's acceptance by their peers, we must have some measure of parenting that precedes our measure of peer acceptance; parenting (x) → peer acceptance (y). This temporal relation allows us to make predictive statements, such that x predicts y. In order to move from predictions to causal explanation we must try to do what experimenters do; we must control, or eliminate, the effects of extraneous variables on dependent measures while simultaneously measuring the effects of our independent variables. Certain statistical procedures, such as partial correlations, hierarchical regression, and hierarchical linear modeling techniques allow us to do this so that we can control the effects of variables that might affect children's peer acceptance, other than parenting strategies, such as socioeconomic status and child's physical attractiveness. Controlling alternate sources of variance are not adequate, however, to proffer a causal explanation. To make a causal argument we must do one of two things: experimentally manipulate independent variables (in this case parenting styles) or use sophisticated path analytical techniques (like LISERAL) or structural equation models which test a specific theory.

To summarize this section, those of us wishing to observe children in the field can do so by describing a specific group at a specific age. Alternately, we can describe the change processes in a specific group as the group develops across time. This latter approach has the added benefit of allowing us to make predictive interferences about the relations between variables. The relative assets and deficits of cross-sectional and longitudinal designs are summarized in Table 5.2.

In the next section, we begin to consider some very specific issues in planning observational research.

OBSERVER BIAS

Observer bias should be a concern to all researchers (see Martin & Bateson, 1993 for an additional discussion). By *observer bias* I mean the expectations and knowledge observers have about participants that may influence the objectivity of their observations per se and/or the ways in which they treat participants and data derived from observations. Observer bias applied to experimental situations would mean that observers know, for example, to which groups (e.g., treatment or control group) participants have been assigned. Such knowledge may influence results to the extent that experimenters may provide subtle cues to the children about the adequacy or inadequacy of their behavior. For example, an experimenter's smile or subtle nod may encourage a child to continue responding in a specific way whereas a frown or look of surprise from an observer may result in a behavior being terminated by the participant. Thus, observers' biases affect their behavior which, in turn, affects the behavior of the participants.

I stress the belief that these biases probably operate subconsciously on the observer. Most biased observers are not being dishonest, they are simply emitting behavior that reflect their anticipations. One very well-established, and simple, way of alleviating this type of bias is to assure that observers are *blind* to hypotheses or group assignment. *Double blind* procedures involve neither the experimenter/observer nor the participant knowing the treatment the latter has received.

A related problem, that afflicts observations in both the laboratory and the field, involves bias among observers who record and score, or code, behavioral data. This sort of bias, too, can arise from knowledge of hypotheses and/or group assignment. So, for example, behaviorally similar responses from chil-

TABLE 5.2
Benefits and Costs of Cross-Sectional and Longitudinal Designs

Benefits	*Costs*
Cross-sectional	
Short-term	No change/process measures
Cross-age comparisons	Measures are contemporaneous
Longitudinal	
Measures change/process	Costly/long-term
Antecedent-consequence relations	

dren in different groups, such as an experimental and a control group, might be coded differently by a biased coder. Observers might be more likely to code a child's behavior in specific ways if they knew he or she was in an experimental or a control group. Such bias can also affect nonexperimental research designs. If an observer knows the research hypothesis, say that boys' play is rougher than girls', then the observer may be biased toward describing boys' and girls' behavior in ways that are consistent with the hypothesis.

Relatedly, bias often results from observers being aware of participants' status on other measures. This knowledge may influence the ways in which observers record and code behavior. So, for example, if the same researcher collects sociometric and behavioral data on the same children, their knowledge of the children's sociometric status may influence the ways in which they code ambiguous behavior. If the researcher knows that a specific child has been frequently nominated as being "disliked" and "nasty" by his or her peers, the observer may more readily code an ambiguous behavioral act, such as rough-and-tumble play, as aggressive for that child. Another child, receiving numerous "liked" and "kind" nominations may have exhibited similarly ambiguous behavior, but because of observer bias, that behavior is coded as rough play, not aggression. In other words, the observer's coding of behavior is being influenced by his or her knowledge of children's reputations.

The issue of bias is a very important one to the extent that such biases have real effects on children and the ways in which observers categorize their behaviors. The children's play literature has some very interesting cases in which very well-recognized effects of play on dimensions of children's creativity were seemingly due to bias. In two very frequently cited studies (Dansky & Silverman, 1973, 1975) it was suggested by the researchers, respectively, that forms of play with objects facilitated creative object use and problem solving. None of these studies, however, controlled for observer bias. That is, experimenters interacting with children in the experimental and testing conditions and observers coding children's responses, knew the specific hypotheses and children's group assignment. This knowledge probably affected the ways in which they interacted with the children in the training and testing situations as well as the ways in which they coded children's responses. In subsequent studies, in which observer bias was controlled, the Dansky and Silverman (1973, 1975) studies were not replicated by Smith and Whitney (1987). Using blind procedures, observers should check their undue influence on participants' behavior.

REPLICATION

One way in which to guard against the acceptance of unreliable empirical findings is through replication. One way to define *replication* is, generally, when an attempt is made to attain the same results using the same measures with similar participants, in similar situations. The null hypothesis is rejected (i.e., we can say that there are reliable difference between groups) only when similar results are obtained in both groups. Remember, the case of cold fusion when researchers could not replicate the original findings; the original findings supporting cold fusion were consequently disregarded.

Literal replication can be accomplished within a research team or across different research teams. Within one research team a replication sample design can be utilized such that two, parallel, groups are studied for each question rather than single groups. Results are accepted by the researcher if they are similar across the two samples. Smith and Pellegrini (Pellegrini, Huberty, & Jones, 1995; Smith & Hagen, 1980) utilized replication samples in studying the effects of play deprivation on preschool children's motor behavior outdoors and the effects of various classroom ecological arrangements on children's and teachers' behavior (Smith & Connolly, 1980). In these cases, two separate groups of children were assigned to different treatment and comparison groups. Graphically, the research design might look like that presented in Table 5.3.

Results are accepted, that is, replicated across samples, if the treatment versus comparison differences exist in both Groups 1 and 2. Although exact, or literal, replication is very difficult an attempt can be made by one group of researchers to reproduce results of another group under reasonably similar circumstances (Lykken, 1970; Martin & Bateson, 1993). In this vein, researchers attempt to draw a sample and reconstruct the situation and procedures in ways that are similar to the study they are trying to replicate. The researcher then compares his or her results to those of the original study. This sort of replication was conducted by Simon and Smith (1983, 1985) and Smith and Whitney (1987) discussed previously in the section on observer bias.

Bronfenbrenner's (1979) notion of ecological validity of experimental results is relevant here. Although not treated as replication per se, ecological validity has one research team comparing the results of an experiment with naturalistic results. So, for example, children could be observed interacting with peers and toys in their preschool classrooms. Then the same, or similar children, would be observed playing in similar social groupings with similar toys in an experimental analogue to that classroom. The similarity, or replication, of the results across the two settings determines the ecological validity of the experiment (see Pellegrini & Perlmutter, 1989).

Yet another form of replication, labeled *constructive replication* by Martin and Bateson (1993), involves very different samples and methods converging with

TABLE 5.3
Replication Sample Design

GROUP 1	*GROUP 2*
Treatment 1	Treatment 1
Treatment 2	Treatment 2
Comparison	Comparison

similar results. For example, in studies of relations between preschool children's oral language and early literacy Dickinson and Moreton (1991) and Pellegrini and Galda (1991) studied preschool children in the Northeastern and Southeastern United States, respectively, in very different classrooms, and using different measures of language and literacy. Despite these differences, their results converged on the finding that specific types of language and symbolic play predicted early literacy. Thus, similar results were obtained by different groups examining a similar question in different ways.

Replication is a conservative approach to accepting research findings. It is also a safeguard against accepting empirical findings prematurely. Indeed, replication should be instituted as a component of our research models and designs. This becomes a particularly important issue when we consider that so much of our child study data have policy implications. Think of the folly involved, not to mention the effects on the lives of children and their families and resources wasted, when we design specific projects, such as "whole language" reading curricula, based on limited research bases. Replication should be a hallmark by which we accept or fail to accept a finding. It is part of the scientific enterprise. Replication should be put, again, into the foreground of observational research; we have our own lessons, as in the cases of the nonreplication of the above presented play findings, which point to its importance.

SUMMARY AND CONCLUSIONS

In this chapter I have pointed out some particular issues that we see as important in designing any observational work. As stressed in earlier chapters, it also should be clear from this chapter that a fair amount of preplanning is necessary. Some of the more basic issues to be resolved involve observer bias, which probably requires using multiple observers, and issues of interdependence. If these issues are not considered prior to the actual observations the data generated will be of limited use. These problems can be particularly insidious because they all lend themselves toward confirming pre-existing conceptions of what we think we will find. Specifically, bias generally operates to confirm our hypotheses, whether they are stated as such or not. To my mind, research is conducted to find something out, not merely reinforce what we already think we know. We, as researchers, students, and teachers should keep an open mind and objectively seek answers to our questions, even when the answers are other than those we want to hear.

SOME THINGS TO THINK ABOUT

1. What are some traits of children that you consider continuous? By way of hint, height is continuous.

2. What are some traits of children which are discontinuous? (Hint: The Piagetian concept of intelligence is discontinuous.)

3. What are some ways in which teachers and other practitioners can guard against bias in their observations of their students?

4. Select children from more than one classroom defined by their teachers as "very smart" and "not so smart." Next, videotape each child while he or she engaged in some cognitive task, such as doing a puzzle or writing. Show the videos of the children to the teachers whose classrooms these children *are not* in. Tell some teachers that specified children are smart and not so smart; you, as the researcher should mislabel some kids and accurately label some kids for the teachers viewing the videos. Have the teachers, individually, tell you why he or she thinks the smart kids are smart and the not so smart kids are that way. Then, assemble teachers in a group and compare their descriptions of the same children who you initially labeled as *smart* and *not so smart*. Do we sometimes make inferences about behavior based on our attributions?

6

Initial Considerations: Entering the Field, Looking Around, and Refining the Plan

TAKING THE FIRST STEPS INTO THE FIELD

In this chapter, I discuss the initial stages involved in conducting observational research. Although we are typically motivated to undertake an observational study for practical or scientific reasons, the specifics of the observational process per se remain vague until we actually enter the field that we are planning to study. No matter how well-formulated our ideas may be, those ideas must interface with the specific situations in which we observe.

Often times, as many observers will tell, the specific contingencies of observational sites necessitates reconsideration, sometimes major, of original plans. For example, we may find out, by initial observations, that specific room arrangements preclude the use of video equipment. More basically, we may find out that what it is we are interested in observing does not occur with any regularity in the situations in which we thought it would occur. Taking an example from my own work, I found, only after a substantial period of observations, that aggression on the playground of a particular school was virtually nonexistent. Although this was very good news for children, parents, teachers, and school administrators, it left me without a study site. A recent vigorous campaign at the school to eliminate fighting (through the uses of more playground supervisors, parent newsletter announcements, and strict enforcement of rules) had been successful: My initial observations certainly supported this conclusion!

In many, if not most, cases, however, we conduct observations in someone else's territory. For example, we may be observing in someone's classroom or in a doctor's waiting room. In these cases, observers must come to terms with key personnel, or infrastructural personnel, occupying the observational site. Becoming familiar with the infrastructural personnel is an important phase in the early phase of field work, so I address it first. Next, I discuss the ways in which initial observations are useful in formulating questions, behavioral category definition and measurement, and habituation of subjects to observers' presence.

Two other important aspects of the observational plan also require preplanning: Deciding when to observe and deciding how much to observe. Specifically, we discuss when data should be collected. The time of the day and the day of the week have obvious and important implications for the sorts of data collected. Mother–child interactions collected on Monday mornings before school and work would look very different from observations of the same folk on Saturday morning. Lastly, the amount of data that should be collected is discussed. The amount of data collected, both on individual cases and across individuals, has important implication for the representativeness of our data. Deciding when and how much to observe, then, is a sampling issue of sorts. That is, we are deciding what part of the day is best to observe those things that we are interested in observing. The "how much" aspect, too, can be considered an aspect sampling. How much data are representative of the phenomena of interest? What amount is required to make reasonable inferences?

The precautions outlined in this chapter should be considered before you begin your project. That is not to say that you will not have to make adjustments during the actual data collection portion of your work, of course; the precautions outlined in this chapter represent some of the more common problems that can be anticipated.

BECOMING FAMILIAR WITH INFRASTRUCTURAL PERSONNEL

Researchers entering a site to conduct observations are guests at that site. As guests, their status is always tenuous but particularly tenuous at the start of the project. One version of this tenuous arrangement has been labeled "mutually voluntary and negotiated entree" by Schatzman and Strauss (cited in Corsaro, 1981) when key personnel grant permission to the researcher to conduct his or her business at the site; this permission can be revoked at any point thereafter. Thus, familiarity with key personnel at the observational site is very important. In some cases they are "gatekeepers," to use Corsaro's apt (1981) term, because they exercise control over access to the site; teachers, administrators, and often custodians are gatekeepers in schools.

Besides the issue of initial and continued access to the site, this phase of the observation is important for ethical and practical reasons as well. Some useful hints, which are discussed later, for initial encounters with infrastructure personnel are displayed in Table 6.1.

Ethically, many researchers, but particularly ethnographers, such as Hymes and Corsaro, argue that the research enterprise should be a collaborative venture between participants and researchers. This stance, as Hymes (1980a) noted most forcefully, can democratize the research process to the extent that interpretations of both participants and researchers are considered and given equal consideration in the planning and interpretation of the project. Indeed, many observers who have conducted research in institutions such as schools, communities, and hospitals often meet initial reluctance. This reluctance is often the result of their previous experience with researchers who have come into the site, imposed their

TABLE 6.1
Interacting With Infrastructure Personnel

1. Schedule meetings as needed
2. Present versions of tentative plans
3. Be democratic/seek input
4. Have a collegial relationship
5. Co-authorship
6. Material rewards

way of looking at the site on the situation (often without much of a preobservation phase), collected their data and left, without further contact.

Such exploitation of participants by researchers can be illustrated with a very simple and common curiosity that is typically ignored by researchers. While negotiating entree to the research site, the researcher, of course, assures participants that they will share the data and final reports. Frequently, however, researchers "forget" their obligations after they have data in hand and have left the site. First hand, I have experienced this, at the hands of one sort of behavioral observer: newspaper reporters. Reporters sometimes call me to get information on a story they are writing. I give information contingent upon their agreeing to clear with me the ways in which that information is used, before publication. Unfortunately this rarely happens. Not only do I resent being misled but I feel exploited. Such exploitation is indeed unethical. Thus, researchers should treat others as they want to be treated. Simple enough.

Open communication between observers and infrastructure personnel also has practical advantages. Certainly exploitative actions, of the sort outlined previously, will not result in the particular researcher, or indeed other researchers, being invited back. Thus, continued access to a data site is at stake. Additionally, getting to know the key people at the site enables the researcher to gain a valued data source. At one level, specific individuals can serve a key informant role. As the meaning and function of specific aspects of the situation being observed may be tactic, in order to unravel the meaning a key informant may be necessary. Relatedly, key personnel can serve as sounding boards for our ideas. For example, they may provide insight into our interpretation of certain events. At another level, insiders can provide valuable logistical information. For example, if a researcher is interested in using a specific type of recording device, teachers may be very helpful in suggesting specific locations where recorders can be placed.

Perhaps the best way to proceed with this phase of the observation is to first present the plan of the research to the key infrastructural personnel. It has been my experience that researchers conducting field research should have variations of their research plan, ranging from the ideal plan (from the researcher's perspective) to the bare essential plan. Researchers should first prepare an explicit statement of the question that they are interested in studying. Next, they should present various versions of the plan (from the ideal to the bare essentials) to the group. Researchers should remain tentative, remembering their status as guests, not wanting to be intrusive. Preschool, primary, and middle-school teachers and the parents of these children are usually very eager to please. Indeed, they typically take on difficult and cumbersome tasks and scheduling regimens if they feel as though they have a stake in the project.

By having a stake I mean that they should be given an opportunity to provide input at various points in the project. They could have input into the planning of the observations and in some cases, in the interpretation of the results. For this reason, researchers should keep in contact with personnel to make sure that things are "running smoothly." Although too many meetings and communications can be a nuisance in the busy lives of our hosts, we must maintain a good balance here.

Different degrees of participation in the research can also be rewarded differentially. In the field of education, it is becoming quite common for university researchers to enter into collaborative relationships with researchers at field sites. In these cases, joint authorship of papers is in order. This strategy, although recommended by Heath (1983, 1985) and Hymes (1980a) a number of years ago, has taken hold in the field of early literacy research in school settings (e.g., Heath, 1985).

Other types of rewards can be offered for participation in research. It is common, for example, for researchers to build financial or material compensation (e.g., books and computers for the school) into their proposals for funded research. As noted in the chapter on ethics in research (Chap. 3), we should use caution that in offering rewards for participation. Specifically, there is a fine line between rewards and bribes.

A basic safe guard is to treat people well and with respect. Do what you promise to do. Offer rewards if people are willing to participate; do not offer them as an enticement to participate. By following these simple rules, you will not only maintain a good relationship with the personnel at the site, but you will probably also collect better data and have more valid interpretations of the data. In short, the lesson of this chapter, presented in advance, is: Do not be in a hurry to begin formal data collection; plan for a specific period of preliminary observation. The time and effort expended in this phase will pay high dividends later.

THE NATURE OF THE QUESTION

Any observational project, indeed any research, should be motivated by a specific question or series of questions that the researcher is interested in answering. The questions may be of scientific interest, such as charting the development of children's ability to read, or of practical interest, such as developing an effective method of teaching young children to read. By the nature of the examples given, it should be clear that the distinction between *basic* and *applied* research is in some cases artificial and in others very blurred. In all cases, the aim is to understand the ways in which children and adults carry on in their everyday lives. Thus, I use the term *research* to include both basic and applied dimensions of the enterprise by which we come to know about phenomena.

Generally, the questions that motivate our research are, at first, pretty global. For example, we may be interested in studying the occurrence of aggression on the playground or children's use of oral language in their preschool and primary school classrooms. Preliminary observations should be conducted in the situation in which we think they occur. Further, we should observe the phenomena according to our current conceptualizations. Obviously, our conceptualization of the research question, the methods we plan on using, and the specific behavioral and verbal categories that we plan on using should all based on a thorough reading of the research literature. That is the starting point.

So, taking the oral language example, we might start observing children in specified classrooms across the school day. These preliminary observations should help us to formulate more explicitly our questions regarding the oral language of specific classrooms. We may find that in one classroom there is a lot of oral language, and very different types of language are used use when talk with their friends compared to when they are talking with peers who are not friends. In another classroom we may find that children's oral language is limited to answering teachers' questions. Thus, at one level, we have reformulated our question to consider three types of discourse participants (teachers, friends, and nonfriend peers).

Correspondingly, preliminary observations may enable us to develop specific hypotheses about the ways in which language is used in specific situations. We may, or may not, then choose to make specific predictions about the ways in which specific types of oral language is used in different situations.

Thus, the preliminary observation period will enable the observer to specify, more exactly, the nature of the question guiding the research. Without such an entry period, the observer is assuming that what they have read about other research projects is all they need to know to study their specific situation; this is probably not the case. The orientations of those researchers whose reports we have read may be very different from ours. That we are motivated by different concerns necessitates that we formulate our questions specifically in situations that are most meaningful to us.

A useful way to organize our preliminary observational notes has been suggested by Corsaro (1981). In his initial observations in a preschool classroom Corsaro organized the notes he took on the situation into the following categories: Field notes (FN), Personal notes (PN), Methodological notes (MN), and Theoretical notes (TN). Generally, FN are behavioral recordings of the participants and their locations. With preliminary observation, this may involve writing descriptions of the situation after you leave the field; to record in the field may be too obtrusive. MN notes include comments on logistics, such as the ability to use a specific type of equipment or coding scheme. PN give insight the observer's personal reaction to specific situations and people, for example, noting that one of the teachers may be feeling left out of the research process. Lastly, TN are larger considerations relating to the nature of the question being posed or the (re)formulation of a specific hypotheses.

Although the researcher may initially think it unnecessary to record observational phenomena that occur repeatedly and are quite obvious, record of all relevant phenomena should be made. It is often the case that what seems obvious and unlikely to be forgotten is often forgotten after hours of observation. In short, records should be kept of what we consider important, no matter how obvious. Organizing initial observations into relevant categories, such as those suggested by Corsaro, seems very sensible. It allows the observer to consider the multitudinous layers of information into separate categories. This level of organization should make the final observation plan more organized and debugged.

MUTUAL HABITUATION: GETTING USED TO EACH OTHER

Conducting systematic observations can be obtrusive. By this I mean that when we, as observers, decide to examine someone closely for a period of time we inevitably have an effect on them. If we are interested in describing the natural lives of our participants, it is imperative that we minimize any obtrusion. The period of initial observation is crucial in this regard to the extent that it gets participants and observers used to each other. The extent that they take each others' presence for granted is, in turn, related to the unobtrusiveness of the observational procedure. Generally, participants do habituate to obtrusion as time progresses. Of course the more obtrusive the observer or procedure, the longer the time needed for habituation.

Probably the least obtrusive is the participant observer, especially if he or she is a natural part of the observational setting, such as a teacher who is a participant observer in his or her own classroom. In this case, the observer is part of the natural scene and thus, minimally obtrusive. What may be obtrusive in this situation, however, is procedure associated with the observation. For example, the participant observer may use recording devices, such as computers, videocameras, or portable radio microphones, or note-taking strategies to which the subjects must habituate.

In the case of a researcher wishing to take a participant observer role, although not one corresponding with actually being employed in the setting, it makes most sense to be at the setting when the focal subjects first enter the setting. So, for example, if we are interested in studying children in schools, observers should be situated in the classroom on the morning of the very first day of class. In this way participants associate the observer with the normal setting.

Participant observers should decide, in advance, the stance they wish to take as participants. Do they want to be treated as if they were children (see Corsaro, 1981)? Do they want to be treated as teachers' aids? Because the specific details of the participant observer approach will be not be discussed in great detail, the interested reader is referred to the following excellent sources: Corsaro (1981) and Fetterman (1998). Suffice it to say that participant observers want to be considered as part of the natural setting; thus, they should attend when the participants attend. Correspondingly, introduction of any sort of recording devices should be put off until the observer thinks participants have accepted them in their role.

The strategy with nonparticipant observers is very different. By nonparticipant observer, I mean an observer who wants to maintain objective distance from those being observed. In the best of all possible worlds, a nonparticipant observer wishes that he or she could be a fly on the wall of their research settings. Thus, these researchers try to conceal themselves behind blinds or one-way viewing screens, or in inconspicuous locations within a research setting. In some cases, so to minimize the effects of their presence, researchers some times leave tape recorders in room to collect language data (see Dunn, 1988, for an interesting example of this approach).

It has been my direct experience that researchers must spend a fair amount of preliminary time in the setting so that participants get used to them and their procedures. With time, however, children do get used to such procedures. By way of illustration, in one project colleagues and I (see Pellegrini & Galda, 1991) had preschool children wearing radio microphones in vests so that we could record their oral language as they played in their classroom. We also video-recorded them from an adjacent observation room through a "one-way" viewing screen. When children put on the vest we also asked them to say their names so that we could have a voice print when we coded the data so that we would be able to distinguish the voice of the focal child from others. Initially children performed for the microphone to the extent that they used exaggerated and loud voices. After numerous observations per child, however, we knew that they were getting used to them in that some youngsters, when huddled in a corner, would use "nasty" language. (Judy Dunn, 1993, also mentions this as a criterion for children being unaware that they are being observed!) I don't think they would have used such language had they been conscious of being recorded. That is not to say that children habituate totally to such devices, I mean that the devices become less obtrusive with time.

Similar time and caution is needed when observing from behind blinds. In cases these blinds may be permeable. Another personal example: Both of my children, as preschoolers, attended the University of Georgia preschool. Each classroom has adjoining observational rooms and one-way screens through which children can be observed. If was my habit, as part of my picking-up-children routine and being a compulsive child-watcher, to drop into the observational room to see what they were doing. On numerous occasions, a child in the classroom would look directly at me through the screen and then say: "Adam, Anna, your Dad's here."

In short, we as observers must take time to have participants get used to our presence. Again, I am not suggesting that participants totally habituate to us. What I am suggesting is that, with time they act in a way that approaches the way they would act if we were not there. The preliminary observation period, thus, is indispensable in this process. Data collected before a reasonable habituation period are questionable at best. They do nothing to advance our understanding of the phenomena under consideration. In the fields of developmental psychology and education this type of data become part of what Bronfenbrenner (1979) described as those collected for as brief a period as possible under strange conditions. This is, at best, a questionable enterprise.

WHEN TO OBSERVE?

The design issues discussed in the next two sections of this chapter (i.e., when to observe and how much to observe) are very basic yet must be given clear consideration and forethought. As noted earlier in this chapter, some preliminary observations may be necessary to determine when the time that specific behaviors can best be observed. We simply cannot observe all participants all of the time. We must determine the best times for observing target behaviors and then determine the appropriate amount of data to be collected. These issues are clearly sampling issues, and related to the representativeness of our data.

Although some of us jokingly respond to students' queries about time and frequency of observations with: As often and for as long as possible, there is some value in this advice. First regarding the *when* to observe, laboratory researchers, generally have eliminated this problem by observing participants during the whole experimental period. There are variations on this procedure: One such exception is where dimensions of the observational period are sampled. For example, in one study of parent–child interaction we (Pellegrini, Brody, & Sigel, 1985) observed parents reading books to their children. Although the whole session was video recorded, only 5 minutes were coded: The first and last 2 minutes and the middle 1 minute. Although I discuss the nature of sampling later in this chapter, suffice it to say for now that one should have good reasons for sampling specific intervals. In other words, observers sampling choices should be guided by some theory: What is it that we think these sample intervals represent? In the book reading example, we decided that most teaching probably went on at the beginning and end, thus we sampled longer from those points.

A related *when* issue for both experimenters and field researchers is the length of the specific observations periods. This issue overlaps with issues concerning *how much to observe*. The variation in the durations of the observation periods in various laboratory and field observations is striking. Some laboratory researchers observe children and parents for a 10- to 15-minute period, whereas others conduct more and longer observations. Similarly, some field observations involve single observations, say in the home, around one event, like book reading. Others, most notably Wendy Haight and Peggy Miller (1993) conduct long (approximately 5 hours) and repeated observations.

The issue of when to observe is related to the representativeness of the observations. That is, do the observations capture what we want them to capture. For the experimentalist, representativeness can probably be maximized by conducting multiple observations of participants in each context of interest; these multiple observations, then, should be aggregated so that there is one score or context. So for example, if we observe children playing with blocks twice and with dolls twice, the two blocks observations should be aggregated into one score as should the two doll scores. Repeated observations and aggregation have the effects of minimizing random variability, and consequently, error in our data analyses. In short, laboratory observations should choose a time interval based on some theory; then they should observe that phenomenon on more than one occasion and aggregate across occasions. Continuing with the parent–child book reading example, length of individual observations periods could be based on the average time parents spend reading a book to their children at home.

The issue of when to observe becomes more complicated for the field observer. The first concern to be addressed by field researchers is to determine when it is during the day that the phenomenon of interest usually occurs. For example, we may be interested in observing the ways in which young children encounter mathematics at home, yet initially, we have no idea when this happens or with whom. Although we discuss in a later chapter various ways of addressing the issue of inventorying children's actions throughout their day with spot sampling and diary techniques, the *when to observe* issue can and probably should be addressed in the preliminary stage of the observation.

Martin and Bateson (1993) offered specific strategies that may be helpful in answering the *when to observe* question during the preliminary stage. These strategies are displayed in Table 6.2.

First, observers could continuously observe in a specific context, such as a home or by following a focal child, for a full 24 hours. This tack is not very practical for most of us to the extent that numerous observers are probably necessary and further, it would most likely meet opposition from participants. By way of compromise, we could sample the 24-hour period by making separate observations during morning, afternoon, and evening sessions. This sampling of different times should inform the observer as to the time and place that the phenomenon of interest occurs.

Once we know when the phenomenon of interest occurs we could make then concentrate on observing during those periods. If more than one period is relevant, such as morning and evening, then, the observer must decide, after extensive observation, the extent to which data from each of those periods are similar or dissimilar; if similar, observations could be conducted at either place and then aggregated. If they are not similar then observations should be collected systematically at each and not aggregated.

The second recommendation is to observe systematically across different parts of the day and then to aggregate these observations (Martin & Bateson, 1993). This approach allows the observer to construct a reasonable picture across

TABLE 6.2
When to Observe?

1. Continuous for 24 hours
2. Sample different parts of the day
3. Observe only one part of the day

the whole day. Obvious limitations to this approach are logistical; for example, will participants tolerate observers in their presence at all times of the day and night. From the observer's perspective, scheduling observations at different times is both time consuming and difficult.

The third approach ignores the problem and observes only at one time of the day, say dinner time (Martin & Bateson, 1993). Such a strategy, we might label this the *strategy of maximum convenience*, is limited to the extent that results can only be generalized to that part of the day. More troublesome, however, is the real possibility that the phenomena of interest may not be occurring at that time or if it does occur, it may take a different form in other parts of the day.

If the observer chooses limited time periods within each day to conduct observations, that is, Strategies 2 and 3, some guidance is needed as to the length of time to observe. Wachs (1985) suggested that a minimum of 1½ hours per observation for field observations. As previously noted, numerous observations should then be conducted and they should then be aggregated at the appropriate interval, such as mornings only or across the whole day.

HOW MUCH TO OBSERVE ?

How much observational data are necessary? This issue relates to the number of participants in the study, the number of observations for each participant, and the duration of those observations. Despite this variety, there is (at one level) a rather simple answer to this question, like the answer to the when to observe question: as much as possible. There is one reason behind the similar answers to the two questions: Larger samples, whether they be samples of participants or samples of different times of day, have the consequence of more closely representing that population of people or universe of behaviors to which we hope to generalize.

If, on the other hand, we are only interested in studying a small group and not making inferences about a population, a larger sample of observations, compared to a smaller sample of observations, more closely approximates the universe of the behaviors of those specific participants. In short, one reason for more being better is that more is usually more representative of the population than is less.

More is also better in terms of statistical analyses of observational data. Larger samples of participants and larger numbers of observations usually result in less sampling error and error variance, where sampling error is the degree of uncertainty about a sample; as the sample increases, error decreases (Suen & Ary, 1989). Sampling error may be particularly problematic in cases of a heterogeneous, or very diverse, sample compared to homogeneous sample, or to having a sample with very similar participants. Because homogeneous samples have fewer differences, there will be less error, therefore we can get away with smaller samples.

SUMMARY AND CONCLUSION

In this chapter I have discussed the importance of preliminary observations. This phase of the observational process is indispensable. It is indispensable because, without it, we would probably have limited access to data collection sites, asks poor questions, collect unreliable and invalid data, and then go on to proffer even more off-base explanations. Thus, the scientific integrity of our work depends on careful preliminary observations. Correspondingly, preliminary observations allow us to enter into a dialogue with our participants. Not only is this a basically democratic act, but it also helps us make more informed decisions.

In this chapter I have pointed out some particular issues that I see as important in implementing any observational work. Based on preliminary observations we should have some idea as to when to observe. The issue of amount, or how much to observe, is more closely relate to issues of sampling and reliability, presented in later chapters. Again, preplanning is necessary. If we ignore preplanning, the quality of the data collected suffer. For example, when we have a limited number of observations of a group or we observed them only at a few specified time, our data are limited. The time of our observations, like the categories themselves, should clearly relate to the questions we have in mind.

7

Observations: Coming Up With Categories

CATEGORY CHOICE AS A THEORETICAL ACT

In this chapter I consider how we arrive at a category system to be used in observational research. I consider using extant systems as well as developing one's own system. As part of this process I discuss the importance of keeping categories and the data derived from each independent of each other.

A coding or category system is a way in which we organize those aspects of the stream of behavior that we choose to study. As noted at various points thus far, interaction between and among individuals is very complicated; there are lots of things going on at many different levels. To illustrate the levels of complexity, I will take for example, the case of a mother and baby interacting around a storybook at bedtime. At a microlevel, we could be concerned with the gaze coordination of the mother and baby and develop a coding system that extracts aspects of the interaction that relate specifically to this issue. At another level, we also might be interested in the heart rate of each participant at different points of the interaction. At a more macrolevel, we might be interested in the ways in which mothers end the stories and say good night to their children and develop a coding system that captures those aspects of the interaction.

Three points are immediately relevant here. First, interactions are immensely complex. Second, because of this complexity, you must choose specific aspects of the interaction to study; we simply cannot describe everything. Third, and as a direct consequent of the first two points, all coding systems *abstract* aspects of interaction. That is, by taking behaviors from the context in which they occur and putting them into some coding or category system we lose some information. It should be the case that we are aware of what is lost and that loss is irrelevant to the questions we asked. So, if we are interested in the ways in which mothers end bedtime stories, coordination of gaze and heart rate throughout the story may be irrelevant and, thus disposable, information.

All of this is to say that our coding or categorization schemes should be driven by our questions and the ways in which these questions interface with the specific situation in which the observations will be made. Though this point may seem obvious it is often lost, so it seems worth some extended discussion. We may choose to develop our own coding system, to reflect specific questions we have in mind and our research context, or we may choose to use or adapt a coding system already developed by someone else.

CAUTION: If you choose someone else's system it may not fit. Very often researchers develop systems that reflect their own theoretical orientations and the specifics of their own situations. As noted by Bakeman and Gottman (1986) a coding system is a theoretical, and personal, statement; thus, to choose someone else's coding system assumes that you, too, share that orientation. Because of the implications of such a choice, it makes ultimate sense in choosing a coding system, even if it is borrowed from someone else, to do so only after you have determined the match between your specific research questions and those specified in extant coding systems.

USING AND ADAPTING SOMEONE ELSE'S CATEGORY SYSTEM

With all this said, a brief word about adopting, adapting, or borrowing extant category, or coding systems is necessary. As noted previously, the use of a coding system should be theoretically consistent with other dimensions of the observational project. Further, be aware of the degree to which the specific questions being asked by you and the originator of the scheme are so similar that they can be answered with the same observational scheme. Lastly, use of the same coding system is obviously appropriate in cases of replication. With those conditions met it is also necessary that the coding system be usable in your specific situation. In short, the choice of an observational coding system should be integrated with all aspects of the study. If not, the results are of very limited utility.

There are numerous places where the student or researcher can find observational coding schemes, and then determine their appropriateness. The most obvious place to look would be current research periodicals in which observational research is utilized. Some of these journals are *Animal Behaviour*, *Child Development*, and *Journal of Educational Psychology*. More dated, but useful source books include the edited volume by Blurton Jones (1972), which includes numerous, microlevel coding systems. More recent schemes for children's social behavior, language, and play are included in Pellegrini and Bjorklund (1998).

A Sad Tale of Inappropriate Borrowing

By way of illustration I provide an example in which a coding scheme was borrowed with little thought to these details. The example is from the area of children's play where a very popular coding scheme to capture the cognitive dimensions of preschool children's play was developed by Smilansky (1968). It included functional, constructive, dramatic, and games play. This system was developed based on preschool children's play in classrooms.

What would happen if a researcher, also interested in the study of children's play, were to use this system, with little preplanning, to study the play of elementary school children's outdoor play on playgrounds? Well, the first thing that would happen is that we would find most forms of behavior on the playground do not fit into this system. For example, on playgrounds we have lots of examples of running, climbing, chasing, and play fighting. Where do these fit in the Smilansky system? They don't, yet they are still probably play!

Further, elementary school students often engage in games with rules and very infrequently engage in functional and constructive play; dramatic play occurs but infrequently. Thus, 75% of the categories (i.e., functional, constructive, and dramatic) are less than appropriate for our target age group.

In short, borrowing of a system with little preplanning is a mistake. As was shown in this example, if an observer were to borrow a coding system without first having asked the appropriate questions, he or she would have wasted time and energy. The observer would have spent considerable time actually collecting observational data only to find out that the behavior being observed did not fit into the system; thus, the data were close to useless. If one chose to use the data anyway, its low quality would be readily apparent and thus probably unacceptable at most levels (i.e., unacceptable as a course project or as a published research report). A better strategy would have been to spend time initially on those steps that are necessary in choosing or developing a category system. In what follows, I explicate a process that will minimize falling into this trap.

WHAT'S THE QUESTION?

The role of the research question is central to the scientific enterprise of inquiring into the nature of things. The initial question, obviously, puts the observer on a track of seeking its answer. Thus, questions determine what we see as relevant and what will be coded; consequently, the question and the resulting coding scheme are important (theoretical) acts. The process by which a question is developed or adapted is cybernetic in nature to the extent that questions are posed, refined, and then reposed. This process is represented in Table 7.1.

Initially, the question posed should be a general one and (obviously) one that is interesting to the investigator. For example, a primary school teacher may ask the question: What role does recess play in the classroom attention of my students? The nature of the questions asked are often the result of a number of interrelated processes: reading the research literature relevant to the question, discussions with colleagues, children and parents, and insights and hypotheses derived from experience.

TABLE 7.1
Question Formulation Process

1. General questions
   Based on reading and experiences
2. Specific questions/hypotheses
   Based on reading and preliminary observations

With these general questions in mind, students should then move toward specific questions. Movement from general to specific questions occurs in the context of more reading the of the research literature relevant to your question and preliminary observation. That is, the specificity of the questions you ask about the general problem can and should be guided by what others have done in this specific area and your general observations. Reading about the ways in which other researchers have answered related questions enables you to begin to understand the nature of the problem more clearly and the theoretical assumptions behind specific questions and coding schemes.

Take the example of recess and classroom attention that we introduced earlier. By reading the related research literature we find out that many observational systems focus on children's level of physical activity when they are on the playground. For example, some researchers code the level of vigor of children's activity along a 7-point continuum (e.g., Maccoby, 1998). The theoretical assumption behind this type of system is that the level of physical activity exhibited on the playground should relate to (antecedent and subsequent) classroom behavior. Theoretically, these assumptions are based on variants of "Surplus Energy Theory" whereby excess energy must be expended so after confinement and thereafter, children can attend to sedentary seat work.

The initial question also becomes refocused based on general, or preliminary, observations with this question in mind. As discussed in the previous chapter, observing relevant situations with a general question in mind will help to refocus the question. For example, you may observe that children are particularly restless (e.g., more physically active and less attentive) in class during a rainy week where there has been no outdoor recess. Additionally, you may observe that on days when children have had unusually long recess periods, they became bored toward the end of the period and an unusually large number of arguments occurred. Thus, you are now concerned not only with the presence or absence of recess but also become more focused on the duration of the confinement period before recess and the recess period itself.

So, the question is now refocused such that you are now looking at the relation among: duration of preceding sedentary task (like sitting at a desk in the classroom), attention, and activity during that time, activity at recess, and attention and activity when children go back into the classroom after recess. The refined question then becomes: "What is the relation between previous confinement and activity in classrooms and on the playground?" Based on this refined question, you then must pay closer attention to the activity dimensions of recess and classroom tasks. Before you can proceed, however, you must decide on the level of specificity of the coding system necessary to answer our question.

COMING UP WITH CATEGORIES

After developing specific questions that we wish to answer, we must next, consider the level of category specificity. There are at least three levels of description that we can consider in developing a coding scheme: Physical

It would be interesting, depending on the nature of one's question of course, to combine various types of categorization systems. For example, we might combine relational and consequential systems to examine the extent to which groups are integrated by gender when they engage in certain types of activities, like chase or games with rules.

At this point we should have a general idea, based on our reading and some informal observations, of the questions we will ask and the type of categories that we will use. Now we must enter the field to look at the behaviors related to our problem. This will allow us to generate a specific coding scheme.

Categories From Preliminary Observations

With knowledge of the question in mind, as well as consideration of the level of specificity to which you aspire, you enter the relevant field to generate a specific coding scheme. Again, decisions about questions and possible dimensions of coding systems are tied to the related observational and theoretical literature. As noted in the preceding chapter, however, it is important before this stage, to determine whether the phenomena of interest are observable at a particular site. With this question being answered affirmatively, we are ready to observe.

Hanging Out. The first stages of the observational process involve "hanging out," or spending lots of time in a setting looking at a variety of things. You, as an observer, take with you into the field your research questions and the level of categorization to which you aspire. With these "sensitizing concepts" (Patton, 1990, p. 218) in mind, you look at those things that you think will be interesting. Again, I stress the fact that you cannot observe everything; there is simply too much out there. Further, you do not go into the field *tabula rasa*; you have these guiding concepts, questions, and category levels to provide some structure to your observations.

It probably makes most sense, in the very first observations, for the observer to not use any types of recording devices, such as paper and pen, tape recorder, or video camera. This rule is especially important to follow where observers will actually be in the field of observation, as compared to a remote site, such as a one-way viewing booth or filming from a distance. The reason is straight forward enough: You want the participants to get used to you before you introduce yet another (i.e., besides yourself) strange entity.

During this hanging out time you should be thinking about your question and categories the ways in which they are realized in these preliminary observations. Are the categories capturing the essence of what participants are doing? Are the categories too involved? Not involved enough? Further, you should be noting the participants who exhibit those behaviors in which you are interested. Also note the location of these acts. Immediately after you leave the field you should either write out or dictate into a tape recorder your thoughts on these processes.

Writing (Saying) It Out. After participants have gotten used to you, you can start recording behavior in the field. To this end, most students of behavioral observation suggest that you write out, in expository form, what it is you see. In some cases, and after participants have gotten used to your presence, it may be easier for the observer to whisper these descriptions into a tape recorder than to write them out. In my own observations of children on playgrounds, I have used tape recorders, not notes, because the tape recorder enabled us to record more information, relative to writing. Further, we did not have to take time to look at the paper to record thoughts; we could keep my eyes on the subject matter at hand. Again, we cannot write or record everything, so we let our questions and category levels serve as our guide.

The form that these notes or dictations take should be such that objective descriptions of participants behavior is recorded, as well as our own interpretations and notes on the phenomena (Corsaro, 1981; Patton, 1990). Objective descriptions of behavior (or low inference if objectivity is questioned) are those where the level of inference made by the observer is kept to a minimum. Indeed, this level is close to noting physical descriptions of behaviors. In Table 7.3, I outline a number of contrasts between objective and subjective language used to describe the same behaviors.

The objective descriptions in the first column are physical descriptions of behavior with minimal inference. By that we mean, the observer is not inferring intent or motivation for specific acts; he/she is describing in terms of movements as seen. Objectivity in the descriptors chosen is crucial at this stage.

Objectivity is crucial at this stage to the extent that you, as a new-comer to a specific field, may not understand fully what it is you are observing. Objective descriptions help you reformulate your questions to more accurately reflect the nature of the phenomena being observed. For example, if you initially considered a description by consequence category system, you may have grouped behaviors inappropriately with inferential descriptors. Objective descriptors allow you to evaluate the degree to which your initial categories are true.

Let us take, for example, the use of the terms *constructive play* and *putting blocks in a row* as contrastive cases. Obviously, in using constructive play to describe what a child is doing you are making inferences about what he or she is doing; you are inferring a consequence of an action or set of actions. This inference may

TABLE 7.3
Objective/Subjective Descriptors

Objective	*Subjective*
Wide smile	Having fun
Open hand hit at	Fighting
Paints on paper and table	Sloppy painting
Putting blocks in a row	Constructive play

be based on the fact that the child is alone, and thus not vocalizing about his or her actions, so he or she must be constructing, not doing something else. Thus, you may have incorrectly classified this set of behaviors. You may later observe that the same child exhibiting the same physical behaviors with a peer seems to be engaging in pretend play!

Putting blocks in a row, on the other hand, describes the same action, with minimal inference. Such a description, when tied to other description, such as, the child moving a block around the floor saying "brmmmmmm," would allow you to reconstitute your constructive and dramatic play categories. You can maximize the likelihood of your descriptions being objective if you describe the actual behaviors involved. Direct quotes from participants are also very helpful in generating initial descriptions.

It also may be helpful at this stage to use the observational procedures recommended by Corsaro's (1981), and defined in the previous chapter, when entering the field. For example, methodological notes can be used by the observer to supplement the objective descriptions. As suggested in the preceding chapter, these notes are good complements to the descriptive notes in that they provide some guidance to the ways in which the observations should be conducted in the future. From the aforementioned case of blocks, a methodological note might suggest that children playing alone with blocks is not necessarily constructive because children do not often talk when they are alone. When children are alone, we should look for other indicators to determine the type of play the child is engaged in.

Personal notes also complement initial descriptions (Corsaro, 1981). You might note, for example, that you have a very difficult time observing in the blocks area because it is too dark; thus, you cannot distinguish different types of behavior very well. Theoretical notes, too are helpful. In this case, you could note that the frequently reported finding that children playing alone with blocks engage in constructive play may be misleading. It may be due to the fact that when alone, children do not talk, thus, you do not code the behavior as dramatic because we do not have utterances indicating fantasy.

After these descriptions, and various notes, are taken you should then try to square this new information with the questions you asked and the level of categorization that you have considered. You are now ready to outline some specific categories.

THE SPECIFIC CATEGORY SYSTEM

The first rule of thumb in generating a specific category system is to keep the system tied to the specific question. The second rule of thumb, is to keep the system only as complicated as is necessary to answer the question. In this section, I pose two separate questions and walk through the process by which a coding system is developed. But before that is done, however, we must address some technical properties of categories.

Technical Properties of Categories

Categories should be homogeneous and mutually exclusive, and sometimes exhaustive (Bakeman & Gottman, 1986; Martin & Bateson, 1993). By *homogeneous*, I mean that all subcomponents of a category should be related to the same construct. That is, they should be providing different exemplars of the same phenomenon; there should not be any lumps, or outliers. By way of simile, we can compare the homogeneity of a bottle of homogenized milk with nonhomogenized milk. In the former case the cream is evenly distributed throughout the bottle. In the latter case, the cream and the milk are separate, although both in the same bottle (for those of us old enough to remember such things). The components of individual categories should be like the homogenized milk, with individual components all being part of the same whole. For example, a homogeneous category for rough-and-tumble play might include: smile, hit at, and run. All these behaviors co-occur and note different dimensions of the same category.

A nonhomogeneous (heterogeneous) category would include the components already noted as well as outliers, like bite and punch. Again, you determine category homogeneity empirically (i.e., to what degree to they actually co-occur) and theoretically (i.e., can they be related for some plausible reasons). If categories are not homogeneous, they are confusing and invalid; by aggregating across dissimilar components of categories you may be hiding systematic patterns in the data.

Relatedly, categories should also be mutually exclusive. By this I mean that the individual categories should be measuring only one thing at a time, not more than one thing; behaviors should fit into one and only one category. Thus, a behavior cannot simultaneously be coded both as rough-and-play and aggression; it goes into only one category. Similarly, take the case of having two categories: social interaction and conversation. They are certainly conceptually, and probably empirically, interrelated to the extent that conversation is a subset of social interaction. In this case, you would want new codes. Either you would collapse conversation into social interaction or have two social interaction categories: verbal and nonverbal. That categories are mutually exclusive is particularly important for data analyses. If different categories are measuring the same, or related, categories we are limited in our ability to say anything about the separate categories.

It is often the case, however, that one set of behaviors can be coded in a number of different ways. For example, rough-and-tumble play can be also be categorized as vigorous play or cooperative play. With preschool boys much of it can probably be coded as dramatic play. That we choose to categorize it as R&T, rather than the alternates, is a theoretical matter. In terms of mutual exclusivity of categories, by extension, we should not have vigorous play or cooperative play categories defined such that R&T could fit into either.

Lastly, category systems could be exhaustive. By exhaustive I mean that we have categories that can account for all of the behavior that occurs in our particular setting. I say categories "could be," rather than "must be," because it is really optional. It is nice to have an exhaustive system if we want to construct an ethogram of a particular context to the extent that we have a full index of behavior in that area. Exhaustive systems are necessary, however, if you want to look at sequences of behavior. Specifically, if you want to look at the probability of an individual behavior following another, you must have categories for all possible behaviors that could be observed. A short cut here could involve having a *dust bin* category, such as *Other Behavior,* which accounts for less than relevant behavior. Alternatively, observers could also note unusual behaviors that occur but are not coded. In short, you should think of coding behavior into categories that are homogeneous and independent of each other.

Two Examples of Category System Development

In this section, I walk through the process of developing two separate coding systems. In the first case I address the way in which an observer can use a variant of an existing coding system to answer a question. I chose this specific scenario because it seems to be fairly common for observers, at all levels, to adopt an existing model. In the second example, I walk through the development of a system from the bottom up.

Starting With an Extant System

Let us say that you are motivated to conduct an observation because we are interested in the ways in which different preschool-age children play together with different toys. You, as kindergarten teacher, may be concerned with using play and play centers as a way in which to stimulate children's development. That query serves as the initial, general question. With this general question in mind, you, then, start to read the play and toy literatures. As part of your reading you find out that play is defined in various ways; thus, your initial reading is aimed at a more exact definition of what is meant by play. This clarification of a definition of play is crucial as it will, in turn, provide a basis for a way in which you will code play behavior. That is, the components of a definition of play could also serve as dimensions for codes that define play.

As you read the definition of play literature you find out that the play of preschool children has been extensively described according to both social and cognitive dimensions in a relatively simple scheme generated by Kenneth Rubin (see Rubin, Fein, & Vandenberg, 1983). The components of the scheme involve a description of play along cognitive dimensions (functional, constructive, and dramatic) and social dimensions (solitary, parallel, and interactive). This scheme, as you find out, has also been used to describe the sophistication (in cognitive and social terms) of the different forms of play. For example, you find out that children engaging in interactive-dramatic and solitary-constructive play tend to score higher on social and cognitive measures than children engaging in solitary-dramatic play. You also find out, by both reading and observing children in your classroom, that specific contextual configurations, such as specific toys, influence the levels of play on this scheme.

At this point you reformulate your question to reflect your new knowledge. It becomes: How does the social-cognitive level of play vary in different play settings? Thus, you seem to be working with a very general, and inferential, definition of play, (i.e., a description by consequence). You take the observation scheme and begin to use it to conduct preliminary observations. Thus, you have these nine categories (i.e., three cognitive categories by three social categories) in your head as you observe children and write down descriptions. Indeed, you may have even constructed a matrix, as displayed in Table 7.4, by which to classify the behaviors.

As you observe, however, you recognize that some things that children do not seem to fit very well into those nine categories; for example, where do we put children's playful wrestling? In this case, we may want to add a category called *rough play*; now you have 10 categories. You also observe that there seems to be tremendous within-category variability for one category: interactive-dramatic. For example, within the interactive-dramatic category, you notice that some children's make believe play is very well-integrated. Other children's play, while being interactive-dramatic, is more fragmented, or consisting of a series of minimally related play themes. Thus, the problem becomes that the system seems to be too macro for you: It does not differentiate children's level of pretend coordination within the interactive-dramatic category.

Now you need to come up with a complementary coding system. That is, you may use the nine code system plus the R&T category and develop a complementary system. That complementary system, in turn, is based on your reformulated questions: What are the social cognitive dimensions of children's play with different toys? How integrated is the interactive-dramatic play of children? You, then, will review the literature specific to integrating play themes while observing. You may then decide that integration is best measured by interconnected language. Thus, your complementary coding system includes linguistic measures: response and nonresponse sequences, topic match between initiation and response, and disagreements. If the original nine plus one categories and the complement to the interactive-dramatic category are sufficient to answer your question, you now have a coding system. You should recognize that your system is homogeneous, exhaustive, but not mutually exclusive. The interaction catego-

TABLE 7.4
An Example of a Play Coding Matrix

	Solitary	*Parallel*	*Interactive*
Functional			
Constructive			
Dramatic			

ries are a subset of interactive-dramatic behavior; thus, these categories are interdependent and should be used as dimensions of one construct: interactive-dramatic play.

Developing Your Own Category System

In this case I begin with the general question of whether children's R&T escalates into aggression. To answer this question, again, you begin by reading the literature on R&T and aggression because you will need to have categories for observing each. We find by reading and observing that aggression and R&T have been conceptualized as very different constructs, where R&T is playful and fun for children and aggression is harmful; you also observe that when children are doing the former they often smile or laugh (a dimension of a coding system) and in the latter they often frown or grimace. Further, R&T play, generally, has children alternating roles, say between the top and bottom positions in wrestling; aggression is not reciprocal, it is unilateral. Both R&T and aggression, however, involve vigorous physical contact (e.g., hitting) and large motor activity (e.g., running). At this point, based on initial readings and observations we have the skeleton of a coding system that involves affect (smile and frown), roles (reciprocal and unilateral), and physical contact behavior. The components of these categories are both micro, to the degree that some describe physical behaviors and smiles, and consequential, to the degree that roles are being described.

With this level of categorization in mind, you continue your preliminary observations, looking specifically for behaviors that meet your criteria. As you observe you may find that there are different types of R&T. For example, you find that certain vigorous behaviors tend to co-occur: smile, push, hit at, run away from, run after. In other cases, other physically vigorous behaviors co-occur: smile, hit at, kick(ed) at, grapple, roll on ground, top position, bottom position. You seemed to have arrived at a new distinction (and consequently, two new categories) in rough play: chase and play fighting. Could it be, you refocus, that play fighting, not chase, is likely to escalate into aggression? At this point, you have three categories (*chase*, *play fighting*, and *aggression*) that are homogeneous and mutually exclusive. The level of description is, for the most part, at the physical description level. You seem to have your categories and are almost ready to observe.

I say almost because your question was a sequential question to the extent that you asked about the escalation of R&T into aggression, that is, the probability of different forms of R&T leading to aggression. As noted earlier, in order to answer sequential questions, your observational system must be exhaustive. At this point you must decide the degree to which you are interested in describing all of the other behaviors that you have observed. If you are interested in this, your question has changed to include not only the relation between R&T and aggression, but also: What are all the behaviors which occur on the playground? If you are not interested in the larger question you should merely code an *other* category. So, our system would include: *Play fighting*, *chasing*, *aggression*, and *other*.

MEASURING CATEGORIES

Now that we have our category system it is time to consider the ways in which we can measure them. In short, how can they be counted? Specifically, in this section we first discuss independence of our units of analysis. Units of analysis refer to our choice of the unit that will be subjected to statistical testing. For example, in studying children in a classroom we may have the category: *student question*. The unit of analysis becomes the way in which we count occurrences of this category: Do we use the individual child as the unit of analysis, or the classroom. As we will see, such choices have important implications for the meaning of our data and has important effects on the reliability (i.e., representativeness) of our data.

Independence of Measurement

The notion of independence of behavioral measures is an important one. By independence we mean, generally, that people or behaviors being observed are assumed to be unrelated. This assumed independence is particularly important for students utilizing parametric statistical procedures. These statistical procedures assume that individual observations and individual participants have been sampled randomly and thus, are independent; any relations among the variables should be due to hypothesized relations. The implications of violating independence assumptions is that within group error variance is minimized and, correspondingly, we raise the probability of rejecting the null hypothesis (see Applebaum & McCall, 1983, for a more detailed description of the statistical implications). Again, the null hypothesis assumes that there are no between group differences or no associations between measures. The null is rejected when differences or associations are found.

In everyday language this means that violating independence assumptions often results in finding between group differences to be statistically significant and generalizable, even when this is not so. Independence violations are quite common. In this section I outline some of the more commonly occurring threats to independence as well as some ways avoid them. These threats and some possible solutions, in the order in which they will be discussed, are displayed in Table 7.5.

The *pooling fallacy* was a term introduced by Machlis (cited in Martin & Bateson, 1993, pp. 34–35). Pooling occurs when separate observations, not individual participants, are treated as the unit of analysis. So, for example we may have 25 third graders ($N = 25$) being observed 10 times during their recess period, for a total of 250 observations. The pooling fallacy would treat the N as 250, not as 25. In this case we want to generalize our results to children not observations, so N should be 25 participants, not 250. The separate observations of each child are not independent of each other and should not be treated as such. Specifically, each individual's behavior should be related from observation 1 though 10; individual children should be different from each and they should be treated as the unit of measurement, not the individual observation. To treat indi-

TABLE 7.5
Some Threats and Solutions to Nonindependence of Observation Scores

Threats	*Possible Solutions*
Pooling	N = Subjects, not observations
Contiguous observations	Aggregate within session
Interrelated categories	Keep mutually exclusive Recognize subscore dependence
Litter/group effects	Group as unit Deviation scores Individual & group factors

vidual observations, not children, as separate units violates the independence assumption.

A related issue involves contiguous observations on individuals and whether to treat these individual scores as separate scores or to aggregate the multiple observations on each participant for specific sessions. Continuing with the example of recess observations, suppose that each of the individual children in the class were observed every 2 minutes for a 20-minute recess period; thus, each child is observed 10 times per recess period. The issue here relates to the way in which we treat the individual observations of each child. Do we treat each of the 10 observations on each child as a separate score for that child or do we aggregate all 10 scores into 1 observation? Certainly, the latter approach is more conservative to the extent that a child's behavior across a 20-minute recess period are probably interrelated and should be aggregated. For example, if we have a child playing football at Time 1, he or she probably will be playing football at Time 10; thus, each recess period would yield 1 observation per child. Treating separate observations within the recess period as distinct measurement point assumes that each is independent. In this case, they probably are not independent.

It becomes an interesting empirical problem, however, to determine what time lag between observations is necessary before we can treat separate, contiguous observations of individuals as independent. Although time is an issue, it is unclear as to what time span is enough. Certainly, the nature of the task itself is relevant here. We may be able to treat free behaviors as one set of separate observations and a teacher lead games during the same period as another set of observations. As a rule of thumb, we might consider aggregating individuals' contiguous behavior within theoretically or empirically, distinct behavioral categories or events.

Determining the extent to which behavioral categories are independent is another issue. As I discuss in a later chapter, observational categories should be homogeneous (i.e., comprised of interrelated components) and mutually exclusive (i.e., not different ways of measuring the same construct). Of course two distinct categories (e.g., physical attractiveness and peer popularity) can be interdependent for reasons other than redundancy. Here, we are concerned with behavioral categories that are interdependent because of behavioral overlap. For example, a category labeled *smile* shares similar behavioral attributes with a category labeled *positive affect*. Thus, these two categories should probably be aggregated into a more molar category called: *positive affect display*.

Categories can also be interdependent because of the ways in which we measure them. For example, in my own research (Pellegrini, 1993) on children's R&T, I measured the relative frequency with which children engage in R&T (i.e., the proportion of total of an individual's outdoor behavior which is R&T) as well as the variety of the behaviors comprising R&T (i.e., the number of different R&T behaviors exhibited by a participant). These two measures, obviously, are interdependent in that the variety measure is derived from the proportion measure. Now, we may want to consider these measures as separate for theoretical reasons, but we should not lose sight of their statistical interdependence.

The last independence issue, labeled *litter effects* by Martin and Bateson (1993), is probably the most commonly violated. Although litter effects refer directly to the interdependence of behavior of litter mates, say of siblings, they can also refer to the interdependence of nonkin individuals who are part of the same social grouping. For example, it is common in one branch of educational research, labeled as *product-process research*, to observe quartets of students interacting around a task. Typically in this research tradition, individuals' utterances and behaviors (i.e., the processes) are coded and then related to some dimension of task performance (i.e., the product). Furthermore, if there are 10 groups of 4, the *N* is typically treated as 40, not 10. Thus, individuals within each group are treated as if they are independent of the other individuals, utterances, and behaviors in that group. This seems problematical: To say that the behavior and language of the individual children in the quartets are independent of each other is like my saying that the following two utterances by two members of a group are independent of each other.

Speaker 1: What time is it?
Speaker 2: 3:30.

Obviously, when people interact with each other as part of a group, individual behaviors are related to the behaviors of the group members. Thus, in this example, the quartet, not the individual, should probably be treated as the unit of analysis.

Similar problems of interdependence are faced when conducting observations in classrooms. Individual children's social behavior within one classroom is probably interrelated to the extent that each child has an effect on other children. Additionally, each individual child is influenced by the classroom teacher. In this case, the classroom may be the appropriate unit of analysis.

Addressing the Problems of Interdependence

Obviously these issues put the observer or researcher against some logistical problems, such as having to observe a larger number of classrooms, rather than observing individuals within fewer classrooms. The implication of this choice is working with a research designs utilizing smaller samples, such as classrooms rather than children within classrooms, or if independence assumptions are violated, having a larger sample, say 25 children from each of two classes for an *N* of 50, rather than 2. Alternately, the two classrooms could be treated as replication samples. In this case results would be accepted in they replicated in both groups.

There are situations, however, when we are interested in the ways individuals within groups interact and thus, it is important to untangle group and individual effects. For example, if we have a male and a female interacting, on separate occasions, with male-preferred and female-preferred activities, we might want to know the way in which each of the groups of individuals interact with the specific activities. This would not be possible, however, if we were to treat the dyad as the unit of analysis. A number of solutions have been proffered to address this issue, and two are discussed here: deviation scores and treating individuals within groups as separate factors in data analyses.

More technically, statisticians have developed a technique, hierarchical linear modeling (HLM; Bryk & Raudenbush,1992) to address units of analysis that are embedded in larger units; for example, children are embedded in classrooms and in schools. Thus, children within a classroom and within a school are influenced by these other hierarchic factors and these factors probably affect their scores in a systematic way. HLM enables a researcher to separate and examine these effects. The interested reader is referred to Bryk and Radenbush.

Deviation Scores. Deviation scores involve using individual scores for a specific behavior minus the group score for that same behavior. Following the boy–girl dyad example previously discussed, myself and Jane Perlmutter (Pellegrini & Perlmutter, 1989) studied same- and mixed-gender dyads of preschool children playing with different toys and coded their play along nine dimensions (e.g., interactive-dramatic and solitary-constructive) and their utterances along six dimensions (e.g., commands and imitations). For the same-gender dyads, dyads were the unit of analyses; that is, scores from both individuals within the dyad were aggregated to yield a male score for male dyads and a female score for the female dyads. For mixed-gender dyads, however, deviations scores were calculated for each dyad such that an individual's score for commands, for example, would equal his or her score minus the commands for that dyad. In this way the individual's behavior is considered as a dimension of the group processes. Others, such as Cronbach (1976), have also discussed variations of the deviation score method.

Individuals Within Groups as a Factor in Analyses

Separate Individual Scores Can Be Treated as Individual Factors. This specific procedure is relevant to those researchers using factorial designs and analyses of variance in their data analyses. Because this is not a statistics book, we only touch on this briefly, and the interested reader is referred to Applebaum and McCall (1983) for a full and very understandable treatment of data analysis techniques. Following the play example, we would have two factors in our analyses, gender of target (2: boys and girls) and gender of partner (2: boys and girls), as well as the type of toys. In this way we can examine the extent to which boys, when girls are their partner, give commands while playing with male-preferred toys.

In short, it is important to consider the interdependence of participants in social interaction. Observers, however, cannot assume that all social groupings result in interdependent social behavior; thus, some preanalysis, both theoretical and empirical, are necessary. Borrowing from Applebaum and McCall (1983), the exam scores of a group of undergraduates in a class should, hopefully, not be treated as interdependent scores. On the other hand, their discussions in the classroom, after and before the exam are almost certain to be interdependent. In short, much, but not all, of group behavior is interdependent. When this is the case, care needs to be taken so that the individual's and group contributions are untangled.

CONCLUSIONS

In this chapter we have outlined a process by which you as an observer come up with a set of categories by which behaviors will be categorized during observations. We also considered problems associated with interdependent categories. The most basic concern in developing a category system is in the nature of the question being asked: The categories that are used should be aimed specifically towards answering that question. Asking a question is a very personal, and important, process in that it is what you consider to be interesting. This question, in turn, determines the way in which you will conduct your subsequent work in this specific area. So, to borrow someone else's coding requires a great deal of thought. You can borrow only to the degree to which you and the originator agree on very important issues of theory and method. Thus, it makes most sense to spend lots of time explicating a good question. Is your question similar to those who have already developed observational systems? Are the children of the same age and social circumstances? If so, use of an existing scheme may make sense. There are no shortcuts.

You may choose, on the other hand, to develop your own category system. These categories should reflect your specific question/theory as well as the idiosyncracies of the situation in which you are observing. Categories systems should be sensitive to all of these demands in order to capture what it is the participants are doing. In this regard observers who use inductive category systems are trying to develop systems that are maximally sensitive to the observational context. Thus, at this level, there is minimal difference between insiders' and outsiders' approaches to observational methods. We should also consider the independence of our categories as results our skewed toward accepting our hypothesis and rejecting the null hypotheses when categories are interdependent.

SOME THINGS TO THINK ABOUT

1a. Take the case of reading books to children before bedtime. Generate a list of three *general* questions that could be use as a basis for an observational study.

1b. For each general question, generate one more specific question.

1c. For each specific question list five general behavioral categories that could be used to help answer each question.

1d. For each general category, list three specific observable behaviors.

2. Take each of the nine categories of the social cognitive play matrix discussed in this chapter. For each, list five possible physical descriptions and five possible relational descriptions.

8

Measuring Behavior and Rules For Sampling and Recording

In this chapter I address some very specific procedures involved in measuring behavior. As discussed in the preceding chapters, basic choices are made by researchers in the ways in which they choose to measure behavior. Issues of category independence are especially important. In this chapter, I continue this discussion by describing some of the ways in which categories can be measured. By *measure* I mean different ways in which categories can be quantified. Next, I describe the ways in which the categories can be sampled from the stream of on-going behavior and then recorded. Specific measurement concerns covered include: frequency, duration, latency, pattern, and intensity.

MEASURING BEHAVIOR

I discuss five ways in which behavior can be measured: duration, frequency, pattern, latency, and intensity (Martin & Bateson, 1993; Suen & Ary, 1989). These measures, with corresponding definitions and examples, are displayed in Table 8.1.

Although there are variations on the measures of behavior presented previously, these five measures are a sound basis by which to measure behavior and develop more refined measures.

TABLE 8.1
Measures of Behavior

Measure	*Definition*	*Example*
Duration	Time of a behavior pattern	R&T bouts are 20-secs
Frequency	Number of behaviors/time unit	3 hits/hour
Pattern	Behavior across time	hit/push/hit/bite
Latency	Time from x to behavior	10-secs from seeing word to reading
Intensity	Degree of amplitude	Vigor rated 1, 2, 3

To begin with, we, as observers, should note the time period or session length during which the observations are occurring because it is an important qualifier of the measures we generate. As observers we may be concerned with sampling either specific behaviors, such as aggression when ever it occurs during a specified period, or we may be interested in sampling behaviors across a specified time period, say aggression during a 20-minute time period. In both the behavior and the time sampling cases, the issue of session length is relevant. Let us say for the purpose of the examples presented here that we are observing children during 20-minute free play periods in their classrooms.

With this as background, let us start with the first measure: duration. *Duration* is a measure of the length of a behavior during a specific session and it is usually measured in terms of seconds (and parts thereof), minutes, and hours. Duration can refer to the interval from the onset (or beginning) of a behavior to the offset (or termination) of that behavior. Taking the 20-minute session length noted previously, we might say that for a specific child the duration from onset to offset of drawing was 4 minutes. This could be expressed as 4 minutes per 20 minutes, and defined as total duration.

Mean durations are averages of total durations, across individuals or within individuals, across sessions. Let us say that we observed four children whose total durations of drawing were: 3, 2, 5, and 10 minutes. The mean duration would be the sum of these four durations (20 minutes) divided by 4.

Relative or proportional duration is the duration divided by the session length: 4/20 or 0.20. Although the relative measure is a timeless index of specific behavior, the total and mean durations are explicitly stated in terms of time (Martin & Bateson, 1993).

A complement to duration measures is the measurement of frequency. *Frequency* is a measure of the occurrence of specific behaviors within an observational session. So during our hypothetical 20-minute session, we observed 6 R&T bouts. Discussion of frequency in relation to the length of the observational session becomes very clear again. Without consideration of the session length, the number 6 becomes almost meaningless. Does the 6 mean that it was observed 6 times in 1 minute, 5 minutes, 30 minutes, or 3 hours? Obviously, the 6 has very different meaning in each of the cases. Frequency, then, should be discussed in terms relative to the session length; thus, frequency could really be expressed as a rate to the extent that we measure frequency/time unit. In the aforementioned examples, we would have different rates of R&T/minute.

Frequency and duration are very common measures of behavior. Indeed, it is often interesting to collect both types of measures on behavioral categories. Obviously, the nature of one's questions should drive the type of measures used but frequency and duration can sometimes provide complementary information for specific behaviors. Both, for example, are excellent measures of what individuals spend their time doing and, correspondingly, the degree to which individuals expend resources. Frequency tells us something about the rate of expenditure whereas duration tells us the extent to which the expenditure is sustained. It may be the case, for example, that children frequently, in the course of recess, run, but the duration of each bout is brief. Longer durations may be exhibited in other types of behaviors, such as games.

Patterns of behavior are measures of specific categories of behavior across time. These patterns may not, however, be expressed in terms of a specific time interval; their order of occurrence may be noted with no mention of time between acts. For example, during our 20-minute observation session we may observe that children's play is patterned in the following way: chase, push, chased, hit at, chase. Although we note that this took place during a 20-minute session, we may choose not to note the actual duration of the components of the pattern. If we chose to add a temporal dimension we could add the duration of each of the individual play components and to the total play bout. The time dimension may be useful, and with the use of mechanical recording devices it is increasingly easy to record time. By tying patterns to a temporal dimension we come closer to representing its actual occurrence.

Latency, like duration, is specifically a measure of time. With latency, we measure the time from when the focus individual is exposed to a relevant stimulus to his or her behavioral response. Some very common examples of latency measures, from the education and cognitive psychology literatures, respectively, include *wait time* and *reaction time*. Wait time is the latency between when an instructor asks a question of a student and when the teacher talks again, assuming that the student does not talk in the interval. The latency in this case is a matter of a few seconds. Reaction time is a measure of the latency between the presentation of a stimulus, such a word to be read and the child's reading of the word. Reaction time is usually expressed in terms of microseconds. We assume that longer latencies are indicative that mental processing is occurring. So in the cases of 10- and 15-microsecond latencies to two presented words, we could assume that the second was more difficult for the children to the extent that he or she took more time to process it.

Intensity is the last measure to be discussed and it is probably the most difficult to measure. *Intensity* is a measure of degree or amplitude, rather than frequency (Martin & Bateson, 1993). Following the R&T example, intensity could be measured as high, medium, and low. Because such judgments can be very subjective, and consequently unreliable, it is very important to specify the ways in which we differentiate levels of intensity. Martin and Bateson suggested using local rates as one measure of intensity. By *local rates* they mean the number of components of a behavior that occur within a certain time interval.

Take the case of R&T again where it is defined as having 10 components (e.g., tease, hit or kick at, chase, poke, sneak up, carry child, pile on, play fight, hold or push). A local rate could be the number of those components that occur within a certain period, say 2 minutes. More intense ratings would be those that had more components than less intense ratings. Of course this type of measure (implicitly) assumes that individual components are equal in terms of intensity. That is, by adding together different units, they are all treated as if they all make an equal contribution to the whole. This may be problematic, however, when individual components are not equal; for example, if we had run and walk as components of chase we could not treat them as equal as run is more intense (e.g., evidenced by a higher heart rate) than walking.

One way to address this issue is to measure intensity by consequence (Martin & Bateson, 1993). In such cases we could measure the result of a specific behavior. Take the running–walking example from earlier: We could measure the distance covered during an interval, the number of calories burned, or heart rate as consequential measures. Although some of these measures may be problematic and obtrusive to use (e.g., taking heart rate), others, such as distance are not. Distance can be measured, for example, by dividing the observation area into graph-like plots so we can note the number of plots covered during a specified time. A bit more difficult, and obtrusive, is the use of actometers. *Actometers* are mechanical devices attached to a foot or hand that record level of activity. Such measures may, however, be both impractical and undesirable to use, thus compounding the problem of objectively measuring of intensity.

One way in which I have dealt with this conundrum in my own research is to use definitions of intensity that have been objectively related to these more obtrusive measures in previous research (i.e., the validity of the measures was established by relating it concurrently to another measure). Specifically, in our research on children's recess behavior we are interested in the level of vigor of their behavior, a measure of intensity. Although vigor can be most objectively measured with an actometer or heart rate, it can also be measured by drawing on research that measured vigor with observational criteria and then related those criteria actometer readings.

In our case, we coded vigor along nine dimensions, as illustrated in Table 8.2. In a system derived from Eaton and Enns (1986), Categories 1 to 3 were coded when the participant was lying down with high, medium, and low ratings assigned to specific sets of behaviors. Categories 4 to 6 and 7 to 9, respectively, referred to sets of behavior while participants were sitting and standing. Each measure also had a corresponding caloric expenditure value. Thus, intensity could be an interesting, but difficult, measure of behavior to measure objectively.

In this portion of the chapter I have addressed specific ways in which behavior can be measured. As noted, these measures are generally concerned with behavior along temporal dimensions and along frequency dimensions. At one level, these measures can be described in terms of *states* or *events* (Bakeman & Gottman, 1986; Martin & Bateson, 1993). States and events are differentiated in terms of duration. States are usually longer in duration than are events. For example, R&T bouts may be considered states while a cry may be considered an event. Events are used measured along the frequency and intensity dimensions whereas states are usually measured by time and pattern dimensions.

We stress that the relative nature of specific measures should be considered. For example, in reporting frequencies, frequencies relative to a specific time interval are important to note. Similarly, relative scores may be necessary in cases in which individuals have been not all be observed for equal periods. In this case, relative scores, too, are important. Behaviors relative to total observational time for each individual could still be used. In other cases, individual components of

TABLE 8.2
Rating Scale for Estimating Caloric Expenditure

Posture	*Intensity*	*Weight*	*Description*
1. Lying	Low	1.9	Lying motionless or slight change in position; includes stationary position on hands and knees
2. Lying	Medium	3.7	Lying with slow gross motor movements; slow crawl or creep; rolling over; hanging by hands or knees from support; slowly pushing objects on hands and knees
3. Lying	High	4.5	Rapid crawl or wrestling on ground or floor; rapid pushing object on hands and knees; hanging over a swing and using feet
4. Sitting	Low	7.6	Sitting, kneeling or squatting with fine movement only with slight changes in position on chair, bike, or swing
5. Sitting	Medium	27.9	Clapping, rocking, pedaling, sliding, pushing or throwing while seated; swinging with some arm and leg movement
6. Sitting	High	57.5	Vigorous gross motor (e.g., waving arms, rapid swinging or cycling)
7. Standing	Low	8.9	Stationary standing with minor position change; bending
8. Standing	Medium	34.5	Walk, slow climb, hanging motionless, standing on swing, throwing, or pushing without great effort
9. Standing	High	75.0	Running, scrambling, rapid climb, whole body throw

Note. From Eaton & Enns (1986, p. 275).

behavior, such as push, can be reported relative to the sum of all other behaviors. These procedures simply aim to equalize children's scores in cases of unequal frequency of observations.

In the next section I discuss those sampling and recording strategies used to extract behaviors from their stream so that they can be measured.

SAMPLING AND RECORDING BEHAVIOR

Sampling

The notion of *sampling* is crucial to understanding one specific way in which behavior can be studied. Sampling, generally, refers to the degree to which we choose to observe all that can be observed. All that can be observed is referred to as the universe of behavior. We sample behavior because it is neither practical nor necessary to observe all behavior.

By way of example, take the familiar example of watching television on election night. We view the television with predictions being made about who will win in a certain area before the election is over. How can this be done? Through sampling. That is, surveys are conducted on a sample of all voters. Inferences about all voters (i.e., the universe, or population, of voters) are made based on what a sample of the voters does. So, we can make an inference (or prediction) of what the whole group will do based on our knowledge of a sample of that population.

Obviously, the more we sample, the more we approximate the universe; therefore, larger samples are generally more accurate than smaller samples. By accurate I mean more accurately reflect the nature of the whole universe. Size of the sample, however, is not enough to guarantee an accurate sample. Systematic rules of sampling must be followed. Correspondingly, specific sampling rules are necessary to derive the measures outlined at the beginning of this chapter. Following Martin and Bateson (1993; see also Altmann, 1974, for another and often cited discussion of these issues), I separate sampling rules, or those rules followed to extract behavior from its ongoing stream, from recording rules, or how the behaviors are recorded.

Sampling, like the measures discussed earlier, can generally be grouped according to behavior or time sampling. Behavior, or event, sampling involves observing all occurrences of a specific behavior. Thus, we become concerned with a specific behavior occurring or not occurring within a certain observational period. Behavior or event sampling is most useful when we are interested in a relatively infrequently occurring behavior; thus, we look for it and only it and record it when it occurs. Aggression is commonly studied with event sampling because it does not occur that frequently (at least in some contexts). Furthermore, event sampling is useful when we are interested in the structure of the event itself so we want to record it from beginning to end.

The time oriented methods are concerned with dividing up the observational period into time units and making observations (or sampling) within those units. The motivation for time orientation is simple: It is often impractical and indeed unnecessary to conduct observations for long, and uninterrupted, periods of time. Thus, time-oriented sampling involves extracting bits of behavior from their temporal stream. As a result of our taking behaviors out of ongoing behavioral streams it becomes very important to make clear and systematic decisions about the ways in which it will be done. After all, it is this sample of behavior that will be used to make inferences about the universe of behavior. If we choose an unrepresentative sample of behavior it will yield information that does not represent the universe of behavior.

For example, if we choose to sample the life of a university professor only from 11:30 a.m. until 12:30 p.m., Monday through Friday, we will get only one type of information that probably is not very representative of what this person does during the rest of the day. In this case more sampling points, say at 9:30, 10:30, 11:30, 2:30 and 4:30 would give a better, or more representative, picture. The point here is that to achieve representativeness we should have numerous samples of individual both within days and numerous observations across different days. In this way we maximize the likelihood that we are gathering a representative sample of individuals' behavior.

I discuss three sampling rules: *ad libitum* (ad lib), focal person, and scan sampling (Martin & Bateson, 1993). *Ad libitum* sampling is not systematic to the extent that it has the observer not following a prespecified set of rules. He or she observes what and whom he or she sees fit to observe. This method is useful in the initial stages of observational work to the extent that it help the observer get a very general picture of what exists in the observational field. That is, it gives the observer some flavor of the context. The problem with ad lib sampling is that observers tend to see the most obvious and most visible sets of individuals and behaviors. Consequently, this procedure is extremely susceptible to the influence of observer bias.

Focal person sampling involves choosing one individual and observing him or her for a specified period. For example, in R&T research we use focal person (child) sampling for 3-minute intervals such that during a 20-minute recess period we observe in predetermined random order about six separate children. During each 3-minute interval we record all relevant behaviors of the focal child, as well as other children and adults with whom the focal child is interacting; this form of recording is known as *continuous recording* and is discussed later in this chapter.

Choice of an appropriate observational interval depends on what you are interested in. If you are interested in particular patterns of interaction your choice should be at least as long and possibly longer than those types of interaction in which you are interested. So if you are interested in pretend play themes, you should gauge the length of the theme and make your interval at least that long. Often times, however, while you are observing a focal child, he or she disappears; this is particularly true if you observe children outdoors. In these cases, you as the observer must have a rule, such as: Stop observation if child is out of sight for 30 seconds. Consequently, your measures would be a proportion of time observed.

Focal person sampling, especially when tied to continuous recording, is very useful if we want to construct thorough descriptions of your sample. With this method, as seen later, we can derive numerous measures and accurately reconstruct the behavior of our focal participants.

The down side of focal sampling is that it is time consuming (Sackett, 1978). That is, if we are observing a large number of individuals, use of focal sampling involves a number of discrete observations. This problem may, however, be minimized with numerous observers and video-recording equipment (Sackett, 1978). With numerous observers, separate observers can be assigned to separate focal children. With videotapes more than one child can be recorded simultaneously, if they are in very close proximity, such as in an experimental playroom. Both of these options, however, have associated expenses. Numerous, experienced, observers are both expensive and hard to come by. Furthermore, repeated viewing of videotapes is very time consuming. It is often more time consuming to code videotapes of behavior than to code it live.

Scan sampling is less time consuming. In this procedure a whole group, such as a classroom, is sampled very rapidly at predetermined intervals. For example, If you are interested in observing children's attention during various parts of the school day, you could utilize scan sampling. In this case you would observe separate individuals and record their behavior instantaneously. It might take you 60 seconds to record the attention of a classroom of 30 children. You would conduct a number of separate scans, varying the order in which each child is observed, across the relevant period. In this case, we would aggregate all observations for each child during that observation and treat it as one score. Separate scores for specific individuals taken within a short observational period, generally, should not be treated as separate scores because they are not independent of each other. By aggregating across the individual observations we get a whole (and reliable) picture of what individuals do during a certain period. By looking only at specific points, we only learn what they are doing at a specific instant.

Event or behavior sampling, as noted earlier, involves choosing a specific event, or behavior, and recording it either continuously or as having occurred or not and is typically used in cases in which the target behavior does not occur with great frequency, therefore one does not want to rely on time-oriented sampling because of the real risk of missing the behavior. Instead, the observer looks for the target behavior to occur and then records it. When recording an event observers should make note of the specific endpoint, or consequence, of the behavior. Typically, an event recording is terminated when behaviors from another behavioral category begin. For, example, if we are observing aggression, we record those behaviors that comprise the category aggression. When the nature of the behavior changes, such as one child comforts the other, the event recording should be terminated, but we should note that behavior that immediately follows the target behavior. These consequences of target behaviors provide insight into possible functions of the behavior.

Some basic and very general sampling issues apply to the notion of behavioral sampling. As noted in the beginning of this section, sampling is an attempt to gather some information that is representative of larger bodies of information. To maximize the likelihood of gathering representative information a few guidelines should be followed. First, and as noted earlier, observe the same individual at different points within the same day. By observing individuals at different points of the day we get a more representative picture. People do different things at 8:00 a.m. than at 2:00 p.m. Similarly, by observing the same individual on different days we gain representativeness; Saturday-morning child behavior is probably different from mornings before the child goes to school.

By extension, the specific order in which people are observed should be considered (e.g., counterbalanced or randomized) so that the order in which they are observed does not affect, or confound, our measures. In the case of counterbalancing we may have a total of 25 observational sampling slots in an observational period, say 1 per 30 seconds. Order of observation is counterbalanced when each child is observed in each of the 25 observational slots. So on Day 1 John would be observed in Slot 1 and Joan in Slot 2. On Day 2 John would be observed in Slot 2 and Joan in Slot 3, and so forth. In the case of randomized order, the sampling Slot (1–25) for each child on each day would be determined by randomly assigning him or her to a slot. Thus, to insure representative and nonconfounded data the order in which we sample behavior should be either randomized or counterbalanced. The hypothetical list in Table 8.3 provides an example.

Recording Rules

Specific recording rules correspond to certain sampling rules. This correspondence is displayed in Table 8.4.

The quantitative measures that can be derived from each recording rule are displayed in Table 8.5.

Continuous recording rules can be used with focal person and event sampling strategies. With this form of recording, the observer records all behaviors of interest for the duration of the observational interval. As noted previously, in R&T studies we recorded continuously all social behavior and social interactants of the focal child for a full 3 minutes. The quantitative measures that can be derived from continuous recording are frequency, latency, duration, intensity, and pat-

TABLE 8.3
Order of Observations

Focal Child	*Order on Day 1*	*Day 2*	*Day 3*
John	1	4	3
Joan	2	1	2
Fred	3	2	1
Frank	4	3	4

TABLE 8.4
Sampling and Recording Rules

Recording Rules:	*Continuous*	*0/1*	*Instantaneous*
Sampling Rules			
Ad Libitum			
Focal	X	X	X
Scan			X
Event	X	X	

TABLE 8.5
Quantitative Measures Corresponding to Recording & Sampling Rules

Recording Rules	*Continuous*	*0/1*	*Instantaneous*
Measures			
Frequency	X		
Duration	X		
Latency	X		
Pattern	X		
Intensity	X	X	X

tern if the whole behavioral sequence of interest is observed during the specified interval. In addition to the behaviors of the focal child it is also useful to note during continuous recording the other children with whom the target child is interacting. For example, you could note the behaviors the focal child aims at other specific children and the behaviors others direct at the focal child.

Rather than coding behavior continuously, across time, we might choose to sample discontinuously, or sample behavior at different time intervals. The recording rules based on time intervals include instantaneous sampling and 0/1 sampling. But before discussing these recording strategies, we must diverge to discuss the choice of a sample interval (Martin & Bateson, 1993). By sample interval we mean that time interval that will be used to determine the interval at which behavior is recorded. The observation period is divided into specific time intervals; the sample intervals are those points at which behavior is sampled. The point at the end of the sample interval is labeled the sample point.

Take the aforementioned example in which we were interested in studying classroom attention. We could choose a sampling interval of 5, 10, 15, etcetera, seconds in a 10-minute lesson. In the case of the 10-second interval in this lesson, we have a total of 60 sample points, Obviously the shorter the duration the more the sample will resemble the universe of behavior and thus, contain less error. Logistics of conducting observations, however, often limit having a short duration. For example, although we could have a 5-second sample interval to record classroom behavior if children are all seated, this short interval would be less practical if children were moving around the classroom or outdoors. Additionally, the degree of detail in a coding system also affects the sample interval to the extent that more complex codes require more time than less complex codes. Lastly, repeated observations within a restricted time range bring into question the independence of the separate observations.

With all this in mind, let us discuss the particulars of 0/1 and instantaneous sampling. With either of these methods, the observer should make clear to the reader the intervals at which behaviors are sampled. Although we may have a specific sampling interval, say 10 seconds, the exact moment at which we record the behavior may vary according to the rules followed. This section makes clear the way in which you should explicate this process.

For simplicity sake, let us say that our sample interval in 10 seconds. The observer would need some mechanical timer, such as a series of recorded beeps that the observer hears through an earphone, to cue him or her when to record. Beepers on digital watches are also useful, but may be too loud for some locations, such as classrooms. With instantaneous recording (also called point sampling) the observer notes the occurrence or nonoccurrence or level of intensity of the behaviors of interest at the instant that the beeper goes off. Instantaneous recording is used with scan sampling. Obviously, complicated decisions about intensity ratings would impact on the sample interval; longer intervals are required for more complex ratings. Instantaneous recording can yield intensity scores. It can also yield scores that indicate the proportion of intervals during which specific behaviors were observed. It does not yield true frequencies because behavior is not being continuously recorded.

0/1 sampling (also labeled *interval sampling*) is similar to instantaneous sampling to the extent that a sample interval determines when we record. Unlike instantaneous sampling, however, 0/1 sampling simply record whether the behavior occurred (1) or did not (0) during the whole 10-second interval, not at a specified instant. So, a behavior could have occurred 1 time or 10 times during the 10-second interval, but a 1 would have been scored in each instance. Like instantaneous sampling it can tell us the occurrence or nonoccurrence of behavior or number of recording intervals. Consequentially, true frequency scores cannot be derived from 0/1 sampling. The advantage of 0/1, over instantaneous, sampling is that is it easier for the observer; the observer has more time to process information in the former case. Indeed, if the sample interval is short enough, 0/1 and instantaneous sampling rules yield very similar measures (Smith, 1985).

CONCLUSIONS

In this chapter I have outlined ways in which observational categories can be sampled, recorded, and measured. The procedure that yields most information, focal child sampling and continuous recording, is also the most demanding in terms of time. Although other sampling and recording methods are less demanding, they have corresponding limitations in terms of the information yielded. Thus, it is imperative for you to determine what it is you want to know and the types of measures necessary to answer that question. Based on that you should choose sampling and recording strategies.

SOME THINGS TO THINK ABOUT

1. Think of trying to measure intensity some aspect of behavior, such as concentration or initiative.

List five attributes that might comprise a local rate measure.

A. ______________________________

B. ______________________________

C. ______________________________

D. ______________________________

E. ______________________________

2. How might you measure this by consequence?

____

____

____

____

____

____

3. Choose any aspect of behavior that is readily observational, such as game playing on the playground.

Try using different sampling and recording rules for that behavior.

____

____

____

____

____

4. List five behaviors that are most amenable to behavior/event sampling?

   A. ____________________

   B. ____________________

   C. ____________________

   D. ____________________

   E. ____________________

5. List five behaviors that are most amenable to focal person sampling.

   A. ____________________

   B. ____________________

   C. ____________________

   D. ____________________

   E. ____________________

6. List five behaviors that are most amenable to scan sampling.

   A. ____________________

   B. ____________________

   C. ____________________

   D. ____________________

7. Using a diary format keep track of some aspects of your family life, such as house cleaning chores.

What day are they done on?

At what time?

Are reminders necessary?

Who issues them?

What form do they take?

Who does what?

8. Try doing the above in both a narrative and checklist format.

9. Try recording a family event using different media (e.g., a videorecorder and a check list).

Which is more obtrusive?

Why?

____

____

____

____

____

____

9

Reliability

In the preceding chapter I discussed the ways in which categories are formed: sampled, recorded, and measured. Measures, as I noted, are derived in part from the theories guiding our research. Among the most important attributes of measures are their technical properties, or the extent to which they are reliable and valid. Reliability and validity are necessary in the scientific enterprise as they help to insure that our measures are objective.

Although reliability and validity can be applied to any number of measures, such as mental test scores, behavioral observations, physiological measures, and self-report inventories, they are most often discussed in the context of paper-and-pencil tests. Indeed, much of the theoretical and empirical work in these areas has been in the context of mental testing. In this chapter I draw from this work to inform the discussion of reliability as it is applied to behavioral observations.

Reliability is often paired, like twins, with validity, where validity generally refers to the truthfulness of the measure. At a very common level we often hear the dictum: Reliability is necessary but not sufficient for validity. By this I mean that without reliability we cannot have validity but reliability alone does not assure validity. Thus, we can have reliability without having validity. In this chapter I discuss reliability and in the next, validity.

Most generally, reliability refers to consistency in measurement and this can be examined either between different individuals (interindividually) or within the same individuals (intraindividually) (Stanley, 1971). Consistency across individuals, or interindividual reliability, is concerned with the degree to which individuals maintain their relative position, or rank, in a group across different measures. For example, a student may rank 21:25 on observations of aggression and 5:25 on a peer nomination measure of aggression. In this case, there is obviously low reliability.

Consistency can also refer to intraindividual consistency where the same individuals are observed on more than one occasion (Stanley, 1971). For example, individuals' scores on one day can be compared to their performance on another day. The degree to which they have the same scores on these different measurement points is a measure of reliability. Variations in measurement of individuals is typically related to error. Thus, error is central to any discussion of reliability.

RELIABILITY, ERROR, AND CONSISTENCY

Let us take what is probably a very familiar example to address intraindividual consistency in measurement. On Monday at 8:00 a.m. you weigh yourself on the scale in your bathroom and it registers 192. You step off the scale for a second and then get on again and it registers 190. Alternatively, after weighing yourself on your scale you go to your partner's side of the bathroom and weigh yourself on his or her scale: 191. This example, that repeated sets of measurements never exactly duplicate themselves, is what we mean by unreliability (Stanley, 1971). Reliability, then, is the tendency toward consistency from one set of measurements to another.

Reliability of measures within individuals is often affected by error in the measurement procedure per se and these variations in measurement can be due either to systematic or chance error in measurement. In order to get an estimate of the error in measurement and true scores we should assess individuals on the same observational instrument a number of times and plot the distribution of the scores observed. These repeated measurements provide estimates of a true score, or an ideal score, without error. True scores are ideals, and do not exist in fact, but we use these repeated measurements as estimates of true scores.

Staying with our bathroom scale example, we would weigh ourselves 100 times in succession and record each weigh. We then take these 100 scores and plot their distribution. We derive a mean score and a variability score for this distribution (standard deviation and variance). The variability of these scores is an indicator of the error of measurement. The distribution of these scores would then be used to approximate our true weight.

There can be a number of true scores for individuals on a specific construct, depending on a number of factors (Stanley, 1971). For example, there can be a true score of individuals' spelling when they are asked to answer orally and another true score when they are asked to write out the words. In other words, true scores represent aggregates of measurements under specific conditions.

Given the realistic difficulties of repeating a large number of independent measurements, especially with time consuming procedures such as direct observations, we often rely on many fewer observations (two is the minimum) and thus indirectly estimate the true score as well as the error variance (Stanley, 1971). The higher the error variance, the less reliable our measure is.

In another scenario, we address interindividual consistency in measurement. In this case we are concerned with the degree to which our measures are consistent in maintaining individuals' rank order in a group. We could compare individuals' weight rankings after they have each weighed themselves on the same scale more than one time or on different scales. In either case, we have parallel measures of weigh for each individual. Consistency between the ranks is indicated by the correlation coefficient assessing the relation between the two sets of measurements. The higher the correlation coefficient between the measures, the higher the reliability. The importance of having reliable measures in any sort of research endeavor should be self-evident. For example, in cases in which we are examining the degree to which one measure, say observed aggression predicts incarceration as an adult, as indicated by court records. Both sets of measures must be reliable in order to make inferences about the relation between the variables. Without reliability the observed relationships, or lack or relationships, may be due to chance, not what it is we think we are measuring.

Types of Error

Variation in measures can be due to a number of different factors. The evaluation of the reliability of any set of measures is really an examination of how much error is systematic and how much is concerned with error measurement. Systematic error, for example, might be due to the fact that a certain scale systematically under weighs by 3 pounds.

There are number of different ways of expressing score variability. Perhaps the simplest way to capture variations in measurement within any distribution is the range of scores. The range in a distribution of scores is indicated by the difference between the largest and the smallest score. For example, if we had the following weights: 103, 105, 106, 106, 108, 109, the range would be 6.

Although the range does tell us about variability, it tells us only about two extreme scores: the highest and the lowest. Variances and standard deviations are additional measures of variation and they do not have limitations of range scores. Both indicate the variation of scores around the mean. Beginning with variance, symbolized as s^2, and defined statistically as:

$$s^2 = \frac{(X_i - \overline{X})^2}{N-1}$$

$$s^2 = \frac{3(X_i - \overline{X}\ \beta)^2}{N-1}$$

Using the weights from above represented as X_i

X_i	$\overline{X}$	$X_i - \overline{X}$	$(X_i - \overline{X})^2$
103	106.16	3.16	9.98
105	106.16	–1.16	1.34
106	106.16	–.16	.02
106	106.16	–.16	.02
108	106.16	1.84	3.38
109	106.16	2.84	8.06

$3(X_i = 637$ $3 = 22.8$

$N = 6$

$\overline{X} = 106.16$

$$s^2 = \frac{22.8}{N-1}$$

$$\frac{22.8}{5} = 4.46$$

The standard deviation (SD or *s*) is simply the square root of the variance. In this case, the SD would be 2.11.

The variance is the preferred way to express variability of measurement. An important aspect of using variance as a measure of variability is that it allows us to identify both the total variation of the measure as well of the extent to which subcomponents of the measurement procedure contribute to the total variance (Stanley, 1971). For example we can identify the contributions of gender and age as contributors to variations in weight.

Error variance is that variance that is attributed to only one measurement point or procedure. The size of the error variance, in relation to the total variance, contributes directly to the reliability of a measure. The larger the portion due to error variance, the more unreliable the measure. It may be the case that the variability reported in peoples' weighs is due to differences in the scales used.

Not all variation in measurement is attributable to error variation. Specifically, constant error can be systematic and not contribute to error variance. Take the example of a scale which constantly overweighs individuals by 3 pounds. Although this problem results in distortions from a true score, the distortion does not result in individuals being ranked differently from one weighing to another. In all cases individuals are overweighed by 3 pounds. Thus, the added 3 pounds is a constant and does not affect individual's ranking in different measurements.

Error variance, on the other hand is not systematic, but random. Random error is not related in a systematic way to individuals' true scores. The source of the variation, however, have implications for classifying variance as systematic or error.

Sources of Variation

In this section I discuss reliability generally. Much of what is discussed here relates to reliability in both testing and in direct observations. As noted previously, much of the theory and measurement associated with reliability comes from testing. With this understanding, we can then more readily apply it to direct observation.

Variation in scores is a hallmark of most measurement regimens in psychology and education. Indeed, some forms of variation are good. If there is too little, or no, variation between individuals on different observational measures, the magnitude of the correlation coefficients used to measure reliability will be lower than when there is systematic variation For example, systematic variation in scores, say variation in social participation, may be due to variations in temperament, a systematic form of variation.

Although more is said about correlation coefficients in the next chapter, I briefly illustrate the relation between variation and correlation coefficients. Correlation coefficients represent the extent to which to sets of scores co-occur and lie along a straight. If they form a perfectly straight line, the correlation is 1. Variations along an imaginary line through the distribution of scores is reflected in different magnitudes of correlations coefficients.

Although perfect correlations are good for purposes of illustration, they are rare in real life. More likely are correlations of some intermediate magnitude. When two variables are unrelated, such as shoe size and GPA among a class of college students, the correlation will likely be zero. When evaluating a correlation, we are concerned with whether the relation observed is one that is greater than expected by chance. That is, if we randomly paired 5, 10, or 20 scores together, what is the likelihood that a correlation of a particular magnitude would be obtained? As the number of observations increases, the correlation needed to obtain significance (usually set a probability of a chance relation of this magnitude in one of 20 occasions, or $p = 0.05$) declines. That is, there is a perfect correlation between the sample size and the critical value needed to obtain significance. So when dealing with correlations one is concerned with the direction of the correlation (positive or negative), the magnitude of the correlation (i.e., its size), and the significance of the correlation.

In Fig. 9.1 I present six possible sources of variation (Stanley, 1971). I note that although these sources of variation were developed for test data, the are also relevant to observational data.

In the first category, lasting and general characteristics of individuals, we have cases of persistent and consistent sources of variation and should thus be treated as a form of systematic variance. The most common sources in this category involve the general ability to comprehend instructions associated with an assessment regimen and a general form of "test-wiseness" (Stanley, 1971). We can also generalize from this to assume that some participants in observational research are more or less wise to the social desirability of certain, and expected behaviors. For example, mothers being observed interacting with their children in a laboratory play situation might assume that some behaviors, such as being patient, are more valued by the observed, than others, such as using corporal punishment. These factors have an obvious effect on individuals' performance on a test or any similar assessment context. This is especially likely to be the case when the assessment procedure is novel and the instructions complex. Thus, scores are partially attributed to individuals' general ability to understand complex and novel instruction and negotiate complex procedures. Individuals with higher ability are better at understanding complex instructions.

"Wiseness," more specifically, typically is a result of experience with a variety of assessment regimens such that levels of anxiety are low. Further, these experi-

1. Lasting and general characteristics of individuals
   a. levels of ability relevant to the measurement procedure
   b. " participant wiseness"
   c. general ability to comprehend instructions
2. Lasting but specific characteristics of the individual
   a. specific to the procedure test as a whole
   b. specific to particular aspects of the procedure
3. Temporary but general characteristics of individuals
   a. health
   b. fatigue
   c. motivation
   d. emotional strain
   e. understanding the mechanics of the test heat, light, ventilation, etc.
4. Temporary and specific characteristics
   a. specific to the procedure as a whole
      i. comprehension of a specific procedure
      ii. specific "tricks" for dealing with a task
      iii. level of practice
      iv. momentary "set"
   b. specific to a procedure
      i. fluctuations in memory
      ii. fluctuations in attention
5. Systematic or chance factors affecting the administration or scoring of the observation
   a. conditions of the observation
   b. interaction of personality of observers and the participant
   c. unreliable or bias scoring
6. Chance variation
   a. luck
   b. momentary distraction

FIG. 9.1. Sources of variation in measurement.

ences also enable individuals to detect subtle cues in the assessment context that provide cues that are useful in behaving in expected ways. For example, a participant may recognize that in some tasks, individuals may recognize the observer's preference for a specific behavior given their instructions at the start of the session.

The second set of factors affecting variability are lasting but specific characteristics of individuals and are relevant to the specific area being observed, not to observational situations more generally (as was the case with the immediately prior example). An individual may be especially facile at playing with Legos, but not with puzzles. From this view two observational sessions would have very different distributions. Consequently, this sort of variation is also systematic when considered within a specific task or format.

Variation associated with format would be treated as error variance, on the other hand, where a number of different formats are sampled in the assessment procedure. That assessments usually attempt to sample individuals' knowledge or skills across a wide universe, we more typically can consider this sort of variation as error.

Temporary but general characteristics of individuals are common factors affecting variations in scores. Commonly, issues related to fatigue, health, or concern over a problem at home influences performance. All too common we hear stories that a child did poorly on one day of a multiday assessment battery and this was due to some temporary issue that occurred before the child left for school that day. My daughter provides an excellent example of this. During Anna's kindergarten year she was given 4 days of tests to determine her placement in the "gifted" class. On the first 3 days of the test, Anna scored at the top end of the tests but on the fourth day she was near the bottom. An alert school psychologist who both administered and scored the tests noticed the inconsistency and called home that night, asking what could have been the problem with Anna that day, in light of her performance on the previous days. When we asked Anna if anything was wrong in the day's test or if anything bothered her, she was quick to point out that today she sat at a table, not at a desk. She went on and said that you really had to be serious at a desk but not at a table because kids in school do not sit at tables to do serious work! Similar stories are told by parents whose children perform poorly because they had to wear a certain pair of socks to school that day, and they hated it, making for a bad day.

This type of variation should be considered measurement error, as in the preceding case, because we are typically interested in making inferences about individuals' across a number of different days, not on one specific day. Cases of temporary but specific factors influencing variability are usually confined to assessments that are novel or have very difficult instruction. The extent to which students "catch on" may be due to a more general wiseness, and it also may be due to chance. Improvement on such complex tasks may also improve with practice, so performance at any one instance reflects an individual-specific and temporary level of practice on the specific measure. The temporary and transitory nature of this variability suggests that it should be assigned to error variance.

The fifth category is concerned with administration/instructional and scoring factors. These factors lead to error variance. It may be the case that there is an interaction between the participant and the tester. It is well-known that some individuals' performance in an observational session is affected by whom they are being observed. African-American children, for example, tend to exhibit higher competence when they are given instructions by an individual of similar race. Children, generally, perform at higher level when they are familiar with the administrator, relative to being unfamiliar. It also may be the case that on a specific day the administrator or observer did not bring an adequate number of observational sheets to the session, so it was disrupted, and inhibited optimal performance.

The ways in which individuals are scored, too, introduces variation. An inexperienced scorer may code responses in an inconsistent and incorrect way. The result is error variance.

The last category is that variation for which a source cannot be identified. The sort of variation may be the purest form of error variance (Stanley, 1971).

To conclude this section, variation in scores can be systematic or due to error. The sources of variation can be either temporary or persistent features of individuals being assessed and due to specific or general features of the assessment procedure per se. It is important to document the sources of variation as well as the degree to which the variation is systematic or due to error for at least two reasons. First, reliability is maximized when we maximize systematic variation and minimize variation due to error. This sort of information is crucial in designing measurement and assessment procedures.

Second, and at a more technical level, partitioning the variance associated with systematic and error variation, in relation to true scores is necessary to calculate reliability coefficients. These coefficients provide a metric of the reliability of our measures.

Estimating Reliability and Reliability Coefficients

Reliability, generally, is an indicator of the degree to which a person's score will remain consistent from one measurement point to another. Consequently, it is necessary for us to have multiple measurement points on each individual. Recall, in our discussion of true scores and error, we noted that true scores were estimated by plotting individuals' scores across multiple measurement points. From this distribution we could calculate measures of variation, with variance being the preferred metric.

In reality numerous points of measurement for individuals, especially where complex and time-consuming procedures are used, are impractical. Further, by the very nature of human beings, change, or variation, is associated with time, so measurements at different time points presents a number of problems. All of this leads to the use of a minimal number of assessment points to estimate reliability. At a minimum, at least two measurement points on each individual, is necessary in order to estimate reliability.

Parallel assessment forms are often used to establish and measure reliability. Parallel forms of assessment involve using two very similar forms of assessment, often drawing items from the same general sample of behaviors. The assumption behind the use of parallel forms of assessment is that the true score and the error scores for each form are drawn from the same distribution of scores (Stanley, 1971).

In order for this condition to be approximated the procedures displayed in Table 9.1 should be followed.

In each of the procedures displayed in Table 9.1 we have at least two measures of the same individual on the related measures. The reliability of the measurement is documented by the correlation between the two measurements.

TABLE 9.1
Procedures for Establishing Parallel Forms

1. The two measurement procedures of two parallel forms should be administered under similar conditions
2. The same assessment procedures can be administered repeatedly
3. The same procedure can be subdivided into parallel forms

In the first and second cases we have two observations at different times. In the first case we have two parallel forms, both on the same individuals at different times. For example, teachers who wanted to evaluate their students' social competence could generate two versions of an observational instrument. Each version would have the same number of criteria, the criteria would have the same behavioral criteria (e.g., cooperates with toys). Thus consistency of the measure is influenced by *both* the similarity of the two sets of items comprising the parallel forms as well as any factors associated with time, change, and measurement at different points in time. Consistency between scores should decrease as the duration between assessment points increases. Factors such as experience directly relevant to the observational instrument should change with time. For example, if aggression is being assessed, it is probably the case that scores will vary as a function of the temporal proximity to a school antiviolence curriculum. An observation taken on the last day of instruction related to that area should be higher than the same observation given 5 or 10 days later.

Alternatively, one may want to use the two observational instruments to demonstrate the effect of instruction. One instrument would be given before instruction to determine how much students already know about the subject matter, in this case being cooperative and not aggressive. The second instrument would be given after instruction to see how much children have learned. If this approach is taken, it is critical that the two instruments be equivalent in difficulty. For example, maybe Version 1 of the instrument is more difficult than Version 2. To control for this, one half of the students should be given Version 1 before training and one half Version 2, and vice versa, of course, following instruction. This way, any unanticipated differences in the difficulty of the instruments will be controlled for. This is an example of counterbalancing.

Repeated measurements of individuals across time is also more difficult logistically. For example, schools may be unwilling to have researchers or evaluators disrupt the everyday business of teaching with assessment procedures. Indeed, a common, and very real, concern of parents, teachers, children, and politicians is that too much time is spent assessing children in schools and this comes at the expense of teaching.

Relatedly, assessing the same individuals at different time points also opens up the real possibility of missing data. That is, there is a very high possibility that some children will be present at one session but not the other. This factor leads to increased variability as well as fewer data points created by missing data. For example, temporary factors, such as illness, influence the consistency of scores. Similarly, more general and persistent factors, such as being prone to truancy or school absences, also have an affect on consistency of scores.

The second case in Table 9.1 also involves assessing individuals at different points in time. In this case, individuals are assessed on the same measure at different points rather than on parallels. A benefit of this procedure, relative to the first one where individuals were assessed on different, but parallel forms of the same instrument, is that we minimize variation associated with content sampling. For example, if we are assessing individuals' knowledge of behaviors related to math (e.g., counts spontaneously) or reading (e.g., spends free time reading), we ideally sample from the same universe of content. In using different parallel forms there is the chance that an individual's consistency will be influenced by his or her chance knowledge of specific items. That is why counterbalancing the presentation of the different forms is so important. Such differences are, obviously, not a problem when individuals are assessed on the same items.

Sometimes, the reliability of an instrument may be fine, but what a researcher or educator is interested is the long-term stability of an underlying ability the instrument purports to measure. For example, Schneider and Weinert (1995) studied the long-term stability of children's memory ability, for instance, the strategy of organization in free recall memory. Organization in memory is measured by the tendency to remember related items on a list together (e.g., remembering all the instances of tools on a list consisting of different examples from the categories tools, fruit, furniture, and birds). They found that the correlations between 2-year intervals were positive but very low, for example, 0.12 between ages 4 and 6, 0.16 between ages 6 and 8, and 0.12 between the ages of 8 and 10. This suggests that the cognitive ability underlying the strategy of organization is not stable over time and that the cognitive abilities underlying this strategy go through qualitative changes over time. But perhaps it is not the ability that is unstable, but the measure itself. To evaluate this, they gave different children the same test of strategy organization, but over only a 2-week period. In this case, the correlations were much higher (0.64), suggesting that the test was reliable, in that children who take it on two occasions separated only by a brief interval scored similarly. The lower correlations found when children were tested at 2-year intervals reflected a change in mental abilities, not a deficiency of the measure instrument.

Observation-Specific Factors Affecting Reliability. In the preceding section I discussed general factors affecting reliability. Much of the work in this area, as I noted, was derived from psychometric theory and reliability in the field of testing. In this section I discuss factors more specific to reliability as it pertains to observational research.

As I noted in the preceding section a number of factors influence the reliability statistic that is generated. Specifically, I discussed the extent to which behaviors occurred very frequently or infrequently affecting reliability. Also recall in the discussion of occurrence and nonoccurrence agreement indices I noted that high- and low-frequency behaviors are susceptible to chance agreement, and consequently, artificially inflate reliability. In this final section on reliability I address three other factors that have an impact on reliability. They are observer fatigue, category definition, and observer drift (Martin & Bateson, 1993).

First, observer fatigue is the effect of long and sometimes monotonous observation periods resulting in observers not attending fully to the behavior; consequently, unreliable data are collected. Three possible remedies are available. First, the length of the observation session could be shortened so that within session fatigue and boredom are minimized. A second solution, in which multiple observers are available, would be to rotate observers through a variety of observational time slots and contexts. Indeed, counterbalancing observers in this way is a necessary safeguard against confounding a specific observer with a specific data set. If only one observer records the behavior of one particular group or during one time period, then the data from that group and time period may be idiosyncratic to that one observer. Thus, counterbalancing multiple observers avoids a number of problems.

Another way of addressing the problem of observer fatigue and boredom is for observers to record the behaviors in the field with a videocamera and then code it later. Although the use of videotape recorders, and other mechanical recording devices, is no panacea some problems are alleviated by their use.

The second, and related, reliability issue to be discussed is observer drift. By observer drift I mean that observers, in the course of a study code the same behaviors in different ways. Observer drift typically rears its ugly head in protracted studies, where coding goes on across a long period of time. For example, you are observing children's playground behavior across the school year. At the beginning of the year, you train observers to meet a specific reliability criterion for each behavior. Observer drift occurs when, with the passage of time, observers change how they code specific behaviors. They may have started off coding mutual gaze between two children as social interaction but 1 month later you coded that same behavior as nonsocial behavior. They may have implicitly changed their criterion for social interaction to include verbal exchanges only.

To guard against observer drift requires that observers are monitored and retrained. More specifically, in cases of prolonged studies, interobserver checks should be made at various points throughout the study, say every 2 weeks or every month. Further, periodic retraining is also necessary. In our studies of school recess, for example, observers were retrained coding videotapes of recess behavior every 2 months.

The third factor affecting reliability is category definition. Clearly defined categories are more reliable than ambiguous categories. Molecular-level categories are generally more reliable than molar-level categories. So for example, smile would be more reliably coded than happy. As noted in that earlier chapter, molar categories can be used but they should be described to observers in terms of their specific components. Further, it is often helpful to define a category in terms of core dimensions and borderline dimensions. For example, in the category rough-and-tumble play, we might consider hit at, kick at to be core dimension in that they represent the basis of what we consider our category to represent. In this case the core is considered playfighting. Borderline dimensions, on the other hand, belong to the category but their inclusion is less crucial to the definition of the category. In the case of the rough-and-tumble play example, chase may be considered a borderline dimension in that our theory considers nonrough, although physically vigorous behaviors, to be part of the category but not at the heart of it. It is obviously important to decide, in advance, the extent to which observers will include instances of borderline cases.

Intra- and Inter-Observer Reliability: Determining It

In this section I discuss both intraobserver and interobserver reliability. The logic here is that observers must themselves be consistent (intraobserver) in their observations before they can agree with others (interobserver).

Intraobserver Reliability. The degree to which two sets of observations by the same observer are reliable can be conceptualized in ways similar to those which are used to determine the reliability of tests. Indeed, the statistical procedures for measuring intraobserver reliability are derived from various test reliability theories. Here I discuss two techniques derived from Classical theory, test–retest reliability and split-half reliability (see Bakeman & Gottman, 1986 and Suen & Ary, 1989 for more detailed discussions). Test–retest reliability is an indicator of the stability of a score from Time 1 to Time 2, and so forth. The degree to which the same score occurs across time is the measure of test–retest reliability.

The same logic, and statistics, can be applied to repeated observations by the same person. Take the example of affect discussed previously. Let us say that the observations were videotaped so we could determine the degree to which a single observer coded the same behavior, such as smile (as pictured in the following photo), across two separate viewings of 10 separate sessions. In Table 9.2 I display the match and mismatch between two separate codings. The *X* indicates that a smile was scored, and a 0 indicates that one was not. A + in the last column indicates between session agreement and – indicates disagreement.

We could treat, by analogy, the two coding sessions as two testing sessions and the separate sessions as items in the tests. Intraobserver reliability is measured by determining the extent to which the separate testings, or observations, yield the same scores. We sample across 10 different observations, rather than choosing just one observation point. For sampling-related reasons, as discussed in preceding chapters, more samples yield a more accurate picture of the universe of behaviors.

There are various statistical techniques that could be applied to these data to generate intraobserver reliability coefficients. I only name and briefly discuss them here. Most simply, an index of concordance (Martin & Bateson, 1993) or a percentage of agreement can be calculated. This statistic is calculated as follows:

TABLE 9.2
Intraobserver Reliability of Two Recodings Across 10 Sessions

Session	*Coding 1*	*Coding 2*	*Agree*	*Disagree*
1	X	X		+
2	X	O	–	
3	X	X	+	
4	0	X	–	
5	X	X	+	
6	0	O		+
7	O	O	+	
8	X	X		+
9	X	X		+
10	O	O		+

Sum +/Sum + –

In this case we have 8/8 + 2 or 80%. If you choose to use 0.80 instead of 80%, you should note, explicitly somewhere in the report that the measure is a percent measure, not a correlation coefficient or a *kappa* coefficient.

Although the use of percentage of agreement has been roundly criticized on a number of grounds, such as not correcting for chance agreements, being influenced by the number of codes, and not being able to compare percentages of agreement to any criterion, it is still useful at a simple level: It gives us a rough and ready indicator of agreement. Like all measures of percentage, scores range from 0 to 100.

Other measures of reliability applicable to test–retest data are different correlation coefficients, such as the Pearson *r* or Spearman's *rho*. Both correlation coefficients are represented with *r*; the Spearman coefficient is sometimes represented as: *rs*. Basically, correlations coefficients tell us the degree to which two sets of measures, like the 10 separate codings on two occasions, co-occur. Perfect co-occurrence would be expressed as +1.0 and –1.0. Correlation coefficients range from –1.0 to +1.0. So a less than perfect correlation coefficient might be 0.65. Positive correlations indicate that as we observe one measure, say smiling in a father, we also observe another measures, say smiling in a son. A negative correlation, on the other hand, indicates that as one behavior is observed with increasing frequency, paternal smiling, another is observed, say son's smiling, with decreasing frequency. Correlation coefficients, unlike percentages of agreement, have the added benefit of telling us the degree to which a particular coefficient is due to chance. In short, with correlations coefficients we also can determine a *p*-value or probability statement. So we could determine that when $r = 0.65$ with a sample of 10, the probability of us getting this finding by chance is 0.05, so we can be sure that in 95:100 cases, if we were to take a similar sample, we would get an *r* of 0.65.

Next we consider split-half reliability. Whereas test–retest reliability was a measure of stability, split-half reliability is a measure of homogeneity. So rather than measuring across different observation sessions we measure within a session. Let us use the information presented in Table 9.2 in a slightly different way to illustrate the point. Look at one individual coding 10 separate sessions (listed 1,10 in the Coding 1 column) for smile. The *X* on each line could represent "a hit," that is, scoring a smile when one actually occurred, whereas the O represents a "miss," or a coding a smile when one did not occur or not coding smile when one actually did occur. Split-half reliability can be calculated by comparing scores from odd items (in this case, sessions 1, 3, 5, 7, 9) with those from even items (2, 4, 6, 8, 10) or comparing the first 5 sessions with the second 5 sessions. Correlation coefficients between the two sets of scores are then calculated. The degree to which the two sets of scores co-occur, as in the previous discussion, ranges from +1.0 to –1.0.

Another specific procedure that can be used to measure split-half reliability is the Spearman-Brown Prophesy Formula. This procedure measures the *internal consistency* of an assessment instrument. By internal consistency I mean the degree to which two different parts of the same assessment tool measures the same thing. Typically this is accomplished by dividing the test in half and examining the extent to which the scores on the two halves are related. We refer to this as split-half reliability. We would expect, for example, an assessment of self-reported depression to be internally consistent. That is, the different questions should be assessing the same construct. For example, we could divide an assessment instrument into two parts by grouping all the odd numbered items together and then by grouping all the even numbered items into a second part. This procedure, in essences takes one administration and treats it as two by dividing it into two parts.

A potential problem with using two halves of the same test to approximate to measurement points is that the length of the test is being cut in half. Reliability is closely related to the adequacy of the sample. The more items that are sampled, the more reliable, and the more valid, the measure. The Spearman-Brown Prophesy Formula gives the predicted split-half reliability coefficient for a test twice as long as either of the two halves. The formula is expressed as follows:

$$r_w = \frac{2r_w}{1 + r_h}$$

where r_w is the correlation for the whole test and

r_h is the correlation between the two halves of the same test (Kubiszyn & Borich, 2000). As with all correlation coefficients, the values range from –1.0 to +1.0. A perfect positive correlation means that the two halves perfectly concordant. A perfect negative correlation means that the two parts are perfectly measuring opposite dimensions of the construct.

To conclude this section, intraobserver reliability is a measure of the degree to which an individual observer is consistent. Consistency can be considered in terms of repeated scorings of the same events or of different scorings across time. Consistency of an individual observer is necessary in cases involving one or more than one observer. We want to make sure that each individual is consistent.

It has been suggested (Martin & Bateson, 1993) that adding a measure of interobserver reliability is valuable to the extent that it guards against only one person seeing the world in a particular way, albeit it a consistently particular way. In the next section I address interobserver reliability.

Interobserver Reliability. Where intraobserver reliability is a measure of consistency within an individual, interobserver reliability is a measure of consistency between observers. Like the within individual case, interobserver reliability can be determined by videotaping (or audiorecording for oral language data) relevant behavior and measuring the degree to which more than one person agrees on the scoring of a particular behavior or set of behaviors. Alternately, two or more observers can score the same sessions live and simultaneously.

Establishing interobserver reliability is a two stage process. First, intraobserver reliability should be established, following procedures outlined earlier. Being assured that each observer is consistent in his or her observations is obviously necessary before more than one observer can agree. Second, different observers must be chosen in order to check the degree to which they agree on what they describe. Procedurally, this usually involves a set number of observers who are actually collecting the data being checked by a set of external observers or by having the primary observers checking themselves. In the former case, one or more observers, who are not the primary data collectors, can check on the observations of the primary observers. This can be done by simultaneously observing the same phenomena and comparing codes or by recoding sets of tapes previously coded and then comparing codes. In the case of primary observers checking on each other, observers could be assigned to recode (on video or audiotape) the previous codes of another observer. In either case, the reliability checks are conducted on a sample of the total observations.

When some form of time sampling is used, it is necessary that both observers are coding at exactly the same time. To this end, it is necessary that observers each receive an external single, such as a "beep," simultaneously, so that they are coding at the same time. In areas where quiet is necessary, such as in a classroom or in an observation booth, it is best to have a prerecorded tape, with a series of timed beeps. Each observer could have an earphone attached to a recorder playing the tape of programmed beeps. In areas where quiet is not important, the earphone is not necessary and the prerecorded tape could play aloud. Alternatively, the "countdown beepers" common on so many of the inexpensive digital watches do very nicely.

It is often best that checks are made on a random sample of data. In this way representativeness of the sample is assured. For example, in some of my studies I have observers check the codes on 20% of all the codes. The original codes are then compared with the recodings.

Calculating Interobserver Reliability. A variety of different statistical procedures have been developed to gauge the degree to which different observers agree with each other. In this section I discuss some of the more common strategies (Suen & Ary, 1989). They are displayed in Table 9.3.

For a more thorough treatment of the various statistical procedures, you are referred to Suen and Ary (1989). I begin with a very simple procedure, the smaller/larger index (S/L). This procedure can be used when two observers code the same behavior, for example, smiles. Take the example of one observer coding a child smiling 25 times and another coding the same child as having smiles 32 times. The S/L is calculated by dividing the smaller value by the larger value:

TABLE 9.3
Interobserver Reliability Statistics

Smaller/Larger Index
Percentage of Agreement
Occurrence/Nonoccurrence Agreement Index
Kappa

$$S/L = \frac{\text{smaller}}{\text{larger}}$$

$$S/L = \frac{25}{32}$$

$$S/L = 0.78$$

The S/L index although simple, has been criticized in terms of its inability to address the degree to which two observers actually agreed on the behaviors. Even if each observer scored 32 cases of smiling in the aforementioned case, and a perfect index of 1.0 was derived, we would not be sure that the two observers each scored the same 32 smiles. We only know that they scored the same number!

The second technique for calculating interobserver reliability is the percentage of agreement. With this procedure, two observers code the same behaviors and their codes are compared. This procedure was discussed in the section on intraobserver reliability, so I will not spend much time on it here. Suffice it to say that the percentage of agreement statistic, although widely used, has been criticized on grounds that it does not correct for agreements due to chance (Bakeman & Gottman, 1986; Suen & Ary, 1989). In cases of extremely frequently occurring and extremely infrequently occurring behaviors, the probability of chance agreement is inflated (Suen & Ary, 1989). In other words, when behaviors occur very frequently or very infrequently, the percentage of agreement statistic is influenced by observers agreeing due to chance, not necessarily due to their coding the same thing.

It is a useful exercise when examining the percentage of agreement to generate an agreement or "confusion matrix" (Bakeman & Gottman, 1986) so that you can see the specific behaviors that are the most agreed upon, as well as those that are not agreed upon. Such a matrix for two observers coding the following behaviors is display in Table 9.4: smile, laugh, frown, and cry.

TABLE 9.4
Confusion Matrix

					Observer 1
Observer 2					
	Smile	*Laugh*	*Frown*	*Cry*	*Total*
Smile	15	12	0	0	27
Laugh	18	13	0	0	31
Frown	0	0	22	2	24
Cry	0	1	1	16	18
Total	33	26	23	18	100

A useful aspect of this matrix is that we can spot those area where observers agree and those where they disagree. Those areas where there is agreement between the two observers lies along the diagonal from smile down to cry. The areas outside of this diagonal are those where there is disagreement. So, there was frequent disagreement between the observers on laugh and cry. This information is useful for training observers to become more reliable in area which are problematical.

The next procedure to express interobserver reliability, the occurrence and nonoccurrence indices of agreement, takes into account the frequency with which a behavior occurs (Suen & Ary, 1989). The occurrence index is calculated by dividing the occurrence of agreements by the occurrence of agreements plus disagreement, and multiplying by 100%.

Graphically represented as:

%oa = occurrence of agree

= occurrence agree + disagree × 100%

By contrast, nonoccurrence agreement is calculated by dividing the total of nonagreements by the total of nonagreements plus agreements and multiplying by 100%. This can be represented:

%nona = nonoccurrence agreement

= nonoccurrence agreement + agree × 100%.

The occurrence and nonoccurrence indices reduce chance agreement due to frequently and nonfrequently observed behaviors, respectively. Thus, separate indices should be used with different types of behavior. The occurrence index could be used when a behavior occurs at levels of 80% or more whereas the nonoccurrence index can be used when behaviors are at 20% or lower (Suen & Ary, 1989). Take the example presented in Table 9.5.

Let us say that two observers are coding, simultaneously, occurrence and nonoccurrence of mutual gaze by a mother and her son. For the occurrence index, we see that the two observers agreed three times (at intervals 1, 3, and 5) and disagreed 4 times (at intervals 4, 7, 9, and 10). Taking these data and applying them to the occurrence agreement formula (%oa) we get:

TABLE 9.5
Occurrence (1)/Nonoccurrence (0) Codes Between Two Observers

OB 1	1	0	1	1	1	0	1	0	0	1
OB 2	1	0	1	0	1	0	0	0	1	0
Interval	1	2	3	4	5	6	7	8	9	10

$$\frac{3}{3} + 4 \times 100\% = 42.8\%$$

For the nonoccurrence formula, %nona, we have 3 agreements for nonoccurrence (at intervals 2, 6, and 8) and disagreements. Four times, resulting in:

$$3 + 4 \times \frac{3}{100\%} = 42.8\%$$

The next interobserver statistic to be discussed is *kappa*. *Kappa* is a frequently recommended statistic (e.g., Bakeman & Gottman, 1986; Suen & Ary, 1989) because it accounts for chance agreements more completely than the previous procedure. The equation for *kappa* (*k*) (Cohen, 1960, cited in Suen & Ary, 1989) is expressed as:

$$\frac{k = po - pe}{1 - pe}$$

where *po* is the proportion of agreement and *pe* is the expected proportion of agreement. To apply this equation, take the data presented earlier as an illustration. Begin by constructing a 2 × 2 matrix where we tally occur and nonoccur for Observer 1 and 2 (Suen & Ary, 1989). This is presented in Table 9.6.

From the data presented earlier, the matrix is completed by, first, entering in Cell b of Table 9.4 the proportion of intervals both observers agreed on occurrence (3:10 or 0.3); in Cell c enter the proportion of interval where both observers agreed on nonoccurrence (3:10 or 0.3); in Cell a the proportion of intervals where Observer 1 scored occurrences and Observer 2 scored nonoccurrences (3:10, or .30); in Cell d the proportion of intervals where Observer 1 reported nonoccurrence and Observer 2 reported occurrence (1:10 or 0.10). The margins, or p1, p2, q1, and q2, are the sums of their respective rows and columns. To calculate po, in the *kappa* formula we add Cells b + c in the matrix (0.30 + 0.30 + 0.60):

Thus, po = 0.60.

pe is calculated by multiplying margins p1 × p2; then q1 × q2 and adding the two products. To calculate *k*, more simply we continue with this formula:

TABLE 9.6
Occurrence/Nonoccurrence Matrix for Two Observers

			Observer 1		
		Nonoccurrence		*Occur*	
Occur	(a)	.30	(b)	.30	.60(p1)
			Observer 2		
Nonoccurrence	(c)	.30	(d)	.10	.40 (q1)
	(q2)	.60	(p2)	.40	1.0

$$\frac{k = b + c - (p1p2 + q1q2)}{1 - (p1p2 + q1q2)}$$

p1 × p2, or 0.60 × 0.40 = 0.24; then multiply q1 × q2, or 0.40 × 0.60 = 0.24.

$$\frac{k = .030 + 0.30 - (0.24 + 0.24)}{1 - (0.24 + 0.24}$$

or

$$\frac{k = 0.60 - 0.48}{1 - 0.48} = \frac{0.12}{0.52} = 0.23$$

Kappa coefficients, like correlation coefficients, range from –1.0 to +1.0, where the latter indicates that observers agree completely and the latter indicates that they disagree totally. Any negative *kappa* indicates that observers agree at a less than chance level. A *kappa* of 0.60 is considered "acceptable" whereas a *kappa* of 0.80 or above is "good" (Suen & Ary, 1989).

To conclude this subsection, reliability can be considered at two levels, intra-observer and interobserver reliability. Both of the terms relate to the degree of consistency within and between observers, or the degree to which observers see the same thing consistently. There are various statistical procedures that allow us to gauge the level of consistency. The standards vary against which reliability statistics are compared, or answer the question: How good is it? For the S/L index, percentage of agreement, and occurrence and nonoccurrence statistics no standard exists. For correlation and *kappa* coefficients we have probability statements associated with the reliability statistics so that we know the probability of our getting a particular statistic by chance. *Kappa* has the added benefit or accounting for chance agreement between observers. All of these factors converge to the point that *kappa* is the recommended reliability statistic. Although the calculations of *kappa* may be bothersome, there are numerous statistical packages available for both microcomputers and mechanical recording devices which calculate *kappa* as part of their data analysis package.

Although the statistical technique used can affect the reliability statistic that is generated, there are other factors which affect the very reliability of the observations themselves.

CONCLUSION

In this chapter I discuss one of the two foundational dimensions of measurement: reliability. Reliability generally means consistency and is necessary before we can assume that a measure is valid. Reliability is affected not only by the measurement instrument per se, but also by the assessment procedure. So the instrument itself must be considered along with the administration and scoring procedures in determining reliability. In the next chapter I discuss validity.

SOME THINGS TO THINK ABOUT

1. How does your knowledge of reliability affect the way in which you construct observational categories? List three ways.

A. ______________________________

B. ______________________________

C. ______________________________

2. Videotape some kids on a playground. Go through the tape and code social and nonsocial behaviors of that tape. One week later try it again.

Did you agree?

Try doing this with another person.

10

Validity

At a very simple level, validity means truthfulness. Validity is concerned with the basic question: Are we measuring what it is we say we are measuring? Does the meaning that we assign to a measure, variable, or construct really correspond to the empirical meaning? Do the variables we are manipulating in our experiment have a causal relation with each other? Do the results generalize to other settings?

As noted in our earlier discussion on measures and reliability, the meaning of a score does not reside in a specific observational protocol. Instead, the meaning, and by implication the validity, of a score is the result of interactions between those procedures and the participants in the procedures. By participants I mean both the researchers and the research participant as each has an impact on the potential meaning of that which is being measured.

Scores derived from a standardized protocol, whether they be a standardized test or observational procedures, still are affected by the people administering the test (e.g., is the interviewer Black, White, male, female) and the participants being studied (Are they Black, White, male, or female? Are they familiar or unfamiliar with the venue?). Consequently, what might be valid for one group may not hold for another. It may be, for example, that a procedure reported as valid was established with researchers and children of the same race and sex in a very familiar setting. Consequently, the validity of this procedure is in question when these conditions are varied. From this view, validity is a dynamic process. It must be established in different places with different participants. The meaning of data derived in one setting can vary from those derived in another.

The meaning that we assign to a measure can be interpreted either in terms of its descriptive or decision-related implications (Cronbach, 1971). Efforts to establish validity can range from establishing it by proclamation (It's valid because I say it's valid or It's valid because it appears to be so) to a theoretical and empirical exegesis, and all points in between. In the first case, a measure is proclaimed to be valid because, on the face of it, it appears to be valid. Take the descriptive claim: "This is a very trustworthy car," made by a used car salesman! Is this a valid description of the car?

Clearly we can use more objective measures of trustworthiness, such as a mechanic being tested on his servicing of a car by checking of critical parts of service checklist. Scores lower than 95, for example, would be described as not trustworthy and scores higher would merit a trustworthy description.

Generally, the validity of our descriptions is the purview of content and construct validity. In short, how truthful is our description of that which we are trying to describe. The content validity of our trustworthy descriptions might be different for the used car salesman compared to the description based on a mechanics' checklist.

Another dimension of validity relates to the truthfulness of our claims as they relate to making decisions. Criterion-related validity is concerned with the truthfulness of data in making decisions and making predictions. Most typically, aptitude tests, such as the Scholastic Aptitude Test (SAT) or the American College Test (ACT) given in high school are used to predict the grade point average of students at the end of their first year of college. These data are used to make decisions regarding the admission of applicants. Applied to behavioral observations, classroom conduct data may be used as part of a battery to predictor of a young child's conduct disorder and subsequent assignment to a "special class."

Descriptive statements can, however, also be used to make decisions. Beginning with the first of the two examples, the validity of the claim that the car is trustworthy, although it is at base a descriptive statement, has clear implications for decision making. If it is trustworthy I should make the decision to buy it.

We could also use descriptive information in a more specific way to make claims about criterion-related validity. For example, we can use the descriptive score of 95 on a mechanic's checklist as a cut-off for trustworthiness. The empirical question then becomes, is this cut off score a valid predictor of trustworthiness? Of course, as part of this exercise we would have to decide on a criterion measure, such as number of repairs or dollar value of repairs.

This discussion of the descriptive and decision-making dimensions of validity is crucial for a number of reasons (Cronbach, 1971; Messick, 1983). First, we often think of validity (especially content and construct validity) only in terms of the adequacy of description. As shown earlier, descriptions can be used to make decisions. Indeed, descriptive data, such as a children's ranking on an observational assessment of conduct disorder, are typically used to make decisions about that child. For example, it is often used to assign children to a high or low group, or to determine if children will be given special treatment. From this view, we should be cognizant of the adequacy and implications of our decisions. To what degree do children at a certain rank perform as high or low in social competence? To what degree is our description of our car as "trustworthy" predictive of future performance?

In what follows I discuss the usual types of validity: content, criterion, and construct validity. I discuss the meaning of each in terms description and decision making, how we attempt to establish each, and some of the leading threats associated with invalidity. I also discuss validity issues as they pertain to experiments and quasiexperiments: internal, external, and ecological validity. As in the chapter on reliability, much work on the topic has been conducted in the areas of testing and experimentation. Similar to the approach in the last chapter, I discuss validity generally, at first, by drawing on this larger literature. Then I discuss issue of validity that are specific to behavioral observations.

TYPES OF VALIDITY

Validity is a judgement, based on theory and empirical findings, about the adequacy of an interpretation, or meaning, we assign to a measure. As noted earlier, validity is not the province of a test or an assessment procedure but, instead, the meaning of the score (Mesick, 1995). The meaning or interpretation relates not only to the score itself but also to implications, or decisions, for actions associated with the score (Cronbach, 1971; Messick, 1995). The extent to which these meanings and implications hold for different groups and for different assessment contexts, such as behavioral observations, is a basic issue in the study of validity. From this view, the validity of any measure is an evolving and dynamic process into the meaning and consequences of measurement. This broad-based view of validity is applicable to content, criterion, and construct validity.

Let us take a very simple example: The validity of an observational score for attending to a book being read by the teacher. The validity would be derived, first, from the degree to which our measure of attention is consistent with a theory. We, as third-grade teachers, could define attention in terms of gaze directed to the book. This conceptualization of attention could be based on the theory that attention means that the subject should be looking at the task, as a minimum. Empirically, we could relate this measure of attention to others, say heart-rate scores while reading.

In terms of consequences, the validity of this score could be evaluated by examining the relation between the score and assignment to a certain reading group. A high score should relate positively to performance in a high group, and a low score should also be consistent with other students in the low group.

In the remainder of this chapter I discuss the three types of validity commonly addressed in educational and psychological research: content, criterion-related, and construct validity (see Table 10.1).

Content Validity

Content validity addresses the extent to which the content in one assessment context, such as a test, adequately represent the universe from which it was sampled. More specific to observations, do the components of a category relate to the more general category? Thus, the first step in establishing and determining content validity is to specify the universe from which we will sample content. So for example, we may be concerned with measuring the content in a research methods class. The universe of material from which we sample would be specified as the information represented in the class textbook, observations of class lecture, and other assigned reading.

TABLE 10.1
Types of Validity

Types	*Guiding Questions*	*Examples of Uses of Data*
Content	Is the content representative of the universe of content?	Evaluate program effectiveness
Criterion-related	Does the measure predict what it should?	Does performance at Time 1 predict performance at Time 2?
Construct	Does the measure converge with and discriminate from other indicators of the construct?	Are the differences between "high" and "low" performers real?

From this universe we sample content, in the form of test items or responses to questions posed by the instructor. Content validity represents the sampling adequacy, or representativeness, of the content we have chosen in relation to the universe of information.

The extent to which the items in the test or the questions asked by the instructor have descriptive adequacy is related to experts' judgements about the content. If experts' judgements say the items describe the content under review, that the content represents the universe to which we generalize and the items and questions correspond to the objectives, then the measure has descriptive adequacy.

It may be the case that the universe from which we sample contains diverse domains of knowledge. We may, in our hypothetical research methods class, sample from knowledge of statistics, history, tests and measurement, and experimental psychology. Consequently, we would be sampling from a diverse universe of knowledge. This has implications for documenting content validity. That is, we would not expect there to be significant intercorrelations between such a diverse set of domains. Thus, the homogeneity of items is not necessary for content validity (Cronbach, 1971).

Establishing Content Validity. How do we establish the extent to which our measure and procedure is content valid? At a gross level, judgements are made by individuals on the fit between the material in the assessment and the universe from which it was chosen. Our judgements can be systematized by examining the degree to which the content of a test or observational instrument meet the objectives of the course in research methods. In Fig. 10.1 I have constructed a hypothetical matrix. Across the top I have numbered the 10 instructional objectives for the class. The numbers under each objective represent the numbers of categories from an observational instrument that fall under each objective.

Content validity is maximized when the objectives are considered at a very specific level rather than at a more general level. So, a general objective, arithmetic calculations, could be further specified as single-digit addition, subtraction,

Objectives	*1*	*2*	*3*	*4*	*5*	*6*	*7*	*8*	*9*	*10*
Observation Categories	3	4	4	9	1	10	5	3	12	1

FIG. 10.1. Content validity matrix

multiplication, and division. Specificity allows us to write items that bare a close resemblance to the objectives.

The data presented in Fig. 10.1 indicates that all of the instructional objectives in the course were met to the extent that all objectives were covered by the categories. So at the gross level, this instrument could be said to be content valid.

At a more differentiated level, we might, rightly, want to make a more precise content validity judgement. For instance, we might want to gauge the content validity in terms of the correspondence between the ordered importance of the objectives in the class and the number of categories to measure them. In other words, we would want those objectives that we deem to be most important to be those weighed most heavily in the observational instrument.

Looking at the data in Fig. 10.1 we see that the objectives that are most frequently represented by categories: 9, 6, and 4, respectively. The remaining objectives are ordered as: 7, 2 and 3, 1 and 8, and 1 and 10. A stronger case for content validity can be made if the order of importance of categories and objectives correspond perfectly.

In the end, however, the judgement as to whether this instrument has content validity, and if it does, the degree to which it does is still a matter of a value judgement. Is the ordering of the categories and objectives in Fig. 10.1 indicative of content or not? Or does it require a clearer ordering of categories to objectives. It is, in the end, a judgement call.

Minimally, however, it is incumbent on the researcher to specify how content validity was addressed. In the aforementioned case, the researcher would specify the correspondence between categories and objectives as rated by some expert in the matter.

Content validity, as noted at the beginning of this chapter is primarily a descriptive enterprise. Our main concern with description is to be assured that the content adequately samples from the universe from which the test items or observational categories are sampled. These sorts of descriptions can also be used to make decisions (Cronbach, 1971). This case is especially true when we look at uses of assessment strategies in educational settings and in the workplace. I explore using a content-valid achievement information to make education decisions.

Making Decisions With Content Valid Data. Achievement data are descriptive to the extent that they tell us how much information on a topic students have learned. Data can be derived form a variety of sources, such as tests, direct observations, and work samples. Yet, these same data can also be used to make decisions about an educational program. That is, the achievement results inform our decisions about the effectiveness of a particular method of teaching or the effect of a particular teacher on students' achievement. Further, we can also ask about the effectiveness of these methods and teachers in impacting students' learning the most important objectives.

Before these sorts of decisions can be made, however, three issues must be addressed, as specified in Table 10.2.

First, and most crucially, the scales of measurement must measure the desired outcomes. By this I mean that what is assessed in a content-valid measure must contain information that is relevant to the decision at hand. For example, in our observational instrument to assess achievement example, we many be interested in the effectiveness of the extant curriculum in teaching children to solve mathematical word problems. This information could be used to make decisions about the ways in which teachers' should allocate their time to calculations and problem solving.

Obviously, in order to make this type of decision we should have sampled adequately from the universe of mathematical word problems. This process is enhanced by presenting scores at the level of subscores as well as an aggregate score. For example, an aggregate achievement score would also list scores for calculation, mathematical problem solving, reading comprehension, and vocabulary. Specific subscores could be used to make decisions about corresponding areas of instruction.

There is a correspondence between the number of content-valid subscores collected and the breath of decision-making possibilities. Obviously, the broader the base from which we sampled, the broader is the horizon of decision making. Issues of economy, to students, teachers, and tax payers, however, should moderate the extensiveness of the assessment. That is, we should not assess everything possible with some dim notion of how it will be used to make decisions.

The second issue is really a matter of economy. We should collect content-valid information only in those areas that are relevant to the program under consideration and to areas that may impact decision making. Assessment is both obtrusive and expensive, especially if it is perceived as getting in the way of the business of instruction for teachers, students, and administrators. It is also costly in terms of the time needed to implement and interpret the assessments. With all of this said, assessments should be used with specific content and decisions in

TABLE 10.2
Using Content-Valid Data to Make Decisions

1. The scales of measurement must measure desired outcomes.
2. Minimize the use of scales that are not important to the program.
3. The standard of performance must be acceptable to stakeholders.

mind. As in our earlier discussion, there should be a correspondence between what is assessed and the importance of different decisions.

Just as we ranked order the importance of the objectives in terms of descriptive adequacy, so too can we rank order the decisions we want to make with the data. This ordering of priorities should guide our choice of testing coverage.

Lastly, the standard of performance must be addressed and it must be acceptable to the stakeholders in the process (Cronbach, 1971). Thus, it must be decided what constitutes "an adequate level of achievement." Deciding the level of adequate performance is a local matter and criteria for what constitutes adequacy should be made at this level. Should the decision be based on future performance, for example? On teachers' judgements? At the least these criteria should be specified. More preferred would be adding some level of empirical justification to the decision. This level of justification moves us into criterion-related validity.

CRITERION-RELATED VALIDITY

Where content validity was primarily concerned with description and only secondarily with decision making, criterion-related validity is concerned, primarily with decision making. In criterion-related, or predictive, validity we have one variable (a predictor) forecasting performance of an outside, criterion variable. The classic cases of criterion-related validity involve aptitude tests, such as the SATs, LSATs, and GREs taken at Time 1 to predict performance at Time 2, usually grade point average at the end of the first year of college or graduate school, as the case may be. Thus, there is a temporal, predictive, dimension to criterion-related validity: The predictor is an antecedent, in time, to the criterion.

Unlike content validity, with criterion-related validity we can make objective judgements about the validity of our prediction. The relation between the predictor and the criterion variables is typically expressed by a correlation coefficient. Our judgements about the validity of the prediction are informed by the magnitude of the correlation and if it is statistically significant or not.

As I commented in earlier chapters, the magnitude of correlation coefficients (represented as r) range from -1.0 to $+1.0$. A perfect positive correlation, $r = 1.0$, means that for every level of increase in the predictor (e.g., SAT score) there is a corresponding increase in the criterion (GPA). A perfect negative correlation, $r = -1.0$, on the other hand, means that for every unit of increase in the predictor there is a corresponding decrease in the criterion. Please note that the examples provided in the following are for illustration only. They do not represent the actual correlations between GPA and SAT. I use these examples because they are familiar. Further, we exaggerate the magnitude of the correlation coefficients just to illustrate our points simply.

Let us take two sets of data, illustrated in Tables 10.3 and 10.4.

In each case we have eight students' SAT scores in their senior year of high school and the GPA of these same students at the end of their first year of college. Figure 7 illustrates a scatter plot for $r = 1.0$ for the relation between SAT

TABLE 10.3
Positive SAT and GPA Values

SAT	GPA
200	1
200	1
400	2
400	2
600	3
600	3
800	4
800	4

TABLE 10.4
Negative SAT and GPA Values

SAT	GPA
200	4
200	4
400	3
400	3
600	2
600	2
800	1
800	1

and GPA. Figure 8, illustrated a scatter plot for $r = -1.0$ for the same variables. The correlation coefficient represents a statistical expression of the fit of the data along a straight line. The closer the fit along a straight line, the higher the correlation coefficient.

In both cases we are making perfect predictions: For every unit of change in SAT there is a corresponding change in GPA. Importantly, a negative correlation of –1 is no less perfect than a positive correlation of +1.

Perfect correlations are not, of course, typical. More frequently, the magnitude is somewhere between +1 and –1. In Table 10.5 I present another set of data for eight students' SAT and GPA.

The scatter plot for these data is presented in Fig. 10.4.

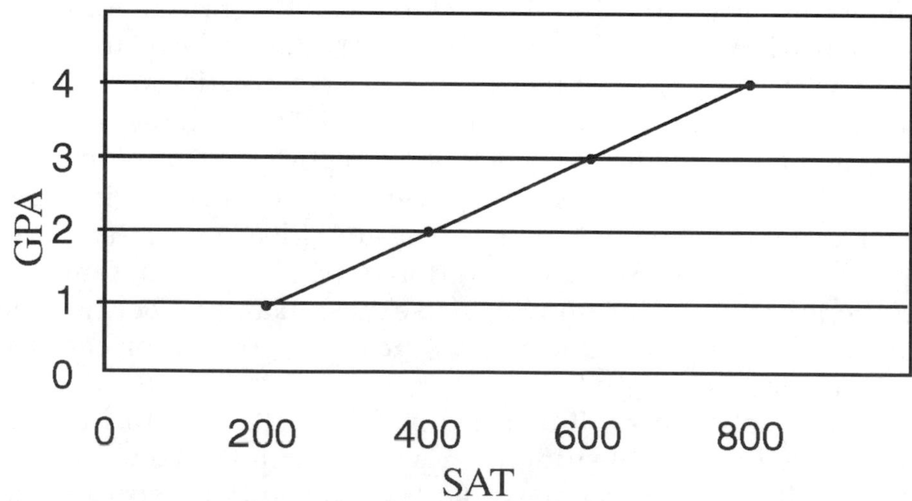

FIG. 10.2. Perfect positive correlation.

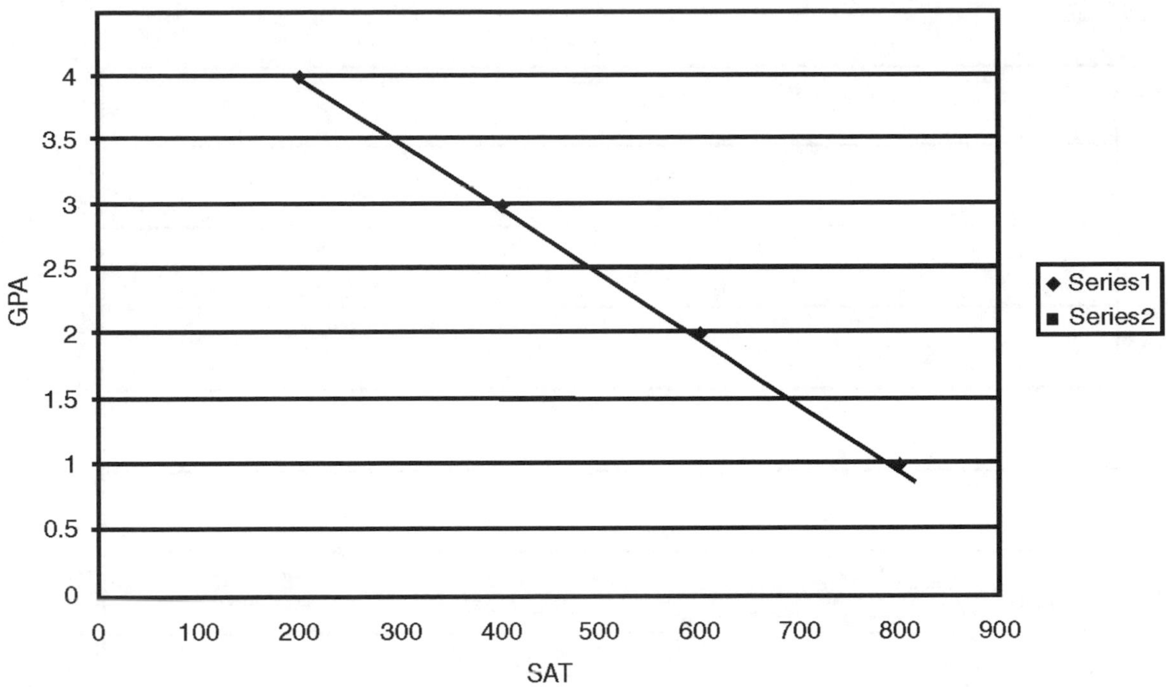

FIG. 10.3. Perfect negative correlation.

TABLE 10.5
SAT and GPA

SAT	*GPA*
520	3.3
330	2.9
410	3.2
450	3.2
360	3.5
460	2.4
590	3.7
290	2.5

The correlation coefficient for the data displayed in Fig. 10.4 is, $r = 0.88$. The importance of a correlation coefficient of this magnitude is determined, first, by taking the correlation coefficient and squaring it: $(0.88)^2 = 0.77$. This value of 0.77 represents the amount of the variation in GPA due to variation in SAT. In simpler terms SAT accounts for 77% of the variation in GPA. Again, note that this exaggerated relationship is for illustration only.

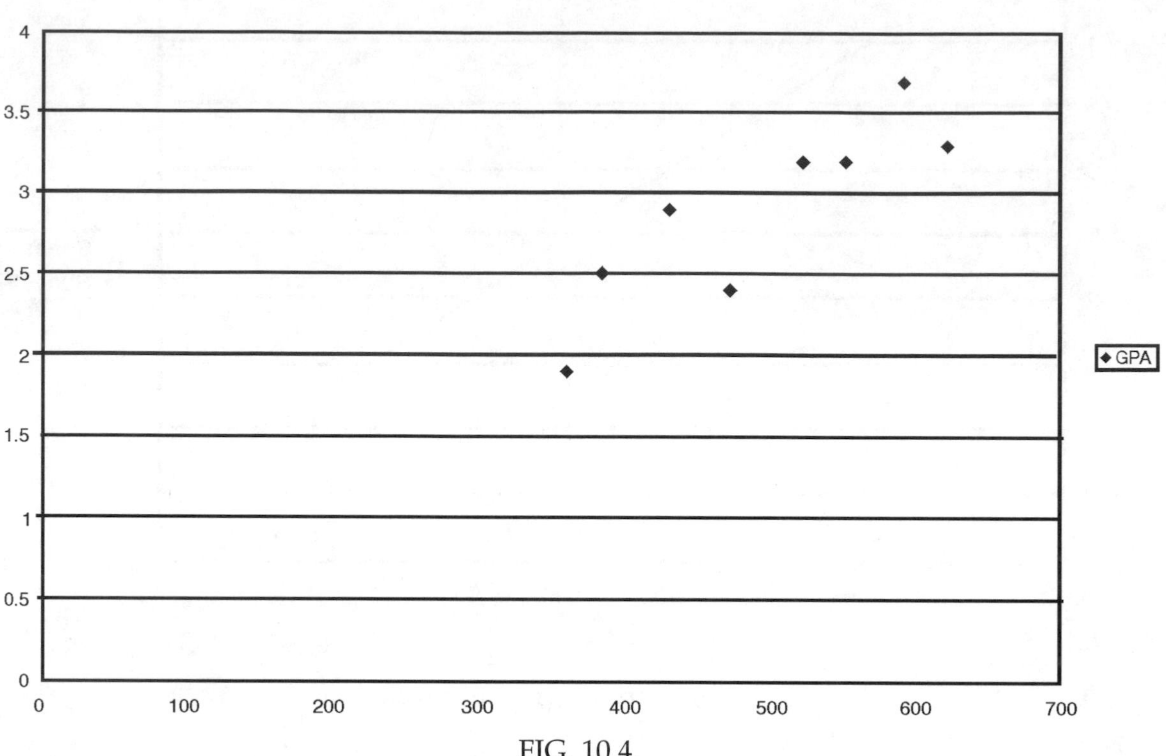

FIG. 10.4.

The other way of judging the importance of a correlation coefficient is related to its statistical significance. That is, to what degree is the value we got, 0.88, due to chance? We determine statistical significance by taking the correlation coefficient, 0.88, and the sample size, 8. In this case, our correlation coefficient is statistically significant at the 0.01. This means that the possibility of this results being due to chance is only 1 case out of 100. In 99 cases out of 100, we get the same results with the same sample.

Statistical significance is determined by the magnitude of the correlation coefficient and the sample size. For example, a correlation coefficient of 0.30 would be statistically at the 0.05 level with a sample of 42 or more. With a sample size of 35, for example, it would not be significant.

Making a decision on how to use SAT scores for college admission becomes quite a bit easier using these two bits of information. First of all, we know that the relation between the two variables is real, it is not due to chance (well in 99:100 cases). Second, the magnitude of the relation and the corresponding R^2 tell us that 77% of the variation in GPA is due to our predictor. Indeed, we can predict very accurately.

There are numerous factors influencing the relation between the predictor and the criterion variables, as displayed in Table 10.6.

Using information at Time 1 to predict performance at Time 2 can be especially difficult with certain populations. For example, trying to predict the perform-

Table 10.6
Factors Influencing Criterion-Related Validity

Factors	*Example*
Age of Subject	Changes in meaning of the construct
Time Between Assessed	Changes in environment
Choice of Outcomes	Tests & judgements
Sampling participants	Restricted range of scores

ance of very young children is difficult because they are changing so rapidly. The implication of this change is that the ways in which we measure a construct at Time 1 (say intelligence) can be very different from the ways in which we measure it at Time 2. Intelligence in infancy, for example, is often measured by observing habituation to novel stimuli (e.g., Bornstein, Ferdinandsen, & Gross, 1981). Intelligence during the preschool years, on the other hand, can be measured, through a variety of means, such as receptive vocabulary size (e.g., Pellegrini & Galda, 1991).

The difficulties with predictive validity in such cases are substantial, as there are matters of both theory and measurement to address. A theoretical case must be made in this case as to why habituation at Time 1 represents a similar construct as receptive vocabulary at Time 2. Next, empirical assessment must document these relations.

When the nature of the constructs changes from Time 1 to Time 2 we are less sure of the relations than when we are measuring the same construct. The relations, or lack of it, could be due to another number of things.

Additionally, the longer elapsed time between Time 1 and Time 2, the lower the correlation coefficient. Lapses of time between assessment points change the relations between scores because other factors intervene. For example, the nature of individuals' environments can change. Individuals can move from an enriched environment at Time 1 to a relatively impoverished one at Time 2. So a test given at Time 1, say at the end of the school year, would not correlate highly with a test given at the end of the summer, at Time 2. The Time 2 score is influenced by the lack of attention to matters relevant to the test, whereas at Time 1 the student is engrossed in these matters. Alternatively, someone could move from an impoverished to an enriched environment, such as from an orphanage to a caring home (or vice versa), and there could also be low intertest correlations.

As noted in the discussion of the changing nature of constructs, the measure we choose as outcomes influence the validity of our predictions. In the fields of education and psychology, a number of outcomes are used in criterion-related validity work. For example, achievement tests and observers' judgments about achievement are used in schools (Cronbach, 1971) and archival information about antisocial behavior (e.g., court records; Moffitt, Caspi, Rutter, & Silva, 2001).

Regarding achievement tests, in many states there are state-wide assessment programs used to measure program impact. The validity of tests as outcomes, however, is influenced by timing and the duration between the treatment and the testing. For example, a test given right at the end of a course of study would probably yield different results from a test given 2 months after the treatment.

The judgements most frequently used in education are teacher judgements, most of which are based on direct observation. To quote directly from Cronbach (1971) on this matter: "The criterion provided by course marks is notoriously unsatisfactory, but the ease of obtaining such data makes them the most common of all outcome measures" (p. 491). Teachers' judgements of students are frequently influences by a variety of extraneous factors, thus making the judgements of questionable validity. For example, female teachers' preferences for female-stereotypic behavior (which is more sedentary than boys') leads them to inflate girls' grades relative to boys (Cronbach, 1971).

This bias also has been observed in the social-emotional realm. For example, Pellegrini and Bartini (2000) compared the relations among widely varying of methods (check lists, direct observations, peer nominations) from different perspectives (teachers, children, object observers) in measuring aggression. Most important for this discussion, teachers and research assistants both rate children's aggression. The research assistants had spent an entire year observing these children so they had an in-depth knowledge of each. The research assistants also were trained to observe aggression reliably. We then compared the relations between each of their ratings with the other measures of aggression. Generally, the researcher assistants', relative to the teachers', ratings related higher to the other measures of aggression. This was due, in part, to the research assistants being less biased in their judgements of individual children and their aggression.

Research dating back 60 years by my former teacher and mentor George G. Thompson (1944) documents this as a persistent problem. He showed that preschool teachers rated physically attractive students as more competent and popular than less attractive students. Thus, the validity of teachers' rating is questionable, given the influence of bias.

The sampling of the students we use in a study also influences the criterion-related validity of our results. Most generally, and as noted in the immediately preceding paragraphs, we have different distributions of scores for different segments of the population, such as boys and girls, poor and middle class, and so forth (Cronbach, 1971). Thus, if the sampling procedures permit, we should have separate predictions for each relevant group.

The validity of the criterion measure is influenced not only by the demographics of the students, but also by the distribution of their scores. Without going into too much statistical detail, the magnitude of the correlation coefficient between the prediction and the criterion variables is influenced by the spread of the scores at each point. If the range of the scores is restricted (lots of very high or very low scores), the correlation coefficient will be low, relative to a case where the scores are normally distributed. So if the validity of a criterion variable was established with normal distributions, subsequent validity judgements should be based on similar distributions, not on restricted scores, such as those represented from groups consisting of mainly very high or very low scoring students.

Construct Validity

Construct validation involves measuring some quality that is not operationally defined (Cronbach & Meehl, 1955). A construct is an abstract representation of that what we are trying to measure. Consequently, and unlike content and criterion-related validity, there can be no direct measure of a construct. Individual measures are used as separate indicators (both in terms of convergence and divergence) of a construct. It is something we approach rather than reach.

Construct validity also relates to the consequences of an assessment. This aspect of construct validity relates to the fact that in all types of validity we should be concerned with both the descriptive and decision adequacy of our validity claims. In other words, how well does an assessment procedure do what it is supposed to do? As part of our evaluation of the adequacy of our decisions, we should also be concerned with consequences associated with the assessments that are inadvertent yet occur anyway. Consequently, construct validity is a unified concept: It encompasses meaning related to the descriptive and consequential dimensions of the construct (Messick, 1995).

In this section I first describe construct validity as a unified concept. But in order to do this, we must break it down into some of its components so that it can be more clearly understood. The components are displayed in Table 10.7 (Messick, 1995).

A construct must have a specified content and specified boundaries. A construct can refer to a domain, such as knowledge of mathematics. A first step in establishing and assessing the content component of construct validity is to assemble tasks and behaviors that represent the domain under review (Messick, 1995). It is crucial to sample adequately the important parts of the domain ad-

TABLE 10.7
Components of Construct Validity

Components	*Evidence*
Content	Content relevance and representativeness
Substantive	Consistency in responses
Structural	Match of scoring of structure to the construct of the domain
Generalizability	Generalize to other groups, settings, tasks
External	Convergent and divergent information
Consequential	Value implications of scores, especially in relation to sources of invalidity

dressed. The universe of the content can be found in curriculum guides, task analyses, and job performance manuals, for example.

It is crucial that the content that differentiates experts from novices be included. It is also important that the most important aspects of the domain be included. The extent to which you have accomplished this is assessed, as in judging content validity, by having a panel of experts review the content of the construct in relation to the domain. Note the resemblance of this procedure to that which was discussed for establishing descriptive adequacy for content validity.

Substantive aspects of construct validity address the processes associated with the domain under review. Keeping with our mathematics example, we would want to document the processes associated with addition and subtraction. This could be accomplished in a number of different ways. For example, we could have experts deconstruct the processes they think are involved in solving addition and subtraction problems. We could also ask individuals to recall what is it they do when they are solving problems. Lastly, "think aloud" protocols, could be used such that individuals talk aloud about what it is they are doing as they are doing it. Specifically, participants are presented with a task, such as playing a game of chess or solving a math problem, and asked to think aloud about their thought processes. Like content and substantive aspects of validity, the key task is to gather a representative sample of processes from the domain.

The structural aspect of construct validity necessitates that the scoring of dimensions of the domain are consistent with the theory guiding the construct. So, for example, subtasks of the same problem should be intercorrelated with each other and each subtask should, in turn, be correlated with the superordinate task.

These scores, in turn, could be generalizable beyond the sample to a large universe of participants, tasks, and times. Generalizability is assessed by correlating the sampled measure with some other measure. Generalizability is maximized, in the original sample if we have adequate samples of content, process, and participants.

One of the ways in which generalizability is documented is through convergent and divergent correlations between the target measure and other, external measures. Theory should specify the extent to which externals measures converge with and diverge from our construct. People scoring high on our measure of mathematics should score high on other measures of mathematics, such as other tests, teacher ratings, or performance on everyday tasks. This is an indicator of convergence. Evidence for convergence comes in the form of positive significant correlations between the measures.

We should also be able to discriminate between measures for our construct and other, nonrelated measures. Measures for our construct should also be distinguishable, and not correlated with, measures of theoretically unrelated constructs. So our construct, mathematics should not be correlated with another construct, reading comprehension. If the two are significantly intercorrelated either (or both) of their labels are inaccurate. Thus, divergence is related to parsimony (Campbell & Fiske, 1959; Cronbach, 1971) to the extent that we want to use the fewest constructs to account for the greatest number of relations. Consequently, we do not want to confuse one construct with another. We do not call it math or reading, we call it intelligence or shared method variance.

Next I present a hypothetical correlation matrix to illustrate this point (see Table 10.8). As we can see, both of the measures of reading (comprehension and word attack skills) and both measures of mathematics (computation and spatial) are highly intercorrelated, at 0.78 and 0.88, respectively. Thus, the math measures converge with the math measures and the reading measures converge with the reading measures. Neither of the reading measures are highly related to the math measures, thus the math and the reading measures discriminate between each other.

The last aspect of construct validity we consider is *consequence*. Consequential aspects of validity include intended consequences as well as unintended consequences that occur. For example, an intended consequence of our construct mathematics is that we are able to identity effective math teachers as well as predict children would are high and low performers in math.

The primary problem associated with this aspect of validity is the possibility of negative impacts on individuals due to construct underrepresentation or construct-irrelevant variance (Messick, 1995). Construct underrepresentativeness exists when our definition of a construct is too narrow and does not include important information. In our hypothetical math construct, we may be sampling from multiple digit addition and subtraction problems only, and not simpler operations as well. In this case the test is too difficult for some children as it only addresses higher level operations, though the construct specifies mathematics at a more general level.

Construct-irrelevant variance is a problem when the assessment procedure has systematic variance associated with other constructs such as shared method variance, test scoring or observer bias, or format biases. Construct-irrelevant variance can result in scores being unfairly lowered or inflated. Scores can be lowered due to tester and scorer bias, for instance. In other cases, the race or gender of the observer may adversely influence the participants' performance.

TABLE 10.8
Convergence and Discrimination Matrix

	2	3	4
Reading Comprehension (1)	0.78	0.30	0.25
Word Attack Skills (2)		0.22	0.18
Math Computation (3)			0.88
Math Spatial (4)			

Inflated scores can result from clues in the observational venue and observer bias. Regarding venue, it may be the case that placing participants in a specific setting affects their performance. For example, when mother and children are observed in contrived situation, their performance is influenced by their notions of social desirability.

Consequences as validity evidence includes both intended and unintended consequences of the assessment procedure (Messick, 1995). An intended consequence of an assessment procedure could be the improvement of placing students in classes. These consequences could be both positive, such as more closely matching instruction to students' levels, and negative, such as inaccurately placing certain groups of students.

To guard against negative, unintended consequences, we should be sure that scores are not influenced negatively by construct-irrelevant variance or underrepresentation. That is, something irrelevant to the assessment should not inhibit individuals from exhibiting their highest levels of competence. For example, we should guard against occurrences where individuals are unfairly scored due to bias.

In short, construct validation involves evaluating scores against all of these levels of concern. This is done by providing a justification as to why a construct can be represented as it has been and evaluating the extent to which the data support this claim for each of the aspects of concern. It is this justification statement that should guide the search for empirical connections between the construct and other converging and discriminating evidence. It is also this justification that guides the hypotheses to be tested in relation to the construct.

VALIDITY: MOLAR AND MOLECULAR CATEGORIES

At this point the distinction between categories involving high levels of inference and categories involving low levels of inference becomes important in this discussion of validity. This section is a very detailed discussed of ways in which to establish validity for these two types of categories and can be read in two different ways. For the student interested in fine-tuned distinctions between different levels of category inference, the section should be read carefully. For those interested in a general distinction between high- and low-inference categories, the section can be read less systematically; instead, students can read *General Comment* sections at the end of relevant paragraphs.

Unobservable constructs, such as romance, have been labeled *signs* by Suen and Ary (1989). They are theoretical categories and the sign represent them. Thus, signs are high inference. A sample, on the other hand, is low inference and can be observed directly and would include such things as: smile, kiss, and hug. (*Sample*, as used here to refer to types of category, should not be confused with use of sampling techniques discussed in preceding chapters.) High-inference and low-inference categories, in turn, can be measured through the use of molecular and molar categories (Suen & Ary, 1989). As noted previously, molecular measures are usually at a physical description level of description and involve a single observable behavior, such as push. Molar measures, on the other hand, represent an aggregate of subcomponents; for example, R&T could be a molar category that is the aggregate of a number of molecular measures such as hit at, push, smile, and so forth.

It is useful to think of the validity of observational data when they are conceptualized along these two dimensions of molar and molecular and high and low inference. The dimensions are displayed in Table 10.9.

Thus, behaviors can be assigned along four dimensions, corresponding to the cells in this matrix. Starting with Cell 1, a molecular/low-inference measure of playfulness might include hit at/open hand. Molecular/low-inference measures have been considered to be, on face value, valid to the extent that little inference about the meaning of the behavior is needed: hit at/open behaviors simply represent what they say they represent, hit at/open hand.

Moving down the matrix, to Cell 3, molar/low-inference measures are aggregates of observable subcomponents. So, R&T is a molar/sample behavior in that it is the aggregate of the molecular sample behaviors. Validity of this category, or the extent to which it really represents the category R&T can be derived from the theoretical and empirical literature. For example, to what degree does extant theory suggest that the behaviors you have listed represent something called R&T. The degree to which these behaviors come together into a homogeneous category called R&T can be established through techniques such as factors analyses.

General Comments: Validity of low-inference categories are established by considering the extent to which each behavioral component of a category and their aggregate into a category are theoretically consistent with our conceptualization of the category.

Moving into more inferential categories, we consider sign-level measures. Recall sign-level categories are unobservable. Working with romance as an example of a sign category, we can say that Cell 2, molecular/high-inference, is affect. In Cell 4, molar/high inference, is an aggregate of the molecular sign behaviors comprising Cell 3.

General Comments: High-inference categories, like low-inference categories, are formed by noting individual components (molecular) and aggregating them into a molar category. The difference between high- and low-inference categories is the degree to which each is directly observable.

As previously noted, the different levels of inference for these categories mean that different validity decisions are necessary for each cell and for each of the different types of validity. In the next section, I address, briefly, the common dimen-

TABLE 10.9
High and Low Inference and Molecular and Molar Categories

	Low	*High*
Molecular	1	2
Molar	3	4

sions of validity. Additionally, I outline the conditions necessary for validity for the four categories outlined.

Different Types of Validity and Molar and Molecular Categories

Construct validity has been considered to be the most basic form of validity, to which all measures should aspire (Linn, 1994; Loevenger, 1957; Messick, 1975, 1983). Construct validity means, the degree to which the behaviors measured represent a theoretical construct; *constructs*, by definition, are not observable, and thus high inference. Construct validity is closely tied to a theory of whatever it is we are trying to measure.

General Comment: If we are not concerned with measuring a construct, such as when we use molar and molecular sample measures, construct validity should not a concern (Suen & Ary, 1989).

When high-inference measures are used, however, construct validity is very important because we are purporting to measure something abstract. With each type of high inference measure, that is, molar and molecular, we must address the extent to which our categories reflect what it is we say they reflect: This is the construct validity question. Construct validity is traditionally established by correlating the behavioral measure with other theoretically relevant measures. It should correlate positively with those measuring a similar construct (convergent validity) and negatively or not all with some measures (discriminant validity). Take the romance example from earlier. The behavioral components of romance should relate positively to related measures, such as positive affect displays, and negatively with measures of inhibition.

General Comment: For molecular/high-inference measures, construct validity simply means correlating that one high inference measure (recall molecular measures have only one component) with another, theoretically related measure (Suen & Ary, 1989). For molar/high inference measures, however, two processes are necessary to establish construct validity.

First, the molecular components of the molar category should be homogeneous, or internally consistent. Without going into detail, establishing internal consistency can be accomplished through a number of statistical routines, such as factor analyses and Generalizability Theory. These procedures are beyond the scope of this book and the interested reader is referred to Suen and Ary (1989) for a detailed, and very clearly presented, technical discussion.

The next level in establishing construct validity is similar to what was done to establish construct validity for molecular/high-inference measures: Each of the components of the molar category, as well as the molar category as a whole, should then be related to other measures purported to measure that construct. The empirical relationship between measures is tested with correlation coefficients.

Content validity is a measure of the degree to which a specific measure represents the components of the variable being measured. Content validity can be best understood if we begin by talking about the content validity of tests, and then move to observational data. Content validity of a test is established by measuring the degree to which the test measures what was taught. The components of the variable of interest in this case (what was taught) are represented by the instructional objectives for the class taking the test. Content validity is determined by the match or mismatch between the test items and the instructional objectives. An instrument is content valid if it measures the same material that is taught. This can be measured by simply noting the match or mismatch between items and objectives.

For observational data, I address the content validity for the four levels of categories displayed in Table 10.9. Starting with molecular/low-inference measures, the measures themselves represent the domain, so like the construct validity case, molecular/low-inference measures are content valid by definition. If we take the molecular/low-inference measure, hit at/open, this measure represents that domain.

For molar/high-inference measures, on the other hand, no one single sign can represent the whole domain in which one is interested; therefore, molecular/high-inference measures cannot be content valid (Suen & Ary, 1989). So, hit at/open cannot represent the domain of R&T because R&T has many more components. Molar/low-inference measures, as noted earlier, are aggregates, of subcomponents. In order to establish content validity of this type of measure we must establish the content validity of each molecular/low-inference behavior first. Then, we must judge the degree to which all of these molecular/low-inference measures, taken together, represent the domain in which we are interested. Take the example of the molar/low-inference measure R&T. In order to establish the content validity here we should be assured that our molecular/samples are representative of R&T. So we should have components that relate the three definitive dimensions of play: affect, such as smiling, vigor, such as run and hit at, and structure, such as top and bottom positions in wrestling. Like content validity in tests, we must judge the degree to which measures actually represent a domain. One way of establishing this would be asking a panel of experts to list the dimensions and gauge the degree to which the two dimensions match.

Lastly, we have the case of high-inference/molar categories. To establish content validity in these cases involves all the procedures utilized in for establishing content validity for molar low-inference measures.

General Comment: Low-inference molecular measures are content valid, by definition. The aggregate of low-inference measures is determined by the extent to which theory or experts consider them as a category. Molecular high-inference categories, on the other hand, cannot be content valid because no one high-inference measure can represent a larger category and a molar.

The final type of validity to be discussed, criterion-related validity, has two components that are discussed: predictive validity and concurrent validity. In both cases we relate our behavioral measure to some other criterion. The difference between concurrent and predictive validity is one of time. In the case of concurrent validity, two measures (one of which is our observational measure) are taken at roughly the same time. In predictive validity, the observational measure is taken at one time and another measure is taken at another time. To gauge each form of criterion validity, correlation coefficients are used. So the magnitude of the correlation between R&T at Time 1 and social role taking at Time 2, for example $r = 0.30$, tells us the degree to which R&T is predictive of social role taking. The fact that R&T is predictive in this way suggests that the R&T measure is picking up something useful in that it relates systematically to other measures.

In terms of concurrent validity, if we think that R&T is a dimension of play, we might correlate it with another contemporaneous measure of play, such as, fantasy. The degree to which the two measures are intercorrelated is the index of concurrent validity.

General Comments: Molecular/low-inference criterion validity is simply a measure of observer accuracy (Seen & Ary, 1989). Alternately, for either molecular/high-inference or molar/high-inference measures we simply correlate our observational measures at each of these levels and then correlate them with either of the behavioral measures of those variables. Alternately, we might correlate them with other types of measures, such as questionnaires. So for example if we have the molar/high-inference measure of R&T, we could correlate it with other behavioral measures of vigorous behavior, such as chasing, or correlate it with a teacher questionnaire that rates children's engagement in different forms of activities, including R&T.

VALIDITY: THREATS TO VALIDITY OF OBSERVATIONAL SCORES

In the preceding chapter I outlined some threats to the reliability of observational measures. As reliability and validity are linked, those threats to reliability are also threats to validity. Two additional threats which are specific to validity and they are reactivity and observer bias. Reactivity refers to the extent to which the subjects of our observations act differently simply because they know we are observing them. For example, if we are observing mothers reading to children mothers could act "un-naturally," or the way they think observers think they should be acting (see Sears, Maccoby, & Levin, 1957). Thus, the validity issue here is concerned with the truthfulness of our observations as representations of mother–child interaction. Observers could be 100% consistent in their coding but still not address the validity issue. As noted in that earlier chapter there are numerous ways to minimize this problem but probably the surest method involves repeated and lengthy observations. As participants habituate to being observed, they will act more naturally.

The issue of observer bias, too, is important. Recall that observer bias exists when observers tend to "see what they want to see." From the play literature we know that when observers are aware of the hypotheses of the study and of the experimental conditions to which children are assigned, researchers code observational data in ways consistent with the research hypotheses. Again, interobserver reliability is high in all these studies, but they were all reliably biased. A safeguard against bias is to use blind and double blind procedures. For example, we should have observers unaware of the hypotheses of the study and if relevant to children's groups assignment. Further, when children are also given tests, interviews, or questionnaires, observers should be blind to these results as they may bias their subsequent observations of the children. For example, if the same person interviewed a child and the results of that interview suggested that he or she was aggressive, that knowledge would probably influence subsequent observations; for example, in observing ambiguous cases, such as making distinctions between R&T and aggression, observer bias may lead the observer to code the child's behavior as aggressive. It also makes sense, where a number of observers are available, to counterbalance observers across sessions and children. That is, different observers should observe different children and conduct observations at different times.

VALIDITY IN EXPERIMENTAL RESEARCH

In the preceding sections I discussed validity as it applied to measurement. These types of validity and much of the discussions surrounding them have been addressed mostly to the contexts of assessment using direct observations.

Important discussions of validity have also taken place in another assessment context: experiments. Indeed, observational methods are frequently used in experimental contexts. For example, Fiske and Campbell (1979) discussed the construct validity of cause or effect to refer to the validity of the generalization of the results of experiments to different settings. From this view, it is a dimension of the external validity of experiments where external validity is defined as the approximate validity of our causal claims from an experiment to different people, measures, and historical time (Cook & Campbell, 1979). In this section I discuss internal, external, and ecological validity in the context of experiments.

Internal validity refers to the approximate validity of our claims of a causal relation between an independent and dependent variable. Ecological validity (Bronfenbrenner, 1979), like Brunswik's (1956) notion of ecological sampling, examines the extent to which the experimental context resembles the everyday context that it is supposed to mimic.

Internal Validity

As noted, internal validity is concerned with the approximate truthfulness of causal claims about the relations between an independent variable and a dependent variable. There are two levels of concern in making this inference.

The first is a statistical inference; that is, we make some inference about the relation between two variables based on the statistical covariation between them. The validity of these statistical conclusions is referred to statistical conclusion validity.

Statistical Conclusion Validity

In judging the statistical conclusion validity of results of an experiment we must determine three things, as displayed in Table 10.10.

TABLE 10.10
Statistical Conclusion Validity

1. Is the study sensitive enough to detect covariation?
2. If 1 is true, is there evidence to infer cause–effect covariation?
3. If 2 is true, how strongly do the two variables covary?

First, a word about covariation is necessary. For our purposes here, covariation refers to the variation, or changes, in each of two variables. So in our earlier example on correlation coefficients and criterion-related validity the covariation between the SAT and GPA was plotted in the two graphs.

The logic is similar with experimental results. Variation occurs in each of a number of treatment conditions and there are corresponding dependent variable scores with each treatment. Treatments and the dependent scores covary. Take a hypothetical example of experimentally manipulating exercise time (the independent variable) and an observational measure heart rate. The data in Table 10.11 and the graph in Fig. 10.5 plots the covariation between the two variables.

Figure 10.5 shows the covariation between exercise and heart rate: Those who exercise longer periods daily have corresponding decreases heart rate.

In order to establish the statistical conclusion validity of these results we must first determine if the study is sensitive enough to detect covariation. This is primarily an issue of power, where power refers to having a sample size that is adequate to test specified hypotheses with specific statistical tests. Thus, sample size and specific statistical tests must be considered in concert. Cohen (1988) offered a useful and widely used guide to power analyses.

After Condition 1 is met, we must next examine the evidence to infer covariation. To do this we must determine the extent to which we are committing Type I or Type II error. *Type I error* refers to the possibility of rejecting the null hypothesis when it should not be rejected. *Type II* error refers to the problem of accepting the null hypothesis when it should be rejected.

The magnitude of the covariation addresses the strength of the covariation. Recall, again, our discussion of correlation coefficients and their varying magnitudes. Similarly, statistical tests of differences between groups in experiments also calculate magnitude by taking into account group means and standard deviation.

TABLE 10.11
Values for Covariation Between Exercise Time and Heart Rate

	Exercise Time	*Heart Rate*
Group 1	30 mins	65
Group 2	60 mins	54
Group 3	90 mins	50

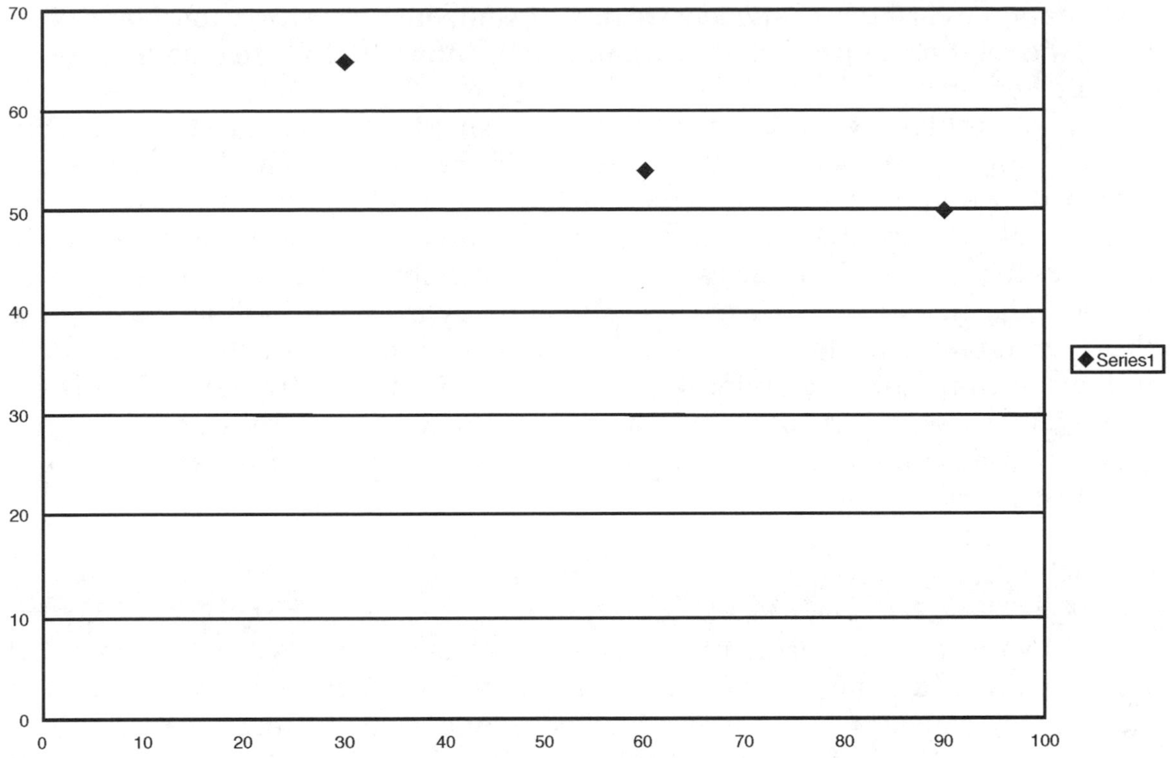

FIG. 10.5. Graph of covariation between exercise time and heart rate.

There are a number of threats to our meeting these conditions, and I only discuss two of the more common threats. A more thorough treatment can be found in Cook and Campbell (1979). First is the problem of violating assumptions of statistical tests. Parametric tests have a number of assumptions and the more assumptions we violate and the higher the magnitude of the violation, the less valid is our index of covariation. For example, most tests assume that participants' are independent and normally distributed. Although many statistical tests, such as the analysis of variance and multiple regression procedures, are rather robust to violations of normality, Type I error problems are associated with measures not being independent.

For example, take the case of four different classrooms of students (20 in each), each class being taught with a separate technique. The problem of interdependence of scores occurs when we treat students within each classroom ($N = 20$) as the unit of analysis rather than the classroom ($N = 1$). Scores within each classroom are not independent, as all students share a number of similar experiences, such as the same teacher.

If we use individuals, instead of classrooms, the statistical tests measuring between group differences assume that variation is due to the treatment, thus the treatment effect is inflated and the risk of Type I error increases. For example, the students in each classroom are interrelated on a number of variables, including their sharing of a specific treatment. These interrelations will be reflected in the systematic covariation between treatment and outcome for each classroom. Thus, the relations with each classroom will be inflated, thus increasing the risk of Type I error.

Second, problems with the reliability of measures are threats to statistical conclusion validity. Measures with low reliability cannot be expected to measure change or differences reliably, as these measures have high levels of error. These error levels, in turn, affect the means and standard deviations, which are used in statistics to measure differences and changes. Reliability can be increased by increasing the size of what we are sampling and by insuring high levels of interobserver agreement. If we are sampling from behaviors, we could have longer and more numerous behavioral observations. Additionally, reliability is increased when we aggregate across measures and methods. So we could aggregate across a number of observations and then aggregate observational scores with test scores.

Internal Validity

Internal validity of experiments pertains to the truthfulness of the claims that one variable is in a causal relation with another. The most basic precondition in establishing causality is the antecedent–consequence relation: $X \rightarrow Y$. That is, X must precede Y in time as a precondition for X to cause Y. Although this sounds very simple, it is not as it can appear that $X \rightarrow Y$ when in fact $X \rightarrow Z \rightarrow Y$.

That is, X may cause Y only through Z. In such cases X does not cause Y, but X causes Z and Z causes Y. Concluding that X causes Y in these cases is a false positive finding; that is, the positive causal relation between X and Y is in fact false. The primary concern for checks for internal validity involve ruling our false positives (Cook & Campbell, 1979).

An example should clarify the process of false positives. We have a treatment X that trains students to be have better math computational skills. This treatment is thought to affect attention during math lessons, Y. The treatment, however, has a direct positive effect on motivation to do math, Z, and it is this motivation, Z, not the training in attention, X, that is responsible for increases in math attention, Y.

The problem of third variables intervening between independent and dependent variables can also result in false negatives (Cook & Campbell, 1979). False negative exists when a true relation between X and Y exist but an intervening third variable disguises the effect. Figure 10.6 displays three cases of false negative relations between X and Y.

Beginning with the case illustrated in Case 1 in Figure 10.6 X has a positive affect on both Y and Z; thus, there is an effect of X on Y. However, Z has a corresponding negative effect on Y, thus masking the effect of X on Y. In Case 2, again an increase in X results in an increase in Y, but a decrease in Z, and a decrease in Z, in turn, causes a decrease in Y, resulting, again, in the masking of the effect of X on Y. In the third, and final case, an increase in X would cause a decrease in Y and Z, both. The decrease in Z would cause an increase in Y.

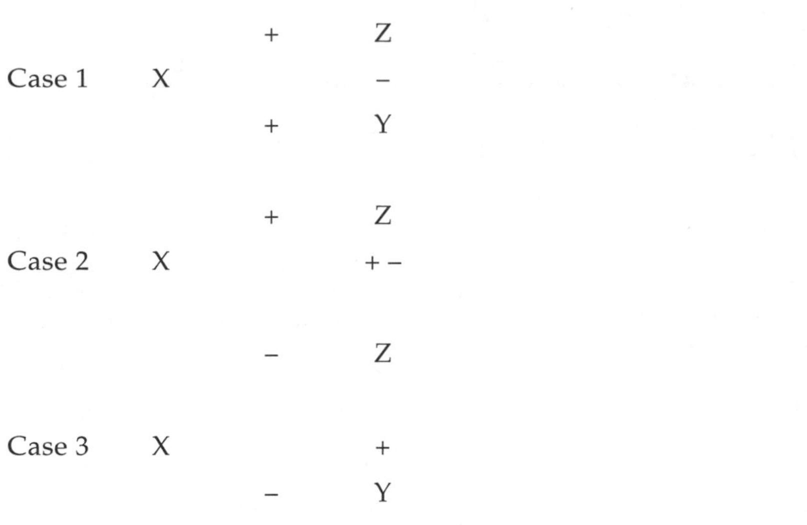

FIG. 10.6. False negative intervening variables.

I discuss one of these examples to illustrate more clearly one way in which intervening third variable can result in a false negative. In model Case 2, it could be that the students chosen to participate in the Treatment *X* are those who have lower initial math achievement scores than the rest of the school population. Thus, the negative $X \rightarrow Z$ relation. In such cases, we would expect students in the treatment to gain slower in achievement than the rest of the students. For the rest of the students there should be a positive $X \rightarrow Y$ relation. The negative effects and positive effects *X* and *Z* would cancel the positive effects of *X* and *Y* (Cook & Campbell, 1979).

In addressing the specific threats to the internal validity of experiments, the still classic treatment of the subject is contained in Campbell and Stanley's (1963) monograph. The interested reader is referred to this work as it is as timely now as it was 40 years ago.

In the remainder of this section we address various threat to internal validity. (Application of these threats to specific experimental designs will be addressed in those chapters on experimental design.) In discussing each case we should conceptualize the threat in terms of the threat being an intervening third variable: $X \rightarrow$ THREAT $\rightarrow Y$. Each of these threats is listed in Table 10.12.

History is the first threat to internal validity. The threat of history takes the form of some event intervening in between the independent and dependent variable to influence results. It may be that in between the *X* and the *Y*, a student received additional, special treatment, such as access to the criteria on which he or she was being assessed.

Maturation is another time-related threat to internal validity. In these cases, however, the mere passage of time and its effects of growth and maturity influence the outcome. So, it could be that the effect of *X* on *Y* is due to the fact that at time point *Y* students are older and have more general experience than at point *X*. The changes could have nothing to do with the treatment at all.

TABLE 10.12
Threats to Internal Validity

Threats	*Brief Definition*
History	Intervening time
Maturation	Intervening growth and experience
Testing	Familiarity with tests and testing demand characteristics
Instrumentation	Changing instruments/measures
Statistical regression	Extreme scores change in opposite direction
Selection	Different effects for different participants
Mortality	Differential leaving of experiment
Contagion	Treatment diffuses to control group
John Henry effect	Control group tries hard
Demoralization	Experimental group tries less hard

Testing is a threat to internal validity when tests are used a number of times for measuring change. For example, increases in scores from a pretest to a posttest could be due to participants familiarization with the assessment regimen, not the treatment.

Relatedly, *instrumentation* also affects measured changes from pretest to posttest. Problems in instrumentation are due to changing instruments to measure the same construct. As discussed earlier, instruments used to measure intelligence in a 1-year-old cannot be used to measure intelligence in a 5-year-old. In another, example, we could have the same instrument giving us different values. For example, in the health club where one of us exercises daily, there are cross-country skiing machines that give a reading of caloric expenditure. Different machines give very different readings for seemingly similar levels of exercise. One, for example, routinely estimates 500 calories expended after 1 hour of exercise whereas another routinely estimates 350 calories for the same duration! Such changes in instruments, not the treatment, may be responsible for observed effects.

Statistical regression (or regression to the mean) is the phenomenon where extreme scores at Point 1, be they very high or very low scores, tend to regress, or move, toward the mean at Point 2. So, regression, not treatment, could be responsible for low pretest scores being followed by high posttest scores. Correspondingly, high pretest scores should lead to lower posttest scores.

Selection refers to the problem of different types of participants being assigned to different groups. The example discussed previously for false negatives is appropriate here. Low achievers were chosen for the treatment group and normal achievers for the control. The perceived negative impact of the program is due to selection bias, not efficacy of the treatment. Selection also interacts with other threats. For example, it could interact with maturation to the extent that participants in selected groups mature at different rates than others.

Mortality refers to problems associated with participants differentially dropping out of experiments. Do, for example, participants in one treatment group drop out at higher rates than those in another treatment? Observed results, then, could be due to the fact that only the persistent participants stayed in the study and their persistence was greater than those in other groups. This led to the between-group differences, not differences in the treatment per se.

Random selection of participants and random assignment to conditions eliminates most of these threats. There are, however, some threats to internal validity that are not solved by randomization (Cook & Campbell, 1979).

First, randomization does not guard against threats to internal validity when treatments are diffused, or imitated. An example from early intervention experiments is illustrative. In early intervention programs for poor children experimental treatments, in the form of preschool programs, were given to some and with held from others (see Lazar & Darlington, 1982). There were, however, cases of program *contagion*, or imitation. In some cases, younger siblings were in experimental treatments and older siblings were in control groups. The treatment was imitated by the parents with their older children. Control children then seemed relatively high, compared to treatment children thus reducing the perceived effectiveness of the program.

Effects between *X* and *Y* can also be diminished when participants know they have been assigned to the control groups and want to "saw up" those in the treatment group. Their knowledge of control group status motivates them to reduce differences with the treatment groups. This is known as the "*John Henry Effect*."

Correspondingly, participants in a treatment group may become demoralized because of the treatment demands, such as having to keep daily records of all they eat and the exercise they take. This *demoralization* may diminish the treatment effect.

To conclude this section, internal validity is basic to trusting the results we derive from experiments. If results are ambiguous, and can be attributed to any number of causes, rather than the effect of *X* on *Y*, then they tell us very little indeed. For this reason, most behavioral scientists put stress on controlling threat to internal validity. After this prime concern has been addressed, we must turn our attention to external and then to ecological validity.

External Validity

External validity addresses the extent to which the results from an experiment generalize to other settings and participants. Although concern with internal validity is primary, external validity cannot be shrugged off as secondary. This is especially true in the social and behavioural sciences, where the aim of most of our work is to understand the nature of people and the ways in which they function. Thus our aim is to understand people in real-world settings.

However, the demands of meeting the threats to internal validity make it all the more difficult to address external validity. That is, internal validity is maximized when we exert strict experimental control and manipulations. These conditions are not usually present in those situations in the situations to which we want to generalize (see Table 10.13).

Problems with generalizability inevitably interact with, or are influenced by, the populations to which we wish to generalize. For this reason, the first threat to external validity is conceptualized in terms of selection problems interacting with treatment. That is, the generalizability of an experimental effect may be limited to the sample on which it was studied, not the larger population. As participants in experiments tend to be different from those who choose not to participate, this is a very real threat. Most basically, volunteers are different from nonvolunteers: Volunteers tend to be more motivated and more educated. Additionally, and as noted in earlier chapters, populations from which samples are often drawn (e.g., university lecture classes or university laboratory schools) are also very different from the populations at large. Again, they tend to be more educated.

Treatments also interact with settings. Treatments occur in specific settings, often laboratories. To what extent can we generalize these results to other settings? Can the effect of an experimental preschool curriculum generated in a university lab school be generalize to the neighborhood Head Start center?

Lastly, treatments interact with history. In other words, is the treatment unique to an historical period, or can it be generalized across time? Is, for example, the efficacy of an antiracial bias program, limited to a period following the widespread notoriety of a horrendous act of racial injustice?

So how do we minimize these threats to external validity? In matters relating to samples generalizing to a population, we should aim for a representative sample. The sample should represent the population to which we wish to generalize. That population can be limited, for example, Native Americans living in the Minneapolis-St. Paul metropolitan area. It can be more general, such as representing all the residents of the state of Florida. There are, as noted earlier, numerous ways, using both random and nonrandom procedures for approaching a representative sample and with the settings for the interactions. We should specify the setting that we want to generalize to and sample accordingly.

TABLE 10.13
Threats to External Validity

Threat	*Brief Definition*
Selection X Treatment	Treatments generalize to specific groups
Setting X Treatment	Treatments generalize to specific settings
History X Treatment	Treatments generalize to specific periods of time

The problem of history interacting with treatment is best addressed through replication. An effect at Time 1 should replicate at Time 2 if it is externally valid. Indeed, the ultimate test of external validity is replication. If the results of an experiment replicate, they have generalized. Indeed, *p*-values in statistical analyses are a short cut for replication. Recall a *p*-value of 0.05 really means that if the same experiment was done again with the same population the result would replicate in 95 of 100 cases.

Ecological Validity

Lastly, we concern ecological validity. Like other forms of validity discussed, ecological validity is concerned with the extent to which our results generalize to other settings and to other people (Bronfenbrenner, 1979; Brunswik, 1956; Cole, Hood, & McDermott, 1978). However, ecological-validity theorists have added substantively to this debate by stressing the role of the congruence between the researchers' and the participants' interpretations of the demands posed by the research setting.

At the level of generalizing to individuals, ecological validity theorists, from at least the time of Brunswik (1956), have stressed the role of researchers' understanding the participants' interpretation of the situation in making validity claims. That is, if we want to make inferences about the meaning of participants' behavior in a certain setting, we should take care that their interpretation of what the research situation means matches that of the researcher. Where there is a mismatch, our conclusions will be invalid.

For example, we as researchers may assume that when we escort preschool research participants and tell them "We're going to play some games," that our meaning of the situation matches theirs. It is incumbent on researchers to document that congruence. That there is incongruence is evidenced in the all too often observed discrepant finding between laboratory and naturalistic studies.

For example, in naturalistic studies of parents' socializing children, we find reliable a sex of parent × sex of child interactions such that fathers, more than mothers, are didactic with sons, relative to daughters (Block, 1983). In laboratory experiments of parents socializing with children, few interactions are founds (Pellegrini, Brody, & Stoneman, 1987). Although differences may be due to other factors, such as the experimenter controlling parents' and children's self-selection into different contexts, the differences could also be due to the fact that the parents' meaning of the experiment differed from the researchers. The researchers assumed that they were observing parents and children in real-life play and didactic situations. The parents, on the other hand, may have interpreted the experiment as some measure of their facility as parents. An important part of this facility, for parents, may have been that they should not be perceived as "sexist" parents. Thus, both mothers and fathers treated their sons and daughters alike.

Consequently, I define ecological validity as "the extent to which the environment experienced by the subjects in a scientific investigation has the properties it is assumed to have by the investigators" (Bronfenbrenner, 1979, p. 29). The simplest way of testing congruence between the researchers' and the participants' interpretations is to interview to the participants directly after the session (Bronfrenbrenner, 1979) or to ask them to talk about what they are doing as they are doing it, as in the think-aloud procedures advocated by Cronbach (1971) in testing the processes participants use. Other procedures include using participant observation techniques, as practiced by ethnographers (Cole et al., 1978). Use of a key informant, also as used by ethnographers, is also useful. In this latter technique, a member of the group under study proffers their interpretation of the research strategy as well.

The cross settings comparisons most often addressed in discussions of ecological validity involve laboratory and everyday settings, where it is often assumed that laboratory settings are less ecologically valid than everyday settings (Bronfenbrenner, 1979). This claim is typically based on the observation that laboratories are less representative of the participants' natural ecologies. Further, laboratories are perceived by participants as strange places and may suppress their levels of competence.

Validity, however, has less to do with the setting of the research than the researchers' claims about the constructs under investigation. Specifically, if a researcher is interested in studying participants' behavior in strange and unfamiliar places, the laboratory is the ecologically valid setting, par excellence (Bronfenbrenner, 1979). Conversely, studying participants in a more everyday, but less strange, setting would jeopardize our claim of validity.

From this view, no one setting has preferred status over the other. If one does choose a laboratory experiment, however, there are two conditions that must be met for an ecologically valid experimental design. These conditions relate to the participants' interpretations and the setting. Regarding participants' interpretations, researchers must make them known, using one or more of the procedures outlined above.

Next, researchers must take care that the laboratory analogue resembles the ecology to which we want to generalize. This could be accomplished by comparing the same or very similar participant in both laboratory and naturalistic conditions. Ecologically valid experimental results would converge with the naturalistic results.

An example of such a procedure is useful. Let us take the case of mothers and father socializing with sons and daughters that we noted earlier. Instead, in our hypothetical case, we could observe, using remote microphones of the sort used by Judy Dunn (1988) in her home-based studies of siblings, and gather a sample of socialization events involving didactic and play tasks. We then use this information to construct an experimental analogue such that each parent and each child are observed in each socialization context. The results from the experiment would be ecologically valid if they were concordant with results from the observational research.

CONCLUSIONS

Validity is a lynch pin in the research enterprise. It addresses one of the most basic, if not the most basic, issue of science and research: Truthfulness. It forces us to specify, measure, and document the nature of our descriptive and consequential statements and the degree to which they are supported by the data. This level of specificity is important for both the advancement of science and policy. Importantly, current discussions of validity recognize that there are both intended and unintended consequences of research. And as part of validity we should include discussions of these consequences. Science and research does not occur in a social-political vacuum, and this is especially true for educational and psychological research.

Validity is also an integrative construct to the extent that it forces us to address both our theoretical conceptualizations of what we study and how we study it and the empirical support for these notions. Thus, exercises to establish and test validity exemplifies the dynamic relation among theory, research, and practice. We need some level of theory in order to begin to specify what it is we consider valid. We then test these notions and use the data to refine our theory. We continue this process as we expand our concerns to different settings and participants.

SOME THINGS TO THINK ABOUT

1. How would you establish the content validity of an observational category, such as social competence?

____

____

____

____

____

____

2. What would be some convergent, divergent, and concurrent behavioral correlates of the measure from Number 1?

A. Convergent: ______________________________

____

____

B. Divergent: ______________________________

____

____

C. Concurrent: ______________________________

____

____

3. Staying with this measure from Number 1, what would be a criterion outcome in a predictive validity study?

____

____

____

4. What is a "sign" level measure for some adolescent behavior?

5. List 3 "sample" indicators of the measure from Number 4.

A. ____________

B. ____________

C. ____________

6. Is internal validity more important than external validity in experimental design?

A. How/Why?

7. How would you design an experiment to minimize both Type I and II error?

11

Indirect Observational Methods

In this chapter I discuss some of the ways in which we can collect observational data indirectly. These techniques are in contrast to the direct observational techniques that have dominated most of this book. Rather than relying on live observational techniques in the field, in this chapter I explore some ways in which we can collect information without actually being in the field. These indirect techniques are particularly useful in collecting information about individuals in nonpublic settings, such as in the home. Thus, these techniques are most usefully to situations where issues of logistics or economics (e.g., traveling to individual homes spread across a diverse area) or privacy-related concerns (e.g., the impracticality of being in homes during the early morning) prevent us from actually conducting direct observations. Instead, we rely on participants' immediate or recollected observations of behaviors of interest. Some of the techniques to be discussed in this chapter include: rating scales, remote or spot sampling, diaries, and remote tape-recorders left at data collection sites. As we see, these indirect methods can be used either by themselves or in concert with direct observational methods. First, I discuss some general reasons why would we choose an indirect strategy over a more direct one.

WHY AND WHEN TO USE INDIRECT METHODS

Probably the most compelling reason to use indirect methods is that of economy. The process of observing individuals, whether they be children and families or individuals in the work place, is exceptionally time consuming. To get a reliable behavioral sample of data takes numerous observations of each participant. These multiple observations of individuals in specific, and sometimes difficult to reach, settings then must be multiplied by the number of participants we are studying. In short, direct observations are very expensive.

The level of time invested can be diminished with some indirect methods, such as rating scales and spot sampling. So for example, if we are interested in an individual's level of social interaction or aggression, we could ask parents or peers to rate them on these dimensions, rather than conducting direct observations. Although the specific positive and negative aspects of such a technique is discussed in the section on rating scales, suffice it to say for now that a positive aspect of this approach is that a large number of participants can be surveyed in a relatively short time relative to the time investment required for a direct observational study.

An additional benefit of relying on information provided by a parent or a care giver is that we can ask them questions that tap their more general knowledge of the child. That is, certain indirect methods, such as questionnaires, can be developed such that they ask informants to provide information on their general and varied experiences with the child. This contrasts with the more context specific information provided by direct observations; thus, indirect methods can provide information on general and diverse aspects of children's lives.

A second reason for using indirect, compared to direct, methods is related to necessity more than to convenience. There are situations in which we simply cannot conduct direct observations and, consequently, we must rely on indirect methods. These situations are those, like those alluded to earlier in this chapter, which are difficult to gain access to. The difficulty in access may be due to children being in remote locations; for example, we might have a sample of children distributed across a large geographic area. Difficulty in access may also be due to participants' desire for privacy. For example, much of the bullying that takes place in schools occurs in bathrooms. We would have difficulty conducting direct observations there; thus we must rely on indirect methods.

The following example illustrates the usefulness of indirect methods in this sort of situation. Consider a case in which we are interested in comparing the routines used by single parents and two-parent families in getting their children ready for school in the morning. It may be impossible for this to be directly observed. On the issue of remoteness of research sites, answering such a question would involve observers going out to individuals' home on numerous occasions. On the privacy level, parents may be very reluctant to allow researchers into their homes during this part of the day. In short, to answer this question would require that we identify numerous volunteers who agree to have us in their homes at a time when most parents rightly choose to keep private. One way around this obstacle is to ask parents to complete a rating scale of their morning routines. That is, we could design questions that we thought were important to their morning routine and ask care givers to complete them. This technique is explored in the next section on ratings scales.

DIARIES

Dairies can be completed by parents or children and can provide objective information on a variety of topics in situations that are difficult to directly observe. Logistically, diaries can be implemented in at least three ways. First, they can be retrospective recollections of key events and behaviors. So for example, at the end of each day or at the end of each week, primary care givers could record relevant information. Second, entries could be made contemporaneously; that is, entries could be made when critical events, such as the use of a specific word or phrase, occur. For example, in one study, the parents of 21 preschoolers were asked to observe their children over a 2-week period and record any attempts they made at imitating another person (Bjorklund, Gaultney, & Green, 1993). Parents were asked to get an estimate of how well children thought they would be able to imitate the behaviors in question (prediction), to describe children's imitative attempts, and after imitating, to ask them how well they thought they had done (postdiction). Figure 11.1 provides three examples from the diaries of three different parents. In general, it was found that preschoolers frequently overestimated their imitative abilities (prediction), and were only slightly more accurate in evaluating how well they had done (postdiction). It was also found a similar pattern of results based on observations during preschool and in a laboratory experiment in which children were shown specific sets of actions (e.g., juggling balls) and asked how well they thought they would be able to imitate the actions (and, after trying, how well they thought they performed). Each of these studies has methodological limitations, but the similarity of findings across the three studies increased our confidence that preschoolers generally believe that they are more skilled at imitating than they really are.

Third, and relatedly, entree could be made on a time sampling schedule. So, at predetermined intervals respondents would make entrees. These predetermined intervals can be marked by using electronic beepers, such as used by Csiksentmihalyi (1990) in his studies of adolescence. For example, in these studies adolescents are typically given preprogrammed beeper, or pagers. The beeps are programmed so that they sample behavior from the course of the day. When the beepers go off, the participants record the relevant information in a diary or log. They could, for example, record the activity they are engaged in or the individuals with whom they are interacting at the time of the beep.

A less expensive alternative to these programmable beepers, is the use of inexpensive digital watches with alarm functions. (I thank Doug Kleiber for this suggestion.) Specifically, these rather inexpensive watches (about $30) can be programmed so that an alarm sounds daily at specific points. At those points, respondents make their diary entrees. In this way we have a time sample of children's activities. Of course these diaries then must be collected and summarized at reasonable points. As noted previously it probably makes sense to collect them weekly so that loss can be minimized.

In one of my projects we had parents and children complete diaries at predetermined times relating to aspects of their morning routine (Pellegrini, Galda, Shockley, & Stahl, 1995). In Figure 11.2, we have an example of a diary used for this purpose in the study of children's literacy practices at home.

These diaries were sent home with first-grade children 3 days per week along with a book across the entire school year. Children were to read the book and respond to it, in the form of talking about it, writing about it, or drawing about it. Using this form, we also obtained a reasonable picture of the social network surrounding children's home literacy events. Did they read alone? Was it with a sibling?

Sample Journal Entry 1

1. Date and time: 3-2-89, 4:00 PM

2. Task and person imitated: Diving in pool; woman in early 20s, on a TV commercial for gum. Patrick said that he could dive into the pool as well as the girl on television "real easy." He took a few running steps and jumped head first in the pool, landing more on his stomach than anything else.

3. Child's prediction: He said he'd be able to do it "real easy."

4. Child's evaluation: I asked him how he thought he did and he said that he did a great job.

5. Parent's review: My impression was that Patrick did a perfect belly flop, but I'd give him an "A" for effort.

Score: Prediction: overestimation; Postdiction: overestimation

Sample Journal Entry 2

1. Date and time: 3-4-89, 3:30 PM

2. Task and person imitated: We were at the zoo watching the chimpanzees swing from the trees. Michael was very impressed by the way the chimps could swing from one branch to another. The next day at home, Michael was on his gym set outdoors, and I asked him if he thought he could swing from bar to bar, like the chimps had done. He said that he couldn't, but I told him to try anyway, with me standing underneath him. He got the hang of it right away, and swung from one bar to another and then to a third, using just about the same movements that the chimps had.

3. Child's prediction: Michael didn't think he could do it.

4. Child evaluation: Michael still thought he hadn't done it very well.

5. Parents review: Although he wasn't in the trees, he actually did a very good job imitating the chimps' swings, even if he didn't think he did.

Score: Prediction: underestimation; Postdiction: underestimation

Sample Journal Entry 3

1. Date and time: 3-5-89, 10:00 AM

2. Task and person imitated: Ryan imitated me diapering a baby. I was watching Ryan play with her dolls. I asked her if she could diaper her doll like she had seen me do with her baby brother. She answered, "Of course." She had many of the right moves, and did get the diaper on her doll so that it stayed, but that's about it. Ryan showed me her doll and I asked her how she thought she did. She said, "It's not as good as yours, mommy. I can do better next time."

3. Child's prediction: Ryan thought that she could do it.

4. Child's evaluation: Ryan correctly observed that she hadn't done as good a job as I had done.

5. Parents review: Ryan was right. She had actually done a pretty poor job, but her enthusiasm was wonderful.

Score: Prediction: overestimation; Postdiction: accurate

FIG. 11.1. Some examples of parents observations and how they were scored.

Child's Name ____________________________ Date ____________ Time ______

Who are you with? Alone_____ or Someone else_____

Who is it? Parent, Friend, Sibling? Another adult?

Book(s) Read

FIG. 11.2. Parent completed home literacy diary.

Using children's diaries, we found that a substantial number of times children reported that they read the book alone when no one else was present. The structure of diary enabled these young children to write their names and the title of the book, as well as check if they were alone or with someone else.

Working with an older sample of youngsters (students in middle school), I also used diaries (Pellegrini & Bartini, 2000). In this case we were interested in the youngsters' aggression and the social context in which it occurred. Diaries were handed out on the same day every week of the school year across Grades 6 and 7. Thus, we sampled youngsters systematically at a pre-established time and across a rather large time interval (see Fig. 11.3).

Additionally, we used a standardize set of responses. Our pilot work and the literature on aggression allowed us to generate a list of possible responses youngsters might have chosen. The standardized set probably increased youngsters' responding because it is often easier to choose a response than come up with one's own. Standardization also probably increased reliability because all children started with the same list that we explained. Thus, individual coders did not have to use children's language, make inferences about what it meant and then categorize it.

Of course, the down side of standardized responses is that we are limited to those responses we provide. Thorough pilot testing and searching of the literature minimize this problem. That children chose one of the responses does not necessarily mean that they shared the same meaning as us. This problem can be minimized by providing thorough instruction and examples before completing the diaries.

WEAKNESSES OF DIARY METHODS

The first limitation of participant-completed diaries and rating scales is the possibility that participants' responses are influenced by the social desirability of certain responses. By this I mean that when participants are asked to comment on their own behavior or that of their children, they often respond in such a way that they tell us what they think is expected of them rather than actual practices. For example, if we ask children about their reading habits, they may profess to reading more (and watching less TV) than they actually do, knowing that this is the type of behavior adults would like to see. Similarly, if we ask parents about their uses of corporal punishment with children, their responses may be influenced by what they think we approve of. This sort of problem has been documented from some of the early studies of child socialization (Sears et al., 1956).

Another well-documented, and related problem, associated with participant-completed rating scales is the effects of the recency of memory. There is a tendency for respondents to record the most recent behaviors rather than those that are the most representative. So, for example, if we are interested in parental disciplinary strategies, parents may record their latest techniques rather than those that they have used for a longer period of time. Similarly, parents may record some events because they are more memorable than others, even although

Your name ____

School Homeroom _________________________________ Date _______________

Please fill out this form and use the WORD LIST (at the bottom of the page) to answer questions. Please be truthful. NO ONE ELSE WILL SEE THEM. WE PROMISE. For completing this form truthfully and accurately you'll get 50 cents. At the end of the year, if you do all the forms, you'll get $15.

Give information for TODAY ONLY, please.

A. Who are the kids you talked with today.

1. Where (Use List)

2. Where (Use List)

3. Where (Use List)

4. Where (Use List)

5. Where (Use List)

WHERE LIST: Coming to school; between classes; at lunch; free time; bath room; locker room.

B. Did you tease or hit anyone? If yes, answer below.

Kid's name	Where'd it happen (Use List)	Why (Use list)	How (Use List)
1.			
2.			
3.			
4.			
5.			

WHERE LIST: Coming to school; between classes; at lunch; free time; bathroom; locker room.

WHY LIST: No reason; They did something to me; I don't like them; Argument; They had something I wanted; Accident

HOW LIST: Tease; Curse/swear; Called name; punch; kick; bite; push; slap.

(continued on next page)

(continued)

C. How many kids were around? No one A few Lots

D. Were they mostly Boys Girls

E. How'd you feel after? No feeling Happy Sad Embarrassed

F. Did anyone tease or hit you? If yes, answer below.

Kid's name	Where'd it happen (Use List)	Why (Use list)	How (Use List)
1.			
2.			
3.			
4.			
5.			

WHERE LIST: Coming to school; between classes; at lunch; free time; bath room; locker room.

WHY LIST: No reason; They did something to me; I don't like them; Argument; They had something I wanted; Accident

HOW LIST: Tease; Curse/swear; Called name; punch; kick; bite; push; slap.

G. How many kids were around? No one A few Lots

H. Were they mostly Boys Girls

I. How'd you feel after? No feeling Happy Sad Embarrassed

THANKS

FIG. 11.3. Diary used with middle school aggression project.

the latter may be more representative. For example, when asking about children's sleeping habits, parents may stress the more memorable patterns, such as early morning waking.

A number of these limitations, however, are minimized when external observers and time-sampling strategies are used. Specifically, problems of selective memory and recency of memory for certain events and behaviors are minimized by systematic sampling strategies. Sampling, as discussed earlier, minimizes these problems by choosing systematically across various periods. Again, the associated costs of observers spending the time in the field necessary to obtain an adequate sample is a real, and nontrivial consideration.

The long-term knowledge that care givers have of their children can be, however, used to the advantage of the observer. Having well-informed raters draw upon their long and varied relationships with participants can be invaluable. That is, scores generated by these raters could represent numerous and varied sampling points, rather than the more limited sampling points of an external rater. Consequently, the ratings may be very stable and accurate indicators of a trait or behavioral tendency. This may be particularly true for rare behaviors. For example, if we are interested in children's imaginary playmates, parental reports may be excellent indicators to the extent that parents probably witness numerous episodes as they occur in different, but limited, settings. Of course, the scores would be valid if the previously mentioned limitations, such as recency and social desirability, are minimized. After I discuss different types of rating scales, I outline some ways in which to minimize some of the problems inherent in rating scales.

RATING SCALES

Rating scales enable observers, be they external observers, participants themselves, or someone close to the participant, to rate the degree to which specific behaviors and characteristics exist. Rather than indicating presence or absence of a behavior (i.e., accomplished by check lists), rating scales, are measures of degree. Consider asking a teacher to rate the degree to which a child concentrates on seat work. A rating scale item for this might take the form illustrated in Fig. 11.4. Different forms of rating scales are outlined in greater detail later in this section.

As noted earlier, another characteristic of the rating scale method is that it can be completed by an external observer, such as an observer in the field, rating spe-

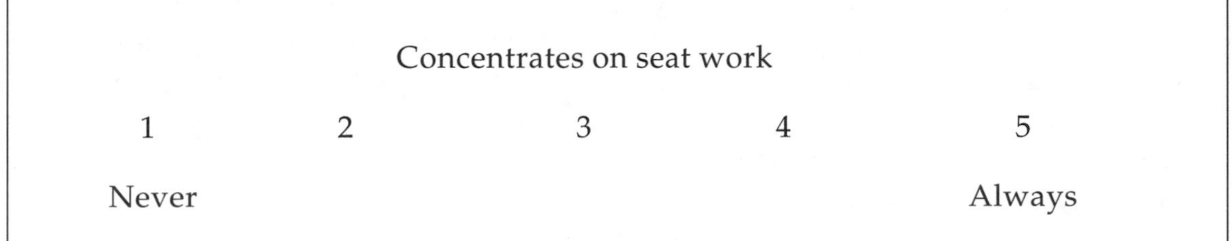

Concentrates on seat work
1
2
3
4
5
Never
Always

FIG. 11.4. Rating scale.

cific aspects of the environment and/or behavior; thus, this method can be used in some of the same ways as checklists. Examples of rating scales scored by external observers include the measures of home environments developed by Betty Caldwell and Robert Bradley (1984). With each of these techniques, the observer enters the home of the participant with a detailed rating scale for aspects of the home physical environment (e.g., the number of newspapers, magazines in the home) and the social environment (e.g., the degree to which care givers respond to child's cries and distress). The external observer can complete the rating scale items either at predetermined intervals while observing in the home or after he or she leaves the site. In the first case we have a form of time sampling, based on direct observation whereas in the second case recollection is used.

In other cases, rating scales can be completed by a participant in the field, for example a parent, a teacher, or a classmate of a focal child. Measures of children's temperament are good examples of the sort of rating scale in which a parent or a teacher is asked to rate children on a number of dimensions, such as activity level and flexibility. Correspondingly, rating scales have been developed for teachers to use as part of the process of diagnosing and treating children with problems. For example, Michael Rutter (1967) developed a rating scale in which teachers rate children on behaviors such as nail biting and hitting that yield, respectively, neurotic and antisocial dimensions of children's personality.

In cases in which rating scales are completed by a participant in the field, ratings are often based on recollections, rather than time sampled observations. Consequently, the scores generated by these scales represent rather global ratings of children, probably based on long and repeated observations.

There are obvious costs and benefits associated with each method of implementing these forms of rating scales. Specifically, a real benefit corresponds to the economy of data collection. As noted previously, by having a number of participants completing rating scales we save on the numerous hours that would be required to collect this information directly. The costs associated with ratings scales and questionnaire completed by participants are obvious.

TYPES OF RATING SCALES

Five types of rating scales are suggested (Guilford, 1954; cited in Irwin & Bushnell, 1980), and they are displayed in Table 11.1.

The numerical rating scale can take different forms, but it generally has the rater assigning a numerical value to a descriptor, such as the one given earlier in this chapter, Example 10. Alternately, individual descriptors representing dimensions of a trait can be listed, and the rater could score one of those, rather than assigning a number to some descriptor the rater thinks the number may represent. In Table 11.2 I use this sort of variation.

The probable benefit of this form of item over the other listed in Fig. 11.4 is that Table 11.2 is more explicit. By this I mean, the rater is told in Table 11.2 precisely what each number represents. In the Fig. 11.4 example, the rater assigns his or her own meaning to each category. This ambiguity is usually not problematic in

TABLE 11.1
Types of Rating Scales

Type	*Definition*
Numerical	Numbers assigned to a descriptive sequence
Graphic	Descriptors on a linear array
Standard	Rated against standardized criteria
Cumulated points	Sum of scores in categories
Forced choice	One choice descriptor

TABLE 11.2
Concentrates on Seat Work

1. Never settles into the tasks
2. Begins task, then losses interest after short while
3. Works through until encounters difficulty
4. Works through unless interrupted by another
5. Works through, beginning to end almost always

extreme categories, such as 1 and 5 ratings, but for the rest it is. The meaning that I assign to a 3 or a 4 may be very different from the meaning you assign to them. Thus, rating scales that have verbal descriptors next to each value are more likely to be reliable than those without the descriptors.

Graphic representations of rating items merely represent the choices outlined for numerical systems along a horizontal or vertical line (Guliford, 1954; cited in Irwin & Bushnell, 1980). Figure 11.5, for instance, provides an example of a graphic representation of a numerical rating scale.

The third type of rating scale is a standard type. By this I mean that the rating is against some standard criterion, such as percentage (see Fig. 11.6). An example

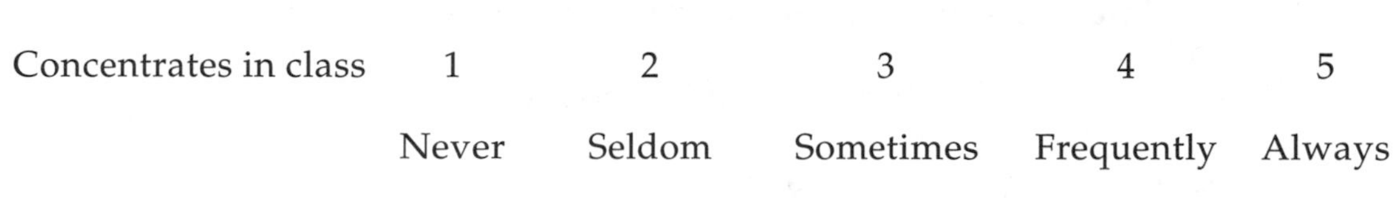

Concentrates in class
1
2
3
4
5
Never
Seldom
Sometimes
Frequently
Always

FIG. 11.5. Numerical rating scale.

TOP 5%	TOP 10%	TOP 25%	TOP 33%	AVERAGE	LOWER 33%
Concentrates					

FIG. 11.6. Percentage rating scale.

would be when someone's ability to concentrate would be compared to other students a teacher has had.

The fourth type of rating scale is a cumulative type. Rather than having the rater score one response to a question, the cumulative type involves scoring as many descriptors as are relevant. For example, a program evaluator many be interested in the extent to which different teachers implement specific program components. Rating scales could be constructed such that each question corresponds to a component and the rater scores the number of components that are implemented; such an example is presented in Fig. 11.7.

Scores for each item would be the sum of criteria met.

A related form of cumulative rating is the *guess who* description. In this case the responder is presented with a list of descriptors, and he or she must name a participant whom he or she thinks best fits the descriptor. This type of rating scale item is currently being utilized in the childhood aggression literature when teachers and children are given descriptions, such as: He always is fighting; he bullies weaker children in class.

Last, we have the forced choice type rating scale. Rather than giving numerous criteria on which to rate participant, scorers must choose only one. An example of this sort of item is presented in Fig. 11.8.

As noted previously, rating scales in their different forms have advantages and disadvantages. Many of the disadvantages relate specifically to the ways in which the scales are constructed. Thus, to maximize their utility we should design ratings scales so that the weaknesses are minimized. A basic problem with many rating scales, and as alluded to in the previous discussion, is that some rat-

1. Individualizes instruction

___ Children work at different rates

___ Children do seat work for different subjects at different times

___ Children choose their own reading books

___ Children choose topics for reports

FIG. 11.7. Cumulative rating scale.

During recess he/she:

___ keeps to him/herself

___ play with one or two children

___ plays in large groups

___ involved in aggressive episodes

FIG. 11.8. Forced choice rating scale.

ing scale items can be very ambiguous. For example when we are asked to rate someone from 1 to 5, we should be given specific criteria, whether they be verbal descriptors or numerical standards, to use as guides.

Another important issue relates to who completes the rating scales, especially in cases when those raters are data collectors rather than participants. Recall in the discussion of observer bias I suggested that biases about certain participants may color the way in which they are rated. For example, if one data collector spent time observing children on the playground at recess for many weeks, he or she probably has a good sample of children's social behavior and social skills and consequently, probably has formed specific beliefs and attributions about those children. If that same data collector were to be asked to complete a rating scale on the same children's behavior in the classroom, his or her knowledge of those children on the playground would contaminate the classroom ratings. Thus, different observers should conduct different data collection procedures. In this way we minimize bias. The bias holds true for raters and interviewers who then serve as observers; the information from the interviews influences the way in which they code their observations.

In order to maximize the benefits inherent in rating scales used by teachers, it makes good sense to give them the rating scales after they have had time to get to know the child. As a rule of thumb, we do not ask teachers to complete rating scales on children until after Thanksgiving. Furthermore, they should have adequate time to familiarize themselves with the instrument and then enough time to complete it. Specifically, teachers should read over the instrument thoroughly, observe the child with the items from the instrument in mind, and then complete the scale. By allowing enough time for rating scales to be completed, you also will minimize inaccurate completion. Often in the rush to complete a large number of long questionnaires, raters do a hurried, and sometimes inaccurate, job. Another way to minimize this is to offer some compensation for their time. For example, money, classroom supplies, and children's books are often greatly appreciated by busy teachers who take time to help.

Last, like most data collection techniques, rating scales are probably best used in concert with other types of measures, such as behavioral observations and psychometric measures. The different techniques typically complement each other. Specifically, Cairns and Cairns (1986) suggested that behavioral observations provide normative data on participants whereas rating scales completed by teachers and parents, even when they are center around the same phenomena, often give us information about children's individual differences. Thus, together, the two techniques give us a fairly complete picture.

Rating scales can also be used as complements to direct behavioral observations. For example, rating scales could be used to help observers locate where and when certain behaviors, or sets of behaviors, occur. Furthermore, in using certain types of questionnaires, we can find out the specific times and places that behaviors of interest occur. In using a form of cumulative items we can locate where young children learn certain types of mathematics (see Fig. 11.9).

Based on the information gathered from this sort of question, observers could then conduct direct observations of the relevant situations. In this way observers' time can be used most efficiently so that they are in the field observing specifically relevant phenomena; the extent to which they are spending time waiting for it to happen is minimized. Pellegrini and Stanic (1993) outlined specific cases in which questionnaire data are used as to locate relevant behavioral events to be observed.

Remote or Spot Sampling Using Telephones and Audiorecorders

In this section I discuss remote, or spot, sampling. This data collection technique, like those discussed earlier in this chapter, is most useful in circumstances in which it would be very difficult and obtrusive for an external observer to conduct direct observations. Generally, this method involves a participant in the field recording what he or she is doing at predetermined sampling intervals. The record-

Rank the situations in terms of frequency in which counting games occur:

___ In the bath

___ At bedtime

___ Watching Sesame St.

___ Setting the table

___ Walking up and down stairs

FIG. 11.9. Cumulative items rating scale.

ing is done in in response to questions asked by a telephone interviewer. It has been used most fruitfully by students of child development who have been interested in what children do at home. These researchers (e.g., Csikszentmihalyi, 1990; Pellegrini & Stanic, 1993) were interested in how children spent their time when they were in situations that were difficult for external observers to observe. Logistically and economically, it is very difficult and expensive for observers to follow participants around in their everyday routines. Spot or remote sampling provides an interesting alternative method to direct observation. In the example that follows, I illustrate how it can be implemented.

George Stanic and I (Pellegrini & Stanic, 1993) proposed the necessity of describing the ways in which preschool children from different groups within the United States come to construct mathematical concepts. In order to understand this process, we proposed describing children's "developmental niche" as discussed by Super and Harkness (1986). The developmental niche is a description of the ways in which cultural knowledge, such as mathematics, develops in children. To this end, it is imperative to provide descriptions of the physical and social dimensions of children's everyday lives. In reality this means following children as they make the rounds of their daily lives, often moving to a number of different locations. Additionally, descriptions of the participants and the processes characterizing these different settings are important. Thus, remote or spot sampling is a good candidate for this job that is all but impossible to execute with direct observational measures.

Methodologically, the data can be collected on children's everyday experience in the following ways. First, I begin with a series of research questions that we are interested in answering. These questions should be translated into a series of questions that can be presented in either telephone interview form or that can be written in a diary or log. In our (Pellegrini & Stanic, 1993) work on locating mathematical competence we proposed having telephone interviewers calling children's care givers at predetermined intervals and asking them the questions that are listed in Fig. 11.10.

In this case we use a time sampling strategy, implemented with telephone interviewing, to determine where children are, with whom and with what they are interacting, and the processes characterizing these settings.

Other researchers, such as Bloch (1989) and Kahana-Kalman, Tamis-LeMonde, and Bornstein (1992), have also used telephone interviews to sample children's development in their everyday context. Specifically, Bloch used telephone interviews to ask care givers to describe the physical locations of their young children's play when at home. She described the degree to which young boys and girls played in the home, yard, or neighborhood.

Kahana-Kalman et al. (1992) used telephone interviews to describe the language development of toddlers. Interviewers called the homes of focal children weekly and asked parents a series of questions about children's language development. For example, as part of their description of children's word comprehension and production, interviewers read mothers lists of specific words and phrase and asked if the child understood and/or used them.

Focal Child ______________ Caller ________________ Date ______ Time ______

Call: Original ______ Callback 1 _______ Callback 2 _______ Callback 3 _______

Questions

Where is (Name of focal child)?

Can you see him/her?

With whom is (name of focal child) with?

What is/are his/her/their age(s)?

What is (name of focal child) doing? OR What are they doing?

What objects are being used?

What is being said?

FIG. 11.10. Questions for telephone interview.

In a further effort to standardize the responses of different people, it is also reasonable to provide a glossary of words to be used in completing the diary. This practice was illustrated previously.

Another remote sampling technique involves the use of remote tape-recorders. With this technique a tape-recorder is left in one location to record the interactions of participants. Variation on this technique have been used successfully by Dunn (1988) in studies of sibling interaction, Tizard and Hughes (1984) in their longitudinal study of home-school relations, and by Wells (1985) in his studies of language use in the homes of families from different social economic addresses. Most simply this technique involves leaving a tape-recorder in one location and leaving it on to record. Obviously, the choice of the location where the recorder is left is critical. It should be left in an area that we know will witness the type of interaction in which you are interested. So for example, children language researchers interested in children's monologues or in discussions with siblings have frequently left tape-recorders in children's bedrooms (e.g., Bruner, 1986). Parents are typically asked to insert tapes and engage the recorder. Tapes, like diaries, are collected at regular intervals.

More technologically sophisticated is the use of the voice-activated tape-recorder. In this case tape-recorders are left in a specified location and they engage automatically when voices are detected; similarly, the recorders disengage when there is silence. There are both costs and benefit of using this sort of machine rather than regular, manually operated recorders are unclear. On the one hand, we are saving a step by having the machine engage automatically. The corresponding benefit of this is that the machines probably are less reactive to the participants, and consequently, the recorded data are probably more representative than those recorded with manually operated machines. The down side of the automatic machines may be that participants forget to change tapes or that data collectors have to go around to the sites to change and collect tapes at regular intervals. Of course, such technology is also more expensive than the manual versions.

In a related vein of expensive but nice technology, one can use tape recorders that automatically engage at predetermined sampling times. So a tape recorder may engage for 15-minutes every day. This sort of technology, used very effectively by Wells (1985), relies on time-sampling strategies to collect systematic oral language samples. Again, tapes are collected and distributed on a regular basis, like diaries. The reader interested in these techniques is referred to Wells (1985) in which the methodology and logistics are fully described.

Recording oral language of this sort provides lots of, and often too much, data. Indeed, you should be selective about the ways in which you are to use the data or else you may be faced with the daunting task of having to transcribe and then code the tapes. If you know what you are looking for, by all means, code the language directly from the tapes. Transcription is incredibly time consuming. If, on the other hand, you are unclear about the coding scheme to be used, transcription may help you to design one, but recognize the large time investment.

Another issue to consider when using remote tape-recorders is the obvious lack of context provided by such a recording medium. That is, tape-recorders record sound and only sound. Thus, we do not know about the corresponding actions, locations, or materials that accompany the utterances.

CONCLUSION

In this chapter I outlined some ways in which we can get at phenomena that are often hidden from observers. They are hidden because they often are embedded in the private lives of those we wish to study. Consequently, they are difficult to access and more indirect methods are called for. I outlined a variety of techniques, ranging from direct observations by external observers using rating scales, to more indirect methods such as diaries and telephone interviews. As noted throughout this book, different data sources are often complementary; that is, different techniques often provide a slightly different look at the phenomena of interest. Thus, where possible the researcher should use a variety of techniques. So, if we are interested in studying the ways in which children's mathematical knowledge develops at home, before school, we might begin by using telephone interviews to determine the time and location of those events that are most relevant to our question. Then, we should probably spend time in those specific setting actually collecting direct observational data, as well as collecting more in-depth diary/interview data from those settings.

SOME THINGS TO THINK ABOUT

1. List three criteria for developing a rating scale to study some aspect of behavior, such as aggression or cooperation.

A. ______________________________

B. ______________________________

C. ______________________________

2. What sorts of diary questions could you pose to get at the same criteria as listed in Number 1?

A. ______________________________

B. ______________________________

C. ______________________________

3. Where is a house, classroom, or other setting could you leave a remote recording device to capture these behaviors?

____

____

____

____

____

____

____

____

____

12

Computer-Assisted Recording and Observational Software Programs

John Hoch and Frank J. Symons
University of Minnesota

Like other areas of technology, software and hardware for observational research have advanced rapidly in the last few years. The software possibilities for researchers to enter observations range from homemade freeware programs developed by other researchers for use in their labs to polished commercial packages costing more than $5000. Most of these programs (except a few special purpose packages with preset codes) allow the user to define the behaviors of interest in a code file. When the observer hits a key or touches the menu on the screen the coded behavior is coded and entered into the data stream along with the time it was entered. Some systems are set up for focal sampling (Roberts, 2002) or interval sampling systems (Greenwood, Carta, & Dawson, 2000; Noldus, Trienes, Hendrisen, Jansen, & Jansen, 2000; Ottoni, 2000). Some systems allow the researcher to enter qualifiers in the data stream such as the person who is receiving the coded action or the intensity of the coded behavior (Magnussen, 2000; Sharpe & Koperwas, 2003). A few packages allow researchers to incorporate data streams from sensors or other devices into the coded data stream (Noldus et al., 2000; Sharpe & Koperwas, 2003).

Options for entering data have also expanded as technology advances. In the recent past, coders used data loggers, laptops, or desktop computers to enter data. Now, there are other options including handheld computers (HP Jornada 720, NEC 770) running the Windows® CE operating system, Palmtop computers running PalmOS (Handspring, PalmPilot, Sony Clio), or Pocket PC (Compaq, Dell Axim, HP Jornada 500 series). Handheld computers use a built in miniature keyboard or touch sensitive screens to enter codes, Palmtops use either an add-on keyboard available in full size or miniature models or the touch sensitive screens. Other systems for entering data take advantage of new technology for voice recognition transcription (VRT) (White, King, & Duncan, 2002) or coding from digital video.

Usually the choice of coding software will determine the choice of hardware because in most cases the software will support only one handheld operating system for mobile data collection. Currently there are no systems for the Macintosh OS. Researchers interested in using observational software programs should invest in Windows compatible machines. Because most of these programs perform similarly in the area of data collection, the analysis options available are the main factors that differentiate software packages. The purpose of this chapter is to review a variety of observational software programs and highlight their application to psychological, ethological, and educational research.

REVIEW OF OBSERVATIONAL SOFTWARE PROGRAMS (OSPs)

Space considerations limit a detailed review of the myriad of the available observational software programs. Interested readers are referred to an overview provided by Khang and Iwata (2000). Caution is necessary, however. Many of the original packages may no longer be in existence due to the fact they were written for hardware that is no longer supported or effective (this should serve as a word of warning to researchers to budget for frequent upgrading of both hardware and software, as progress waits for no one). Within several years of this writing, elements of different programs listed in the Khang and Iwata table will also be outdated as prices and capabilities are always changing. Thus tables such as the one referenced here and even the content of this chapter are intended as a guide to some of the possibilities, but before purchasing hardware or software the reader should investigate any changes. To keep current, readers are encouraged to check issues of the periodical *Behavioral Research Methods, Instruments & Computers*, which often includes publications explaining new options for direct observational coding. In the following section, we offer a selective review of the details of several observational software programs that represent the range of options currently available in terms of recording and analysis features. In subsequent sections, we highlight specific applications of the reviewed programs.

The Observer

Among the widely used OSPs is The Observer by Noldus Inc. (Noldus et al., 2000). The main advantages of this program include an easy to use interface and the automatic tracking of subject data by the program. Once the initial set up is complete, the program allows novice users to easily navigate between subject data and automatically keeps the data organized by subject, observation date or other grouping variables. The Observer can be purchased with the option to collect data using handheld computers and can also include video-coding software and hardware for inputting video taped data. The Observer is well suited to use with ongoing projects that include many subjects and a large staff of coders. Once the system is set up by the researcher, the day-to-day operations are simple and use a familiar Windows-like interface. Another advantage of The Observer is the fact that the output files from this system are something of an industry standard. Many other analysis and coding programs can input The Observer's data files allowing flexibility in analysis (Bakeman & Quera, 1995; Magnussun, 2000; Tapp, Wehby, & Ellis, 1995) This is a very polished program, but the price of the software reflects the fact that it is the industry standard (approximately $2,000 and $6,000 with video component). Another possible limitation of The Observer is that in making the program simple to use, the researcher gives up a level of control and flexibility to work with the data files and make changes in the observation system after the initial set up. Once the codes are specified and the subjects are entered, no changes can be made without recopying the set up files.

Multi-Option Observation System for Experimental Studies (MOOSES) / Procoder Digital Video (PCDV)

The MOOSES/PCDV programs offer a lower cost alternative to The Observer software package (Tapp & Walden, 2000; Tapp et al., 1995). MOOSES includes both data collection for desktop machines and options for analyzing the data. The Procoder software allows users to code from digital video, which can be stopped, rewound, and replayed automatically to code multiple passes. All analysis of PCDV data is done in MOOSES. The MOOSES software will also read and analyze data in the .odf format created by The Observer. For handheld computer use, MOOSES is downloadable and is named MiniMOOSES. This software includes a wide range of analysis options including descriptive data, lag sequential analysis, reports on the total time various combinations of codes are running and easy export of statistical data into Excel or other packages. It creates simple time graphs that show the occurrences of various codes in the data stream (see Fig. 12.1). These programs allow the application of shuffled permutation analysis to compare the sequential dependencies found in the data to 10,000 random combinations of the coded data. The extensive analysis options and flexibility in set up and use make MOOSES/PCDV a good choice. The MOOSES software creates very simple, compact data files and can easily be run on older computers. However, these programs are more difficult to use than The Observer for individual coders. In MOOSES, the user must set up and specify directories in which to store files and be able to navigate the hard drive's directory structure in order to keep track of data files. The interface is not as intuitive as some of the other software reviewed here and most finished graphs will be made with external graphing software. Knowledge of computers and the ability to navigate windows and text files is required for effective use of MOOSES. PCDV is more intuitive to use and follows the common windows methods for navigation and file structure. The ability to replay and recode specific interactions and easily transcribe speech into the systematic analysis of language transcripts (SALT) system (Miller & Chapman, 1997) are also assets of this software.

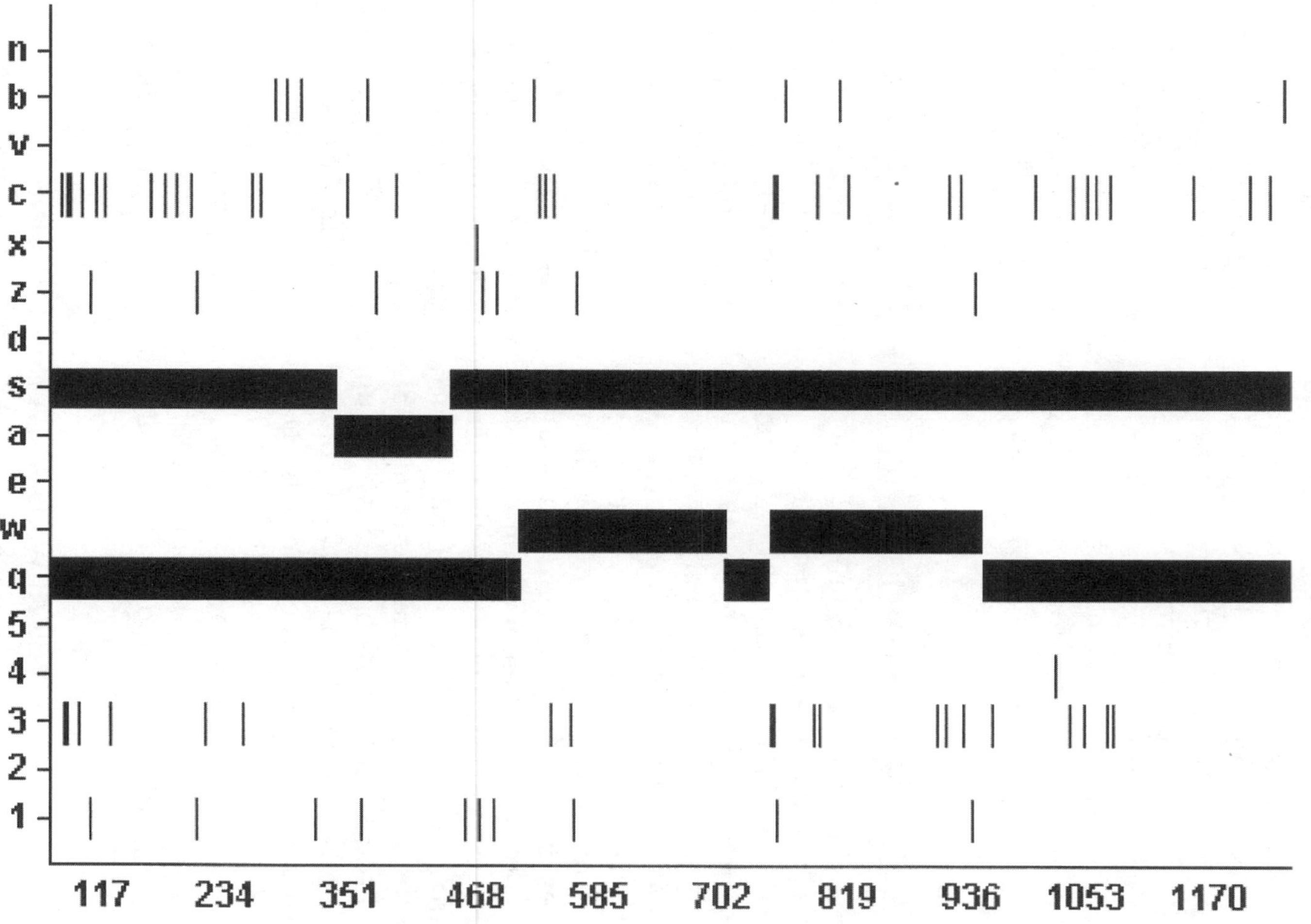

FIG. 12.1. MOOSES visual analysis output graphically displaying the temporal structure of coded events in a time stream.

Behavior Evaluation Strategies and Taxonomies (BEST)

The BEST system offers similar data entry options to MOOSES and the Observer (Sharpe & Koperwas, 2003). The BEST system allows the user to run another program simultaneously in another window and automatically obtain data from external sensors, such as heart-rate monitors and pressure switches to integrate into the coded data stream. It also allows the observer to hold a key down to record duration instead of clicking two separate keys to turn a behavior on or off. It is moderately priced (approximately $500) and supports the use of handheld data collection through Pocket PC or Windows CE. The analysis options in BEST include the basic frequencies and durations, and lag sequential analysis. The sequential analysis in this program returns a data table that gives the rates of occurrence of various chains of behavior. It does not currently allow users to specify two event sequences.

Obswin

The Obswin software allows flexible use of categories and real-time coding of variables using either desktop or a variety of handheld technologies (Neil, Oliver, & Hall, 2000). The data may be collected using interval or real time methods. The data analysis options are wider than usual in this software especially in the graphing possibilities. The analysis options are varied and robust including the usual statistics found in all the software described here (frequencies, duration, interobserver agreement, lag sequential) but Obswin also includes Markov chain analysis, which gives an indication of the common transitions between variables of interest. Autoregression analysis allows the user to determine the point in time or event lags at which a variable of interest is no longer significantly correlated with itself. This allows the researcher to determine a bout length for a particular behavior such as scratching, which would allow the researcher to examine the chains of repeated scratching. Survival time analysis provides the amount of time after which a behavior is unlikely to reoccur. Obswin is menu driven and appears to be stable and intuitive to use for those familiar with common Microsoft® Office programs. The graphing utilities available in Obswin generate very readable and polished looking graphs with many user definable options that reduce the amount of exporting of data into other graphing and statistical packages to obtain finished graphs from raw observational data. The software includes video-coding options and the ability to read and export from and to a wide variety of common file types.

OVERVIEW OF ANALYSIS OPTIONS AND ISSUES IN OBSERVATIONAL SOFTWARE PROGRAMS

When it comes to analysis options, most packages provide descriptive statistics for frequencies and durations of coded events. Most will also calculate interobserver agreement between two data files and report a variety of agreement statistics. Beyond these basic functions the packages differ greatly, some calculate conditional and transitional probabilities of two types of coded events occurring at the same time or following each other (BEST, Ethólog, Obswin, MOOSES, The Observer, HARCREL, GSEQ), others allow the user to perform lag sequential analysis of the data to determine the probability of event sequences (GSEQ, MOOSES, The Observer, Obswin, HARCREL), other programs include log-linear analysis functions or pattern analysis that provide descriptions of patterns of event sequences in the data (GSEQ, THEME). Some specific information on these analysis options and OSPs that can be used to perform them are reviewed in the following paragraphs.

The Generalized Sequential Event Querier (GSEQ) does not offer data collection systems, but it has many tools for analyzing the data. GSEQ and the companion package Sequential Data Interchange System (SDIS) use a command line interface or a series of menus to select between various types of analysis (Bakeman & Quera, 1995). The program is capable of interobserver agreement calculations using a variety of indices and log linear analysis in addition to lag sequential analysis. Log linear analysis allows users to simultaneously examine all of the relations between events in the data stream. The program creates tables of the sequential combinations of codes found in the data and allows the user to test the dependencies in these relations individually or in groups. It also allows collapsing of behavioral codes into larger categories and can analyze data from real time, interval data or even from data records with no time information. GSEQ is built to allow the user to specify relations of interest or to use log linear analysis to simply search the data stream for possible patterns. GSEQ can also be used to perform many of the sequential analysis that MOOSES or the Observer software will perform. It includes a simple text-based graphing capability that shows the occurrences of codes on a time scale. All other graphing is done by exporting data to statistical packages such as Excel or SPSS.

Theme is another analysis package for observational data that is commercially available. It is designed to input data files from The Observer format. It analyzes the files searching for complex patterns based on a comparison to the random distribution of the behaviors in the data stream. The program uses a bottom-up approach, building two event patterns and testing them against a random distribution, then building larger patterns out of the two event patterns. Theme offers a unique method of examining patterns in a data stream and is well-suited to complex coding schemes involving interactions between many actors and a wide range of codes. Theme will output diagrams of the patterns found using a "tree diagram" or export data on the patterns to statistical packages for graphing.

MOOSES allows the user to analyze coded data using lag sequential analysis to phrase specific questions about relations between coded events. MOOSES allows the use of either time lag (how many times did *mother console* follow *child yell* within 5 seconds) or event lag (how many times was *mother console* the next code after *child yell*) data analysis. It also calculates adjusted probabilities and adjusted z scores for the probabilities of chance occurrence of event sequences. Sequential analysis can be run using groups of codes (*mother console* after any type of child behavior) or single behaviors. The user can also perform sampled permutation analysis to determine the probability that coded sequences are occurring more often than chance occurrence by shuffling the observed data up to 10,000 times. MOOSES includes a simple graphing program and will easily export data to graphing software.

APPLICATIONS OF OSPs

To illustrate the possibilities opened up by the use of OSPs, four studies using varying levels of analysis are reviewed here. They reflect a range of research interests and study populations, from sick children to professional soccer players to aggressive cowbirds. By looking at these successful applications of OSPs the readers may be inspired to apply some of the same OSPs to their research questions. New technology can be seductive: The same study may sound more important and advanced using Voice Recognition Technology (VRT) rather than paper and pencil, however researchers should keep in mind that if the use of OSPs will not help in answering the research question or make coding more efficient, or accurate, they may be a waste of time and money that could be better spent pursuing the aims of the research. In some cases however OSPs have allowed researchers to quantify and find patterns in data that would not be possible using paper and pencil methods.

Application of Voice Recognition Technology to Animal Social Behavior

White, King, and Duncun (2002) incorporated the use of VRT to code the behaviors of cowbirds. VRT methodology was introduced as a way to increase reliability and accuracy in observations. The VRT method frees the coder from having to look down at a keyboard or a screen to enter observations. Speech recognition is also faster than keyboard entry so qualifiers may be added to the data record that could not be captured in traditional real-time recording. To compare the use of VRT data collection to paper-and-pencil data collection, the authors collected data using both methods and compared the number of errors and the amount of data recorded using each method.

To collect the VRT data, the authors used hands-free microphones and transmitters to transmit to PC computers (500mhz) running Via Voice software. Via Voice interfaced with a word processing package (Microsoft Word), which added time stamps to each spoken codes. A database program was later used to analyze the data records. The voice recognition software was set up and trained to each user's voice, which took approximately 2 hours. Then researchers trained to at least 95% accuracy in the lab, which usually took an additional 10 hours of training. When the criterion for accuracy had been reached, the coders would enter the bird aviaries where coding was done.

Using both the paper-and-pencil system and the VRT system, researchers coded the colors of the leg bands on any bird within 30cm of the focal bird using seven minute time samples. In separate 15-minute observations, researchers coded the frequency of singing using paper-and-pencil recording sheets. Using the VRT system, researchers recorded instances of singing with additional information on whether the singing was directed at a near neighbor bird and the identity of the neighboring bird. A comparison of the VRT data to the paper-and-pencil data from 30 randomly chosen observations showed that using the VRT system, coders caught more occurrences of singing than when they used the paper-and-pencil method. The authors checked the error rate of the VRT system by searching the data stream for recordings that were not in the code set, but did not perform any structured interobserver reliability check between the two systems. They were unable to send multiple coders into the aviaries simultaneously because of interference problems resulting from the wireless microphones. In future studies a comparison of the interobserver agreement and training time needed should be compared between VRT, paper-and-pencil and computer keyboard coding systems. The fact that coders coded more occurrences using the VRT system does not necessarily mean that the reliability of the system was higher.

This application highlights the potential advantages of using a VRT system to code behavior that is occurring rapidly. Using VRT coders were able to keep their attention on the aviary without looking down to write notes. It also shows that the technology used is effective for field use. There are also potential problems with VRT that are pointed out by this article. Initial start-up time for coders to record samples of all the codes and train the system to their voices took approximately 2 to 3 hours per coder. Approximately 10 hours of initial practice and correction were required to hit 95% accuracy. Correction of the voice-coded transcripts initially took approximately 10 minutes per 15-minute data session, but within 2 weeks the researchers were able to reduce this time to less than 1 minute per session. In comparison, transcribing the data from the paper-coding method into the analysis software consistently took 7 minutes per 15-minute session and did not decrease as the study went on. Like other computerized methods, over a longer study this initial investment in training time is repaid in time savings later, but for shorter projects, paper and pencil would still seem to be the most efficient method.

The Via Voice software will interface with other observational software and may allow voice coding with other observational software. The software will also transcribe sound files from digital or tape-recorded sessions, which may help alleviate the costs involved with transmitter microphones. The use of a tape-recorder (or the audio track from a video recording) also allows a permanent product to be preserved from the observation sessions to check the accuracy and reliability of the coding.

This study offers an initial glimpse into the possibilities opened up by advances in voice recognition software. It shows some of the requirements in terms of initial time commitments to set up the software and train it to coder's voices. Later work will help clarify issues relevant to the use of VRT in human environments such as the reactivity of the subjects and interference from background speech.

Application of Temporal Analysis to Athletic Behavior

Borrie, Jonsson, and Magnusson (2002) used the Theme Software to analyze the patterns of passing and shooting that lead to goals in professional soccer games. Thirteen matches were analyzed including 9 international matches. The data from each match was analyzed individually. To code the matches, researchers divided the soccer field into a grid consisting of 18 cells. The movement of the ball from one cell to the next was coded along with codes for the behavior of the ball carrier such as pass, header, shoot, foul, slide tackle, loss of control (of the ball) and so forth. Coding was done using ThemeCoder which allowed multiple pass coding of digital videos of the matches.

The Theme software uses a pattern detection system known as a T-pattern analysis. The T-pattern analysis searches through the data stream for two event sequences that are not prespecified by the user. It begins by finding two event sequences that occur more frequently than would be expected from a random shuffling of the total number of coded behaviors in the data. Using an example from the soccer study, if a pass from Field Cell 11 followed by shot from Field Cell 15 occurred 3 times in the actual data and only occurred once in a random ordering of all the events that were coded, the pattern would be tested for statistical significance and would form the basis of a T-pattern. After the software makes an initial pass through the data finding two event patterns, it begins to look for larger patterns made up of the previously identified smaller patterns. Patterns that are more fully expressed by larger patterns are eliminated by the software as it builds to longer, more complex patterns. In the soccer study, patterns could include behavior of one team or both teams.

One difference between T-pattern detection and lag sequential analysis is that the user does not define a specific relations for the software to search. Instead, the software begins building patterns that fit the user defined level of significance. The user does not select a specific time window or event window between occurrences of behavior in the T-pattern analysis, so events may occur at varying times and with any number of intervening events and still be part of a pattern. In terms of our simple pattern example, this means that the T-pattern would still detect a pattern if the player passed the ball from Cell 11 to 15, headed the ball, lost control, and then took a shot from Cell 15, or if the player passed from Cell 11 to 15 and shot with no intervening events. As long as the time frame between the pass from Cell 11 and the shot from Cell 15 had roughly the same time spacing on both shots, Theme would find the pattern.

In the soccer example, the T-pattern detected 3 significant T-patterns in one championship match that led to goals twice. Several specific players showed regular patterns of passing the ball back and forth from the edges of the field to the center of the field as they moved toward the opposing team's goals. In another match, a 9-event sequence was detected that involved actions of both teams that resulted in goals both times the pattern occurred. To ensure that the patterns were not due to random distributions of coded events, the researchers created randomized data files with the same number of occurrences as a complete match and then compared the numbers of detected patterns between the actual coded matches and the random data sets. The random matches contained between one half and one ninth as many patterns as the actual match data. Researchers also compared the total amount of patterns detected between club and international matches. Both types of match included roughly equal amounts of coded events, but the international matches showed higher diversity of patterns as well as number of occurrences of patterns than the club matches.

There are difficulties in using this type of analysis in applied settings. First of all, this analysis can give the coach information on the types of patterns that resulted in goals in a particular match but it cannot predict what will be effective in the future. Because it is descriptive and uses correlational analysis, it cannot be used to make causal statements (this holds true to greater or lesser degrees with the analyses shown in the other applications as well). In other words the researchers in this study cannot tell the coach that these patterns caused goals, only that they sometimes resulted in goals. Another applied issue with the T-pattern analysis is due to the length of the patterns created by the software, which may include behaviors emitted by many different participants (both student and staff behaviors may be part of the pattern and may be interspersed through time). Using the soccer example, this difficulty is seen in the fact that the patterns may also include behavior of players from the opposing team, it may be difficult for a coach to convince the opposing team players to join in the patterns that result in goals for his or her team. The nature of the Theme software allows detection of complex patterns that are occurring in the data, but it does not allow researchers to ask specific questions like those performed by lag sequential analysis in software such as MOOSES. This may encourage researchers to go on fishing expeditions in their data, looking for any patterns that exist instead of patterns that answer a specific question.

Application of Sequential Analysis to Naturally Occurring Teacher–Student Interaction

Sutherland, Wehby, and Yoder (2002) applied the MOOSES software package to determine if teacher praise was sequentially dependent with student *opportunity to respond* (OTR) in special education classrooms for students receiving services for emotional and behavioral disorders. OTR was defined as teacher academic questions with wait time for student answers. It was based on previous descriptive research that showed that high rates of both OTR and teacher praise in effective teaching environments. The use of lag sequential analysis allowed the researchers to answer this question in a way that would not be possible using paper-and-pencil methods. Although previous studies had shown that both teacher praise and OTRs occur at high rates in effective classrooms, sequential analysis is needed to show that there is a sequential structure to these interactions.

MOOSES allowed the researchers to quantify these structures and evaluate how often they occurred relative to chance occurrence.

The researchers used handheld computers running the MiniMOOSES software to collect data in 20 self-contained classroom for students with EBD (Grades k–8) in urban classrooms. They coded 15 minutes per classroom, per session of data during regularly planned academic instruction times. These consisted of small group and large group settings and the full range of subject areas (math, reading, social studies, etc.). Two observers coding simultaneously were used in 22% of the sessions to provide information on interobserver agreement.

The strength of the sequential relations between teacher praise and opportunities to respond was indexed by the Yule's Q statistic calculated by MOOSES. Yule's Q allows researchers to examine sequential relations adjusted for the base rates of the codes in the data. In other words, using Yule's Q, the researchers could examine the likelihood that each teacher would praise a student and then give the student an opportunity to respond in each classroom. The study found that OTR was significantly correlated with correct academic responding. They also found that the likelihood of OTR following teacher praise was greater than expected by chance. Most of the teachers had high sequential dependencies of the two event chain ranging from 0.39 to 0.80. These results were also significant using the Liker's Z score that MOOSES provides. The authors suggest that this correlational study could guide teacher training programs to suggest increases in both teacher behaviors by increasing either behavior. The authors also suggest that more research is needed to include additional measures of student success to better show the effects of OTRs and teacher praise.

Application of Real-Time Recording to Parent–Child Interaction During Medical Procedures

Manne et al. (1992) applied GSEQ software to determine how a child's reaction to getting a needle changed as a result of different adult strategies during the procedure. The authors created three categories for the codes relating to child behavior (momentary distress, cry or scream, and cope) and six categories for coded adult behaviors (explain; distract; command to cope; give control to the child; praise; and criticize, threat, or bargain). It is tempting as a reader to wish that the researchers had made many more specific codes for particular adult behaviors and strategies, however it is important to narrow down the universe of things that could be coded to those that are important and that you have reason to believe are effecting the target behavior. This narrowing can come from previous research, observation or theory. Wherever it comes from, it is important to not try to code everything. Previous studies had shown that only children who were distressed before the injection were calmed by explanations; otherwise explanations only increased the child's distress.

In this study the authors videotaped 43 medical procedures with 24 boys and 19 girls (age 3–9 years) who were undergoing chemotherapy that involved venipuncture. In 29 of the 43 taped injections, the mother was present, in four cases the father was present, and in the rest of the cases, both parents or the mother and another relative were present. One fourth of the sessions were coded by two observers to check interobserver reliability. *Kappa* coefficients for all codes were 0.80 or greater.

Each procedure was broken into phases defined as preparation, insertion, and completion. The entire procedure was defined as beginning when the child and parent entered the room where the procedure was to be done and ending when they left the room. As readers might expect, the insertion phase showed the highest rates of child distress, whereas the completion phase showed the highest rates of praise. Explanations by adults were most common during the insertion and completion phase, not during preparation.

The authors also tested the stability of adult and child behaviors across the time of the procedure by testing the correlations between coping, crying, and distress from the preparation phase to the insertion phase, the insertion phase to the completion phase and to compare nonadjacent phases, the preparation to completion phase. Child momentary distress and crying was positively correlated and significant across all three tests (this comes as no surprise to parents, who know that a child who is crying tends to keep crying). The authors then tested the correlations between child and adult behaviors within each phase of the procedure.

All the information obtained by the study up to the sequential data analysis could have been obtained by paper-and-pencil coding and correlating the occurrences of various codes within phases. Procedurally, this would have been laborious and time intensive. The advantage of using OSPs included the ability to record more behaviors more quickly without looking down at a clipboard, the ease and automation of calculating interobserver agreement and running the correlation analysis. Finally, it is unlikely that lag sequential analysis would have been applied in the absence of computer-assisted software technology.

SUMMARY OF APPLICATIONS OF OSPs

The contrast between the study of child distress and the study of teacher–student interactions are an interesting contrast of application of analysis tools. In the teacher–student interaction study, the authors were testing a specific question derived from previous research whereas in the adult–child interaction study, they were interested in discovering what the effects of a range of adult behaviors were on child behaviors. The soccer study also falls in the category of exploratory studies; the coaches of the soccer team did not use the Theme software to ask a specific question (what happens after a bad pass? If we pass through the middle of the field, how often does it result in a goal), they used the software to discover existing patterns. It is important to note that even if there is not a prespecified question, the choice of what to code involves a hypothesis. Because it is impossible to code everything (do not try it) researchers in the soccer study chose to have a code for goal instead of goalie nose scratch because of specific assumptions about what is important in the game of soccer. By the same token, the authors of the adult–child medical procedure study decided to identify three possible responses for each child instead of trying to code each possible type of verbal response. These decisions will help guide your choice of tools and results. Each of the analysis offered by OSPs might apply best to a particular research question. The challenge to you as a researcher is to choose the software that fits your question.

13

The Research Report

In this chapter I talk about writing a research report. Although the writing of the research report can be viewed as culmination of the research cycle, it can also viewed as a more formative dimension of it. By that I mean that the very act of writing about research helps us to clarify and systematize our thoughts about the research process. Indeed the completion and writing up of one research project often leads to more ideas for more research.

Further, the act of writing actually helps this process. Expressing oneself verbally has a way of making explicit what it is we are thinking about. In many ways it forces us to think about our thought processes. For example, talking about material, such as a list of groceries, helps us remember that material and also helps us to organize it (Olson, 1970). For this reason, many psychologists, such as Vygotsky (1962), Pavlov (1927), and Bruner (Bruner, Oliver, & Greenfield, 1966) considered language to be an important instrument of advanced thinking. In this light, then, it is not surprising that writing is viewed as hard work. It is!

In this chapter I begin by discussing how writing can be useful in the process of identifying our research questions and hypotheses in the context of writing a research report. Although there are different audiences for research reports, such as a research journal or a doctoral committee, the format, generally remains constant, and follows rule specified in the *APA Publication Manual*. I follow those rules as well.

But before we can write a research report, we must make explicit our research question.

ASKING THE RESEARCH QUESTION

The research process is motivated by a question. We are motivated to find out something we do not know about. As students of the research process, we should write down the questions we ask at each stage of the process. Writing the questions down, helps us keep track of the questions and to etch them into our cognitive processes so that we can continue think about them and refine them.

A useful format for organizing research questions has been suggested by Salkind (2000). He suggested that questions be written in declarative form first

SOME THINGS TO THINK ABOUT

1. Consider a research question that requires direct observation. First, try to decide what the best recording method might be (e.g., real-time continuous, time sampling, etc.). Next, consider what steps you would be required to follow to use traditional paper-and-pencil methods for recording and answering the research question. Last, consider the steps you would be required to follow to use a computer-assisted observational software program to answer the same research question.

2. List what you consider to be the pros and cons of (a) traditional recording methods and (b) computer-assisted recording methods.

3. Imagine you are the principal investigator on a research grant designed to study prosocial and antisocial behavior in school children. Go online and identify two different computer-assisted observational software packages. Compare and contrast the packages and determine which you would select.

____

____

____

____

and then expressed in terms of the relations between variables. A brief rationale for relating sets of variables to each other should also be made (Cooper, 1998). This rationale can be based on either theory, extant data, or both.

It is also useful if questions are phrased in such a way that they can be empirically tested (Kerlinger, 1992). From this view, the variables identified in the question should be measurable.

It is also important to differentiate research questions from hypotheses. Hypotheses are conjectural statements between variables and expressed in declarative, not interrogative, form (Kerlinger, 1992). Simply, it is an educated guess about what a researcher thinks will happen. Hypotheses are typically derived from theory.

Further, the way in which the hypothesis is stated has implications for the way in will be tested. For example, if we pose the nondirectional hypothesis there will be a difference between boys and girls in their uses of physical aggression. We know we have two groups (boys and girls) and will examine between group differences on a dependent variable (physical aggression), thus a t-test would be used to test it. A directional hypothesis (boys will be more aggressive than girls) would be tested in the same way.

In choosing the labels you use for variables it is important to be concise. In cases in which the same label is used to define a variables that differ in important ways or when different labels are used to describe the same or similar phenomena, those distinctions should be made. For example, in the aggression literature, some researchers study aggressive acts used to damage their peers' social relationships. Some researchers label this *relational aggression* (Crick & Grotpeter, 1995) whereas others label it *indirect aggression* (Bjorkqvist, 1994). Different labels for the same phenomena add to confusion, so a thorough explication of labels is crucial in an accurate understanding and expression of ideas.

In light of inconsistency in labeling, it often makes sense to begin one's search of the literature using a broad-based, rather than narrow, approach (Cooper, 1998). After all the differences and similarities are sorted out you can specify how you define your variables, and how this label relates to the extant research.

Although posing a research question or hypothesis may sound like a rather simple exercise, it can be difficult. Indeed and in many ways it is one of the more difficult dimensions of the research process. It is certainly the area in which one's creativity can be highlighted. Asking a provocative and creative question is something to which many of us aspire. These sorts of questions can guide a field. An examples of this sort of question has been presented by Brian Sutton-Smith (1967) in his study of play. He asked about the role of play in children's novel responses to everyday events. This stimulated a research program into the effects of play on creativity for the next 20 years (e.g., Dansky & Silverman, 1973, 1975; Smith & Whitney, 1987; Sylva, Bruner, & Genoa, 1976).

Another example of a very creative research question that helped to shape subsequent research was Premack and Woodruff's (1978) query about chimpanzees having a theory of mind. This question about chimps' ability to know what other chimps are thinking resulted in one of the most actively researched areas in developmental psychology in the 1990s (e.g., Harris, 1990; Wimmer & Perner, 1983).

Other, simpler and seemingly more mundane, questions are questions of replication. That is, a research question may be guided by skepticism about a certain finding. Replication is important, yet often under valued, venture to the extent that it adds validity to a finding. If a finding is replicated we can have confidence in it. Indeed, some scholars concern replication a more robust test of the validity of a finding than the tradition *p*-value approach (Lykken, 1968).That is, a *p*-value of 0.05 or 0.01 tells us the extent to which a finding is due to chance. Replication is a direct test of the validity of that finding. Of course one of the more famous examples of where a very provocative finding was not replicated involved the case of cold fusion.

As you are trying to explicate your research question, you will probably come up somewhere in between these poles of a novel question and one of replication. Your question can originate in a real life question or problem, such as those faced by teachers and clinicians daily. For example, you as a primary school teacher may have observed that on those days when your children do not have recess they are less attentive than on the days when they do have recess. This could lead to you asking: What is the effect of recess on children's classroom attention. Upon further reading and thinking you find a theory that helps you refined this question into a hypothesis. The theory of massed vs distributed practice states that individuals learn more effectively if the effort on tasks is spaced, or distributed, compared to massing it into larger chunks (Ebinghaus, 1885/1964; James, 1901). This theory leads to the following directional hypothesis: Children in classrooms having recess will be more attentive than those in classrooms with recess.

Alternatively, it can be sparked by reading the research literature. In the course of reading, you may come up with questions that you think need to be asked that were not, or could be asked in new and different ways. There are some areas of psychology and education that are rife with controversy, and thus, have many questions. For example, when I was a graduate student I recall reading Vygotsky's (1962) *Thought and language* and being captivated by his debate with Piaget on the role of egocentric speech in the thought of preschool children. Debates are usually very fertile grounds from which to glean research questions and hypotheses. A dimension of this debate became the topic of my doctoral dissertation.

In either of these cases, an important, and indeed indispensable, part of the process of asking and clarifying a research question or hypothesis is to immerse yourself in the empirical and theoretical literature. The theoretical and empirical literature not only spells out what has been studied and how but it also help you to clarify more exactly the nature of your question. At one level, it tells if something has been adequately studied. It may be that a question has been so thoroughly studied that it has very little interest of worth. For example, a researcher would not want to ask the question: Does phonemic awareness relate to early reading facility? It has been studied to death!

Reading the literature, however, can help you to reshape your originally naive questions into something more interesting. For example, rather than asking about the relation between phonemic awareness and reading we could ask, about the development of phonemic awareness. In the literature we may have found that children's rhyming abilities relate to phonemic awareness (Bradley & Bryant, 1983), so we might want to ask about where children get exposed to rhymes: Does the reading of nursery rhymes effect phonemic awareness?

The literature will further help you clarify your questions in terms of methodological issues. Probably most important, the literature (and the advice of your teachers, advisers, and mentors) should help you keep the question on a manageable scale. That is, you do not want to ask a questions that is so ambitious that it cannot be completed in a reasonable period of time.

Relatedly, the literature should also help you to recognize the different ways in which these sorts of questions have been addressed in methodological terms. This level of concern requires that you read Method sections of journal articles with great care, for it is in this section in which these details are specified. For example, to address directly the causal role of nursery rhymes on phonemic awareness would require an experimental design. In more naturalistic studies, we would have to control factors other than exposure to nursery rhymes that could be responsible for the relation with phonemic awareness. For example, we would want to statistically control children's linguistic facility and IQ as they both probably relate to phonemic awareness. This sort of control is necessary if we want to talk about the relation between exposure to nursery rhymes, not rhymes plus language and IQ, and phonemic awareness.

To conclude this section, asking a research question is a difficult and recursive process. Our question should be written out, re-examined, and revised, always as a result of our reading the theoretical and empirical literature. In the next section we talk more about how to formulate and reformulate your question in the context of a literature. Part of this discussion entails exploring exactly what the literature is and where to find it.

THE LITERATURE REVIEW

The literature review is traditionally the first section of an empirical article. In its best form, it is a well-argued case for why a specific question is worth studying. It embeds the research question in the extant research and theory and specifies the ways in which the study adds to our current understanding. The review should be pointed in that it focuses on the relevant dimensions of the extant literature, such as the specific outcomes, methods, theory, or applications (Cooper, 1998). It does not merely describe studies in the area in a list-like fashion. It uses the findings in the study as data in making an argument for the importance of the study.

In short, it documents the way in which the study advances science because it defines and clarifies a problem in a body of work and points in directions by which these questions can be addressed. To achieve this goal you should keep a working outline of your thoughts on the literature you are reviewing. The outline will help you to organize your thoughts and to keep your writing organized (Bem, 1995).

In cases in which empirical studies are reviewed, the review should synthesize findings from relevant studies that address similar or identical research questions posed in your study (Cooper, 1998). Besides synthesizing the current state of knowledge as they relate to this specific question, the review should point to areas future study is need, and why. The questions should be posed in terms of the theories which might provide guidance in answering them and making sense of the different findings in the literature. This sort of discussion should be the lead in to the specification of your theoretical orientation and to the specific research questions that you pose.

To provide a concrete example, I draw on the massive research literature on aggression and sociometric in the educational and developmental psychological literature (see Coie & Dodge, 1998, for a masterful review in this area). Our research question, generally, is: Why are some aggressive boys liked by both male and female peers?

In this literature aggression is very broadly defined in terms of doing harm. *Sociometric* status refers to the extent to which children are liked and disliked by their peers. The literature is generally consistent in showing that aggression is negatively related to being liked by one's peers (i.e., high aggression relates to low popularity). There are, however, some cases in which these correlations between aggression and sociometric status are attenuated and indeed some cases when the correlation is positive (Graham & Juvonen, 1998a, 1998b). These cases, for the most part, are observed during the period of adolescence, not childhood. Why is this the case? Why are there such glaring inconsistencies?

Next we invoke a theory to explain the differences and then we use that theory to frame our research question and hypothesis. The theory we invoke is a variant of social dominance theory (e.g., Bernstein, 1981; Dunbar, 1988) that states that aggression is often used to establish status in social groups when the group structure is in the state of flux. After a series of aggressive and reconciliatory interactions, a dominance hierarchy is established. These dominance individuals are the group leaders.

The theory can be used to predict, in hypothesis form, the occurrence of high rates of aggression in early adolescence (when youngsters are both changing from primary to middle school, overly concerned with peer status, and exploring new social roles).

CONSISTENCY IN DEFINITION AND METHOD

The validity of the conclusions you draw from your reading of the research literature is influenced by the ways in which you define terms that others have used and use similar methods to collect used in the research reports (Cooper, 1998).

In the very beginning of the literature review, you should define the variables under study. In cases where different labels have been used in the literature to describe similar phenomena or when the same labels have been used to define different constructs, you should situate your definition in this literature. You, for example, could use the term relational aggression, show how it is the same as indirect aggression, and specify that you will use the former to include the latter as well.

One can easily see how the inconsistent use of labels for specific constructs may result in inconsistent findings in the literature. Similarly, different methods used to study the same phenomenon may be responsible for differences, thus you as the reviewer should attend to and document different methods. Indeed, it may be the differences in or concern with methods that motivate your research. I present two examples to illustrate the ways in which different methods can be responsible for different and seemingly inconsistent results.

In the first case, consider the study of bullying among school-age children. Bullying is typically defined as the deliberate and repeated use of aggression by a bigger and stronger youngster against a weaker and smaller victim (Olweus, 1993). Bullying has traditionally been studied by using self-report methods, when individuals indicate the extent to which they have been a bully or a victim. More recently, bullying has been measured through the use of peer nomination techniques, when individuals are asked to nominate peers who get picked on, are mean to others, and so forth (e.g., Pellegrini & Bartini, 2000a; Schwartz, Dodge, & Coie, 1993). In very few cases, bullying is defined in terms of direct observations of individuals' behavior (e.g., Pellegrini & Bartini, 2000). These different methods have different assumption and yield different results (Pellegrini & Bartini, 2000). Specifically, peer nominations and direct observations provide normative information on public behavior, or behavior in the view of peers and omni-present adults. To that degree they are typically intercorrelated and yield similar age trends.

Self-reports, on the other hand, tell us about individuals' private thoughts and feelings on events. From that view they may be more prone to overestimation (in the cases of some paranoids) or under estimation (as in the case of some socially unaware youngsters). The writers can use these differences in methods, then, to either explain inconsistent results in the literature or as a basis for a methodological review.

Given these differences it is important that you systematize the ways in which you search the research literature. In the next section I present one method to aid in this effort.

Coding Research Literature

The validity of the conclusions you make in your literature review are related to the accuracy and specificity of the information you glean from the research articles you have read. Recall our discussion of the ways in which variables can be defined in different ways. Thus when we use a specific label to define a variable, we must be clear about the ways this definition fits into the extant literature. Similarly, different studies probably use a variety of research designs, methods, and types of subjects to examine the relations between the variables of interest. These differences also have implications for different patterns of results. In short, in order to clearly understand the literature on the relations between specified variables we need a clear understanding of some very specific details of each study. This clarity, in turn, will maximize the validity of our conclusions as well as the clarity of our expression.

To aid in this process of deriving clarity of details in research studies we recommend that a coding sheet be used for each research article that we read to collect this information (Cooper, 1998). By specifying exact types of information we minimize errors or omission. A model of such a coding sheet, based on Cooper is displayed in Fig. 13.1.

The report identification information is as basic as it is important. This information is needed so that it can be included in the reference section of you manuscript. There are different sorts of information required depending on the source. For example, for conference papers, the month of the presentation as well as the site of the meeting is required. For both book chapters and journal articles, page numbers are required. Being thorough in the initial identification will save lots of time latter, when it comes time to write the reference list. On more than one occasion, I have spent too much time trying to retrieve the page numbers of a book chapter.

It also may be helpful to keep a text file of all the references you use. These references can be kept in a central place and in APA format and retrieved when needed.

The research design information describes the study design. Specifically, was it experimental or nonexperimental? If it was experimental, you should list the design used. For example, was it a control group, pretest, posttest design. It would most useful if you used a consistent labeling system for these designs. The labels provided in Campbell and Stanley's (1963) are still probably the most common. The use of randomization distinguishes true experiments from quasi-experiments and should be noted as it certainly affect the internal validity of the experiment.

The treatments of the experiment should be described in terms of the duration. Treatments of different durations, should be differentially effective and thus, only those of similar duration are comparable.

There are some issues that are relevant to all research designs, be they experimental, quasiexperimental, descriptive, or correlational. First, we should note the degree to which the researchers were blind to various conditions that might bias the results of the study. Bias might influence the ways in which the participants act (e.g., the Hawthorne Effect) or researchers treat participants such that they influence the outcome. For example, if a participant knows he or she is in an experimental group, he or she may improve just because of this knowledge, not because of the treatment itself. Similarly, if the researcher knows that a participant is in the experimental group, rather than the control, he or she may treat him or her differently, perhaps by providing subtle hints that improve performance. Double blind procedures are used in experiments such that neither the researchers nor the participants know the conditions of assignment of participants or the hypotheses.

Report Identification	
Author(s)	Last name, and initials of ALL authors in the order listed
Title of report	Exact title
Journal	Full title
Book chapter	Give full book title and editor(s) and publisher
Year	Year, and month if relevant (as in conference papers)
Volume	Volume number
Page numbers	
If a conference paper	Name of the meeting at which the paper was presented
Location	Location of conference
Research Design	
If Experimental/Quasiexperimental	
	What was the specific design employed
	Within/Between subjects
	Number of treatments
	Duration of treatments
Randomization	Selection
	Assignment
Control group	Equivalent/Nonequivalent
If nonequivalent	No matching
	Matched on pretests
	Matched on demographics
Counter-balanced	Was treatment counter-balanced
Double Blind	Were participants and experimenters blind to assignment/hypotheses
Venue	Where was the experiment conducted (e.g., classroom, hallway, lab)
If Nonexperimental	
Venue	Where was the study conducted (e.g., classroom, home, playground)
Design	Descriptive (e.g., ethnography, field observation, correlational, action research)
Duration of study	
Double blind	Were participants and researchers blind to participants = status /hypotheses
Participants	**Total number**
	Gender, SES, ethnicity, ability breakdown
Variables	Label used and definition of independent/predictor and dependent/criterion variables

Measures	**Labels and definitions**
	How collected?
	By whom?
	When?
Statistical Analyses	
Descriptive	Range, mean, standard deviation
Inferential	Test used (e.g., t-test, ANOVA)
	Sample size for each test
Significant & Nonsignificant outcomes	
	Effect size
	P-value

NOTES

FIG. 13.1. Lit rev coding sheet.

In more descriptive and correlational work, minimizing of bias is no less important. It is important to note if the same researcher, for example, is conducting behavioral observations as well as testing children. In such cases, information on one dimension may bias the way the researcher treats the participant on another. For example, a researcher conducting sociometric interviews of all children will find that some are rejected by peers (i.e., disliked more than they are liked) and others are popular (i.e., liked more than they are disliked). This knowledge of certain children's sociometric status could, in turn, influence the way in which this same researcher codes behavioral observations of those children. For example, the researcher may be more likely to code and ambiguous behavior, as aggression if he or she is observing a child he or she knows is rejected but code it play fighting if the child is popular.

The venue, or place where the data are collected, is relevant to all research designs. Is it a laboratory? A living room in someone's home? The hallway outside a classroom? A classroom? This information influences the data generated. For example, children will probably act differently if we are studying their play behavior in a laboratory compared to their living room. In the latter case, they may exhibit higher levels of competence, relative to the former condition.

Research venue also influences the external validity of the study. Or the extent to which the results can be generalized to other settings. It may be the case that behavior in a laboratory is not generalizable to a more naturalistic setting, such as the home or a classroom.

Duration, too is relevant here. Is it one observation for 10 minutes in a laboratory or three observations of 45 minutes each at home. Reliability and validity (both internal and external validity) increase as the duration and number of observations increase.

A clear and explicit description of the participants is always important. Information such as age, gender, and SES is important. Depending on the nature of the research, other information on the participants may be relevant as well. For example, in a study of school-size effects on achievement, students' achievement scores are necessary. Again, having this information should help us be more exact about the results we are trying to describe. For example, age and type of school in which children are enrolled is important in understanding trends in aggression. Specifically, physical aggression decreases with age, except during early adolescence and when youngsters are moving from primary to middle school (Pellegrini & Bartini, 2000; Smith, Madsen, & Moody, 1999).

Variable definition, too, is important to clarify. As discussed earlier, there are cases when the same phenomenon has been given two labels, as in relational and indirect aggression. There are also cases when the same label is used to describe two different phenomena. For example, rough-and-tumble play has been described by some as containing both playful and real aggression and by others as containing only playful aggression. This distinction clearly has important implications for the ways in which we interpret results.

The measures used to collect the data by which variables are defined, too, influences their meaning. Measures derived from direct observations tell us one thing about phenomena, such as aggression or temperament, and it is very often different from the information garnered from self-reports on the same phenomena (see Cairns & Cairns, 1986, and Pellegrini & Bartini, 2000 on these issues).

Similarly, the ways in which these measures are administered influences results. I recall a practice in an elementary school in which he taught that is illustrative. In the spring before children entered kindergarten, they were tested (one session) by a strange adult (the Assistant Principal) in a strange room (her office) in the school. That the scores generated by these procedures were considered close to worthless by the kindergarten teachers is not surprising!

Lastly, it is important to record the statistical procedures used and the results as they too influence our interpretations. For example, the use of multiple t-tests, rather than a single analysis of variance increases Type I error, or the possibility that the null hypothesis will be rejected when it should not be.

This coding sheet is not meant to be exhaustive. It is meant to be illustrative. The important point in using such a sheet is that the researcher should list the important dimensions of the research being reviewed and then go about collecting information systematically.

WHERE TO LOCATE THE LITERATURE

We live in the information age. Clearly there is lots of it about. Indeed, we are surrounded by it, but unless we know how and where to look the search can be very frustrating and nonproductive. I recall being a graduate student (In my "first life" studying history) and being sent by my adviser to the British Museum's Students' Room to find information on the Justices of the Peace in the County of Suffolk during the period from 1580 to 1650. There I was in this room, literally surrounded by the information that I needed, but I had no way of accessing it. I knew neither how nor where to look. I spent an entire week looking through endless indexes of documents, and find only a very few that were relevant. When I met with my adviser the following week, he gave me a listing of references for specific documents relevant to the topic. Obviously, my next trip to the Students' Room was much more productive.

This anecdote illustrates the point that although we are surrounded by information, it is useless unless we know how to access it. In this section I provide some guidance through this morass of information. I begin, however, with note the important distinction between primary sources and secondary sources.

Primary sources are the sources that report original research. Primary sources are typically found in scientific journals, conference papers, research reports, and doctoral and masters theses. Secondary sources are those sources that discuss the primary research already conducted. Secondary sources are typically found in review articles, book chapters, and text books. An example of a primary source would be a journal article on a study examining the effect of different ways of measuring aggression (Pellegrini & Bartini, 2000). A secondary source would be a review article in a journal or a review chapter (e.g., Coie & Dodge, 1998) on aggression. Another example of a primary source would reading what Piaget (1983) had to say about Piagetian theory. A secondary source would be a developmental psychological text where his theory is discussed (Bjorklund, 1995).

The processes by which sources are located can be divided into formal and informal channels (Harris, 1998). Informal channels for locating research information do not have rules governing contact between the primary researcher and the person requesting the information. Formal channels for locating research information, on the other hand, are governed by rules that primary researchers follow to get their information into the hands of other scholars.

Informal Channels

Informal channels for accessing research include personal contact and solicitation, and "invisible colleges" (Cooper, 1998). Personal contacts are limited to the researcher and a close group of collaborators. For example, in writing a review on bullying, personal contacts would include our own work in the field as well as that of our students, and collaborators. This channel has inherent biases in it. That is, the information is biased by specific theoretical and methodological orientations governing the work of this group. For example, our ethological bias means that we tend to collect direct observational data and that we interpret our results in terms of evolutionary models. This is in contrast to other researchers in the same field who follow an attribution theory orientation (e.g., Graham & Juvonen, 1998a, 1998b). In the latter case, the use of self-reports is important in understanding of victimization.

Personal solicitations involve the student contacting directly those researchers active in the field. For example, a student might send solicit information on bullying by asking heads of departments of psychology for the names of faculty studying bullying. The student would then contact the faculty directly. These sources are less biased than the personal contact source in that scholars from a variety of theoretical and methodological orientations will probably be sampled.

Informal colleges are a collection of scholars working in the same area and usually linked to each other through the work of fewer influential scholars. For example, there is a group of scholars from around the world who study bullying and they are aware of each others work. The influential people in this network include Dan Olweus and Peter Smith. Contacting these people will result in accessing research on the topic.

Another sort of invisible college can be access through organizational listservs (like the one available in Division 7, Developmental, of APA). The reviewer can put out a query on the listserv and get access to the research of the members of that list. Of course the problem with this channel is that many scholars are being overwhelmed with junk e-mails, or "spam," associated with such lists. Indeed, shortly after the Division 7 listserv came online a number of scholars unsubscribed because of the large volume of junk.

Formal Channels

In contrast to informal channels to access research information, formal channels are governed by rules of access. These rules are typically related to the quality of the research report. For example, the primary formal channel is a research journal and access to that channel is governed by the peer review process. Only those papers meeting the rigors of peer review are allowed to appear. Other formal sources governed by the peer review process include conference papers and e-journals, although these latter source are typically less rigorous than traditional research journals (Cooper, 1998).

From this view, reports available from primary sources are usually of higher quality, relative to those available from informal channels. By higher quality I mean that the papers usually are theoretically motivated and the methods used to address the questions result in reliable and valid results.

Although this bias for high quality is certainly a positive characteristic of information in the formal channel generally and in journals specifically, there is also a less bias desirable. In most research journals there is a bias against publishing replications and a bias against publishing reports supporting the null hypothesis (Cooper, 1998; Kerlinger, 1992). Publishing replications of extant is not news, but they are important to the extent that they provide stronger support for the validity of a findings (Lykken, 1968). Thus by omitting replications, journals may be underestimating the validity of a finding.

Not publishing null results, too, is important. Recall null results support the idea that there is no relations between variables. It is probably the case that null results are not published because they can not be explained unequivocally. That is there can be numerous reasons for null results, none of which can be proven with the data. From this view null results add little to the accumulated knowledge of science. The implication of this practice for the student writing his or her literature review is that there is a bias in the literature toward positive effects being reported, and possibly being over estimated. That is, the reader only sees positive results, not null, results and he or she concludes that the results in a field are probably positive.

There are cases when null results do tend to get reported, however, and this tends to be in the context of a researcher failing to replicate a well cited study. For example, in there are two studies in the play literature which are frequently cited to demonstrate the positive values of play. Dansky and Silverman (1973, 1975) conducted two studies showing that playing facilitated associative fluency, or the ability to generate novel uses for conventional objects. In another study, Kathy Sylva (Sylva et al., 1976) showed how play resulted in children's improved use of tools to solve a problem. When different research teams tried to replicate these results using double blind procedures (Simon & Smith, 1983, 1985; Smith & Whitney, 1987; Vandenberg, 1980) the results did not replicate and were published in high-status research journals.

Formal channels of access are available from a number of sources. Primarily, the research journals of the organizations to which you belong and subscribe should be the first place you look. Organizational journals from the American Educational Research Association (AERA), the American Psychological Association (APA), and the Society for Research in Child Development (SRCD) are but a few examples. It is also useful to peruse the programs of the conferences for these organizations. One can write for copies of conference papers and get information well before it appears in print.

Collections of abstracts are especially useful because they allow you be preview a report without investing too much time. Especially useful collections of abstracts include: PsycINFO and PsycLIT. Both of these are subscription-based services that allow the researcher to access a large computerize data base for a limited time. Educational Resources Information Center (ERIC) and Resources in Education (RIE) are additional sources of research reports in published and unpublished outlets. Lastly, Dissertation Abstracts International and Dissertation Abstracts Online are resources available to access frequently unpublished empirical studies.

Another excellent place to find primary sources is by reading high-quality review articles in the field. These articles typically offer in-depth analyses of the field. The reviews often embed the research question in theoretical and methodological issues surrounding the questions, thus the student is offered not only a list of sources but also a good model on a review. There are a number of journals that specialize in review articles. APA publishes *Educational Psychologist*, *Psychological Bulletin*, and *Psychological Review*, AERA publishes *Review of Educational Research*, and the Association for Child Psychology and Psychiatry publishes *Child Psychology and Psychiatry Reviews*. SRCD publishes review articles occasionally in *Child Development* as does the Animal Behavior Society in *Animal Behaviour*. *Developmental Review* is another source of high-quality review articles addressing issues in developmental psychology. In reading any of these sources, it always makes good sense to use the references lists as a guide to future sources. If something sounds especially interesting and relevant, find the reference to that point, and then access that reference.

The Writing of the Literature Review

It is best to be guided by the outline on which you have been working. An example of such an outline is displayed in Fig. 13.2.

And now that you are ready to actually write the literature review you should also be guided by two stylistic dicta. Scientific writing should be governed by accuracy and clarity (Bem, 1995). Accuracy, of course is represented in the ways in which you report the information gleaned from the research literature.

Your consistent use of terms is part of accuracy. As noted previously, different scholars probably used terms in different ways. You should specify the terms you use, how this usage relates to the literature, and use those terms consistently throughout your report.

Clarity is achieved by simple and direct writing. To this end, you should keep the number of words you use to express an idea to a minimum. Relatedly, you should have a central theme in your review, or a line of reasoning. This line of

I. Literature Review

A. State Problem: The intent of this study is to examine the ....

B. Why is this Important

C. Definition of Terms

D. Research Questions/Hypotheses

E. Summary

FIG. 13.2. Outline for literature review.

reasoning should be clearly expressed and the review should be organized around this argument. Explicate only those points germane to your argument. Keep diversion from that line to a minimum. Such diversions take the readers' minds away from the point you are trying to make.

It order to keep your introduction focused you will want to foreground the analyses that will be forthcoming as they contribute to the argument you're making. Traditionally, we have been taught to write our reviews in such a way that they reflect the a priori hypotheses that we are going to test. In fact, many of us do not write the review of literature until after we have examined the data. That is, the data we have collected tells us what is most interesting and that shapes our argument, not a priori hypotheses (see Bem, in press, for a provocative discussion).

By way of justification of this approach, Bem differentiated between the context of discovery and the context of justification. The context of justification is what we can conclude in our articles and they provide readers with grounds for believing us. The context of discovery, on the other hand, is not governed by rules. This context has us examine the data we have and trying to discover what the data are saying.

The argument you present can be expressed chronologically, or by recounting the history of your research topic. From this view, you would discuss the ways in which the study of a specific topic unfolded across time.

Alternatively, you can organize your review around a specific theory or competing theories. You would state your theory of each of the theories, and review the literature in such as way as to demonstrate the adequacy of each theory to explain the diverse findings in the literature. Your discussion of the literature should lead to the specific hypotheses derived from the theories expressed.

Organizationally, each subsection of the introduction should either begin with or culminate in your stating a specific research question or hypothesis. For example, you could state at the start of a subsection: The second objective of this study is to examine the relation between sociometric status and rates of aggression in adolescence. In the remainder of that section you would build the case explicating why you think such a relation should be found.

Alternatively, you could end a section by noting: In light of social dominance theory we predict a positive relation between proactive aggression and sociometric status in adolescence. In this case, your arguments build to the statement of the question, based on what you have reviewed.

There are a few guidelines to follow which makes this task a bit easier. First, do not begin sentences with a person's name. Ideas, not people should be what you are concentrating on, thus, the ideas, expressed by those people should be foregrounded.

Additionally, when you criticize the work of others, criticize the work, not the people. Personal attacks are never called for and they frequently come back to haunt you. For example, the people you criticize will probably be called on to review your work in the future (Bem, 1995).

No matter what specific format you used, it is important that you remain consistent in the order in which you present the questions. What starts off as the first objective should remain the first objective. Results from the first objective should appear first in the results section and discussed first in the discussion.

When you are writing you should aim to have the manuscript understandable to an educated lay person. To this end, minimize the use of jargon. Also, a case in which you are presenting complicated theories or a complicated set of finding, present them in a step-by-step fashion, using examples to clarify the points you are making (Bem, in press).

Lastly, when you end your literature review, you should present a brief overview of the study you are about to present, based on what you have reviewed. This will provide a transition to the Method Section (Bem, in press).

THE METHOD SECTION

The publication of the APA (1999) specifies the following about the Method section: "The Method section describes in detail how the study was conducted. Such a description enables the reader to evaluate the appropriateness of your methods and the reliability and validity of your results. It also permits experienced investigators to replicate the study if they so desire" (p. 12).

In short the Method section is like an abbreviated technical manual of the research project. This is the section where you explicate exactly what you have done, how you have done it, and with whom and by whom. This section is straight expository text. It should be written in such as way that there is no ambiguity over what was done.

Where the Literature review was written with the educated layperson in mind, the Method section should be written with the naive and educated layperson in mind. By naive we mean a person with little previous knowledge of the methods used. Our methods should be written in such a way that this naive person could use our written text, without previous background knowledge, to replicate the study.

So, for example instead of saying the sociometric interviews were used, the author would specify what was done: Individual children sat with an experimenter outside of the child's classroom. Individual pictures of classmates were placed in front of the child, and he or she was asked to point to each picture and name the child. When the naming was complete, the child was asked to nominate three children they liked the most and three children they liked the least.

If the Methods used are complicated, it may help the reader negotiate the complexity by previewing of the Methods used is presented at the very beginning of the section (Bem, in press). In extremely complicated cases, it is helpful to visually display the data collection scheme.

In Fig. 13.3 I present an example of such a presentation. This figure also presents the different ways in which data were collected across a 2 year period.

Also individual sections should contain examples of questions asked of and instructions given to participants.

Also in the interest of clarity all variables, groups, and operations should be named with clear and easy to remember labels (Bem, in press). Do not use abbreviations as they add to overloading the cognitive resources of the reader.

Year 1	Year 2	
	Time 1	**Time 2**
Self-Report	**Self-Report**	**Self-Report**
Bullying	Bullying	Bullying
Victimization	Victimization	Victimization
Bullying Attitude	Bullying Attitude	Bullying Attitude
		School Transition
Peer Nominations	**Peer Nominations**	**Peer Nominations**
Like Most	Like Most	Like Most
Friendship	Friendship	Friendship
Network	Network	Network
Isolates	Overt Aggression	Overt Aggression
	Isolates	Isolates
	Bullying	Bullying
Teacher Measures	Victimization	Victimization
Emotionality		
Proactive Aggression		
Reactive Aggression		
Dominance		
	Direct Observations	**Direct Observations**
	Bullying/Aggression	Bullying Aggression
	Victimization	Victimization
	Indirect Observations	**Indirect Observations**
	Bullying/Aggression	Bullying/Aggression
	Victimization	Victimization
	Teacher Measures	
	Emotionality	
	Proactive Aggression	
	Reactive Aggression	
	Dominance	

FIG. 13.3. Example of a schedule of data collection.

The APA Manual provides a list of the subsections of the Method section. These subsections should be labeled, and they should appear in the order presented next.

Participants

The first section is *Participants*. Participants are those individuals who take part in the research enterprise; they are the individuals who are studied. A concise description of the number and nature of the participants helps the reader assess the generalizability of the finding (are the findings limited only to middle-class males?). Of course this information is important in any attempt to replicate results. Additionally, explicit information about participants helps the reader make comparisons across different studies in the literature.

Part of this section should also include the ways in which participants were recruited. For example, it could be reported: All children attend the Laboratory Preschool. The population of the school was 150. Participants were chosen from those children whose parents or guardians returned informed consent forms: 125 children.

Major demographic information on participants, such as age, sex, and social-economic status should be reported. In some cases other information may be relevant. For example, if the researcher is interested in ethnicity or if the study is being conducted in an area typified by a diverse population. For example, in many studies of children in urban American schools, ethnicity is relevant. In a recent study in Minneapolis, first-grade classrooms we reported: The children were from the following ethnic groups: 40% Hispanic American; 30% African American; 10% European American; 10% Asian American; 2% Native American; and 3% Other.

If the study has one of these demographic features as an independent or dependent variable in the study, the number of participants in each category should be noted. For example: There were 45 5-year-olds (20 boys and 25 girls).

In experimental research involving nonhuman animals, the laboratory origin of the animals should be made clear. For examples, the hamsters were purchased from LABORARAT. You should also report the genus, species, and strain of the animal (APA, 1999). If captive animals are used, information on their housing should be reported, for example, cage size, type of bedding used, lighting, ambient temperature, and diet (Animal Behaviour Society, 2001). Other demographics may be relevant, for example, the weight and physiological condition may be relevant.

In all cases the researcher should report the extent to which there was participant mortality. Participant mortality refers to the number of participants who leave the study before it has been completed.

Mortality is relevant to as it may affect the validity of the findings. For example, in a study examining a treatment for aggressive boys, if most of the participants who dropped out were very aggressive, it would bias the results. It might appear that the treatment was more effective than it really was only because the least aggressive boys remained in the study.

Ethics associated with recruiting and working with research participants is another important component of this section. It is appropriate to note that the participants were recruited in a manner consistent with the APA ethical standards.

Indeed, when submitting a research report to an APA journal, this should be noted (APA, 1999, p. 14).

In the case of nonhuman animals, ethical consideration, too, is necessary to document. If the study involves captive animals, any certification, say by the APA, should be noted. If wild animals were used in the lab, and then released, length of time held in captivity and the way in which they were returned to the wild should be noted (Animal Behaviour Society, 2001).

Apparatus

The next section in the Method section, according to the APA Manual is *Apparatus*. Apparatus are the special material and equipment used in a study. Complex, customer made equipment should be illustrated. An example of a piece of custom-made apparatus follows. In this experiment children were presented with three sticks, each 0.25 inches in diameter and of varying length: 18 inches; 12 inches; 9 inches. They were also presented with two wooden blocks (1.5 × 1.5) with 0.25 inch holes drilled through each side.

If the material was purchased from a commercial supplier, the supplier's name and address should be mentioned. For example: Children and their parents were observed while they played the board game Clue (Parker Brothers, PO Box 1012, Beverly, MA 01915).

Procedure

The Procedure section details each step taken in the research study, in the order of occurrence (APA, 1999). In this section, the research should summarize instructions given to participants, discuss the way in which groups were formed and the manner in which the experimental manipulations was carried out. Specific to experimental designs, this is the section in which randomization, counterbalancing, and controls are explicated. It also is important to mention, for both experimental and nonexperimental research, the ways in which researchers were trained and how the research protocols were monitored. Use of blind and double blind procedures should also be noted here.

In cases in which well-known tests are used, it is appropriate to reference that test so the interested reader could retrieve it if need be. In cases where an unfamiliar procedure is used, that procedure should be explicated either in the text of this section, or it an Appendix.

In summary, the Method section should be written in such a way that a reader could replicate the study as conducted by the original researcher.

THE RESULTS SECTION

The Results section summarizes the findings of the study. It should be organized around the research questions or hypotheses posed in the Introduction. They should be presented in the same order and using the same labels as used in earlier sections.

In introducing the Results, you should present evidence that you were successful in setting up the study as you conceptualized (Bem, in press). For example, if you wanted to collect direct observational data of aggression by observing children on the playground, you should state that this was done successfully, and present evidence. To this end, you could provide evidence for the ways in which participants habituated to observers' presence. You could talk about the number of observations collected per participant. You could also talk about the interrater reliability.

Information on the technical dimensions of your measures, such as reliability and validity data can be presented at the beginning of the Results section or in the Method section, where you are describing those measures.

This is also the place to explain the ways in which different variables were formed. For example, you would explain the way in which the observational data from each observers was aggregated. You would also explain the ways in which different measures of bullying (e.g., the aggregate of direct observations, peer nominations, and self-reports). For example, in this case you would present a correlation matrix displaying all the significant intercorrelations between all measures to justify aggregation. You then would want to specify the way in which they were aggregated. For example, scores from individual measures were standardized and then averaged.

If the analyses are complicated or have a number of different phases, it will be helpful if you provide an overview to the analyses to be conducted at the beginning of this section.

The writing style in this section is similar to that in the Method section to the extent that it is straight forward, expository text. You are presenting the results in relation to the research questions or hypotheses. This is not the place to try to explain a specific finding.

The Result section should be divided into subsections corresponding to your research questions or hypotheses. This level of organization helps keeps the reader oriented to what you are trying to say, without losing the big picture. Each section should begin with the big picture, first, and then the details (Bem, in press). Restate the hypothesis or question and inform us the answer, clearly. For example, state simply that the hypothesis was supported or that the answer was no. After this point, present the results from the statistical tests that enabled you to reach that conclusion. End each section with a brief summary, restating the findings for that subsection.

In reporting the data for each research question or hypothesis, you should present the data in sufficient detail to justify your conclusions. You should mention all data relevant to the questions or hypotheses, even those that were counter to your expectations. It is usually helpful if descriptive results are presented, in tabular form, first. You should include the range, mean, and standard deviation for each relevant measure. In this way the reader can get a picture of the way the data are described, before they are presented in more inferential ways. An example of a table of descriptive statistics is presented in Fig. 13.4. This figure summarizes some of the descriptive data for the measures presented in Fig. 13.3.

The presentation of the results of inferential statistical analyses (e.g., correlation analyses, analyses of variance) can be presented in the text or in a table. In either case the following information should be included: magnitude or effect size, the value of the test (e.g., $r = 0.69$; $F\ (1.75) = 3.73$), the degrees of freedom for the test, the probability, or p-level ($p < 0.05$), and the direction of the effect (APA, 2000). Effect size is commonly expressed by Cohen's d. In Fig. 13.5 I present an example of the tabularized results of a hierarchic regression analysis. By tabularizing the information, the writer can concentrate on describing the results, without cluttering the sentence with details (although very important details) regarding the p-value or R^2.

APA (1999, p. 16) makes specific recommendations about providing sufficient evidence to help the reader make judgments about your statistical analyses. Specifically, when using parametric tests of location, such as a one-way analysis of variance, sufficient statistics include cell means, cell size, and SDS. For randomized block designs and multivariate designs (including repeated measures), the same information is required, with the addition of a pooled within-cell variance covariation matrix. For correlation and regression analyses, a correlation matrix is required. For nonparametric tests, such as *chi*-square or a sign test, summaries of raw data (e.g., the number of wins vs. losses) are sufficient.

Descriptive Statistics for Victimization, Bullying, Negative Attitude Towards Bullying, and Dominance

		Bully	*Victim*	*Agg-Victim*	*Negative Attitude*	*Dominance*
5th Grade						
Boy						
	M	0.79	1.52	0.98	1.27	16.56
	SD	0.59	0.73	0.54	0.67	9.05
Girl						
	M	0.50	1.44	0.86	1.65	15.65
	SD	0.58	0.64	0.42	0.69	8.49
6th Grade						
Fall						
Boy						
	M	1.01	1.25	0.90	0.92	14.63
	SD	0.96	0.55	0.48	0.69	6.41
Girl						
	M	0.67	1.43	0.92	1.20	12.41
	SD	0.55	0.72	0.50	0.67	5.21
Spring						
Boy						
	M	0.88	1.29	0.86	0.80	
	SD	0.69	0.55	0.43	0.66	
Girl						
	M	0.66	1.44	0.88	1.20	
	SD	0.74	0.62	0.42	0.72	

FIG. 13.4. Example of table of descriptive statistics.

Summary of Step Wise Regression Predicting Sixth Grade Bullying

Variable	*Step Entered*	*Partial R2*	*Model R2*	*F-value*	*Probability*
5th Bullying	Forced 1st	0.21	0.21	31.38	0.0001
5th Dominance	2nd	0.03	0.24	4.68	0.03
Emot × gender	3rd	0.03	0.27	5.99	0.01
Emotion	4th	0.02	0.29	2.82	0.09
Transition	5th	0.01	0.30	2.32	0.12

FIG. 13.5. Example of tabularized result of statistical analyses.

THE DISCUSSION SECTION

In the Results section you presented your finding in a rather straight forward manner. In the Discussion section you evaluate these findings in relation to your hypotheses and the relevant literature. The Discussion section, if it is brief and straightforward, can be combined into a Results and Conclusions or Results and Discussion section (APA, 1999, p. 18).

If the Discussion is to be a separate section, as it often is, it, along with the Introduction will be the most difficult sections of the research report to write. Like the Introduction, the Discussion should be in the narrative or persuasive genre. It should engage the reader and move him or her through the central core of the study. Indeed, it has been recommended that these two sections be written in close proximity, after you have examined your results and know how your story line, or argument, will develop (Bem, in press).

The Discussion should begin with a statement about what we as a scientific community have learned from the study (APA, 1999; Bem, in press). The findings from the Results should not merely be restated but they should be reformulated so that they the results throw light on the broader questions of theory, methods, or policy. As with the Introduction and the Results section, the Discussion should be organized around the subsections corresponding to the research questions and hypotheses.

You should also discuss the ways in which your results fit into the larger literature in the field. Are they consistent? Inconsistent? Why? It may be the case that your results differ from others because of differences in the sample (you made mostly 5-year-old boys and others had 3-year-old boys and girls) or in measurement (you may have used direct observational measures of aggression and others may have use self-reports).

Although this section should mention limitations of the study (e.g., a limited sample) it should also point out the ways in which it added to the literature (e.g., by adding observational data to a field characterized by self-report measures).

Most commonly, Discussion sections end with recommendations for future research (Bem, in press). Indeed, these recommendations should, and often do, result directly from limitations with or ambiguity in findings in your study. In other words, you are recommending what you would do if you knew then what you know now!

TITLE, ABSTRACT, REFERENCES, AND APPENDIX

The title of a research report should convey a concise statement of the topic of your paper and identify the variables under study; for example, A Longitudinal Study of Aggression, Dominance, and Affiliation During Adolescence. The recommended length is 1 to 12 words (APA, 1999, p. 7).

The Abstract is a summary of the contents of the research report. It usually is about 120 words in length (APA, 1999, p. 9). As the Abstract is the first encounter most readers have with the research report, it is very important in the ways in which the paper will be judged.

An Abstract should, first, be accurate. An accurate Abstract reflects the content of the manuscript, and should not include anything that was not included in the paper. It is good practice to compare the headings you used in the paper to the topics covered in the Abstract.

An Abstract should also be self-contained, such that all terms and abbreviations are understandable. Key words used in the paper should be included to aid in the accurate indexing of the paper.

An Abstract should be concise and specific. This is accomplished by the economical use of words. Also the first sentence of the Abstract should contain the most important information to be conveyed, such as the thesis sentence or the most important finding. Subsequent sentences should be maximally informative. The tenor of the Abstract should be nonevaluative, simply stating finding, not commenting on them. Lastly, it should coherent and readable. It should be written in the active voice and third person. These components are summarized in Fig. 13.6.

The Reference section of a research should follow the format expressed by the APA (1999) in their Manual. *The Manual* provides an easy and effective guide for formatting references. There are, however, computer software programs that help with this. Specifically, APA Style help is available through APA and can be used on most word processors.

Appendices are necessary to included when we are using a relatively new procedure or measures. For example, an Appendix could include the list of words or the stories we ask participants to memorize. In other circumstances, Appendices

Components of the Abstract in a Research (APA, 1999, p. 10)

The problem under study

Limit to one sentence

The participants

Specify relevant aspects, such as number, age, sex

Methodology

Design, procedures, measures used

The Finding

Include statistical significance levels

Conclusions

Implications or applications

FIG. 13.6. Components of the abstract.

could include a computer program or statistic procedure we use to analyze our data. We cold also list the behavioral categories we use to observe participants.

EDITING, REWRITING, AND REWRITING

If writing a first draft was not torture enough, unfortunately, first drafts rarely are in a form where they are acceptable by a committee or for publication. Scientific writing is a form of expression that requires you to communicate a number of very complicated, and sometimes controversial ideas to a very critical audience. From this view, it is not surprising that first drafts need reworking.

A common problem, or at least common to me, in many first drafts is that the author is not explicit enough. By this I mean that the author, because of his or her close knowledge of the topic and the paper, often expresses ideas as if the reader is as familiar and knowledgeable of the details of the paper. Consequently, critical ideas, links between ideas, and details of method are often omitted. For example, it might be stated that: "A sociometric procedure was administered to all students." As discussed earlier, this state leaves much ambiguity. Was the procedure administered to individuals or group administered? Were they asked to identity classmates first? Were pictures of classmates used? A class roll? What specific questions were asked? How many nominations were elicited? How were they recorded?

Although this may sound very picky, think of the purpose of a Method section. One purpose is to invite replication. Replication could not be carried out with the instructions as given.

Similar lapses are often observed in the logic of an argument developed in an Introduction. It is often the case that the writer expresses himself or herself in such a way that in order to understand the logic of the argument the reader would have to be immersed in the relevant literature. For example, The author could state: "Accordingly, people who know they will be meeting each other in the future are likely to be more cooperative than those who do not meet." In order to be understood, the author should explicate the connection between repeated interaction and cooperation. Individuals interact with each other according to quid pro quo logic and will cooperate so as to maximize cooperation being reciprocated. Similarly, they will not be aggressive because it will be reciprocated. In cases where there is no opportunity to meet again, aggression pays!

So, how do we put psychological distance between us and our paper? There are at least two options. First, after your first draft, put it down for a week or two. This time lapse should make it less familiar than it had been. More time results in more distance.

Secondly, you should have a colleague read it as well. Although it can be very painful to show what we perceive as less than finished work to a colleague, it really is necessary. After all, the paper will be read by others (e.g., doctoral committee members, journal reviewers and editors), so it might as well be read by someone who is supportive but critical. Give your paper to some one you know will provide a thorough and honest review. Beware of the person who gives you back the paper with the very few comments, aside from a "great" scrawled on the title page. Either the person did not read it, or read it uncritically, or you are a fantastic writer.

It often works well to set up a network of colleagues who read each others' papers. I will read yours and you read mine. The more people who read it and comment on it, the better it will be. If you doubt this, read the acknowledgments in many journal articles, most authors, no matter how senior, acknowledge the comments of their peers.

The APA has offered a checklist to help you edit your manuscript, once you have completed a first draft <http://psychology.about.com.science/psychology/library/howto/htcopyedit.htm>. These steps are outlined in Fig. 13.7.

Having a computer makes this whole process much easier than before computer. It is no longer a big deal to change something. Changing one paragraph no longer means that the whole chapter has to be retyped. Tools such as spell and grammar check forces us to look closely at details that we might ordinarily miss. Indeed, some programs, such as the grammar check in Microsoft® Word offer style hints, such as sentences being too long or complex. Additionally, there is an entire chapter (chap. 2, *Expression of Ideas*) in the APA Manual (1999) that provides guidance on style. As noted previously, additional software can be purchased so that the manuscript is checked for APA format, too! Lastly, the built in thesaurus helps us to vary our word usage.

All of these tools should be accessed after our final reading and revision of the manuscript, and before it is submitted.

1. Spell and grammar check the entire manuscript.
2. Proofread once for writing style and clarity.
3. Check citations for APA style.
4. Check that References are in APA style.
5. Check that the all cited work is in the Reference section.
6. Check spelling of peoples' and organizations' names.
7. Check for APA style of whole manuscript.
8. Read to reduce redundancies.

FIG. 13.7. Checklist for editing a research manuscript.

SOME THING TO THINK ABOUT

At this point there's only one thing to think about: Write the paper, have colleagues read it, and submit it!

14

Summing Up: Using Observational Methods in Applied Settings

THE BEGINNING OF THE END

The theme of this book has been the use of behavioral observations as a method by which we can understand children in their everyday worlds. These places include home, school, playgrounds, day-care centers, camps, and numerous other settings where children spend their time. I have noted repeatedly that most of the descriptions of children available to us are of children in schools, preschools, and day-care centers. These descriptions provide important information for educators and parents in terms of the design, implementation, and evaluation of educational programs (see Pellegrini & Bjorklund, 1998). Although these descriptions of children in various school settings are important, it is also important, as Wright (1960) noted more than 40 years ago, to have descriptions of children in other settings. After all, they spend much of their time in those other places yet we know very little about them. It is probably the case that knowledge of what children enjoy doing and are capable of doing in these diverse settings can provide useful information for educators. Using information about children's competence in everyday settings as bases for educational and intervention programs will provide the core of this final chapter.

In this final chapter I cobble together the different pieces of information presented in this book into a statement about implications for observing children in these various settings, but particularly for applying this knowledge to children in educational settings. Most basically, observational methods are useful to the degree that they provide valid descriptions of children in various settings. This information can be used in program development, implementation, and evaluation. These points are developed more fully in this chapter.

A PRIMARY BENEFIT OF OBSERVATION

In the very first chapters of this book I talked about the ways in which observational methods were useful and how they could provide unique forms of information. Perhaps the clearest and most unique way in which observational methods can be used is by providing good descriptions. Good descriptions, that is reliable and valid descriptions, in my opinion, are the basis of all systematic inquiry. Describing behaviors in terms of physical descriptions and consequences of those behaviors provide important and objective information by which we assign meaning to behavior. For example, we can make inferences about the functions of a behavior by examining its consequence.

Reliable and valid descriptions are also important as a basis for the advancement of knowledge and scholarly interchange. Clear and replicable descriptions of behaviors and their assignment to categories are crucial points in any scientific venture. Clearly stated descriptions invite replication (Blurton Jones, 1972). Convergence between different researchers is an important indicator of the objectivity of our findings. This level of description is necessary, it seems to me, before we can do other types of research, educational intervention, or evaluation. If we do not have clear descriptions, we probably do not have clear categories; without such clarity we cannot design studies with meaningful variables (i.e., categories). By extension, without clearly stated and objective categories we cannot design meaningful educational programs and evaluation strategies.

For example, if we want to implement a play-oriented curriculum in a preschool or use play as an evaluation construct we first need clear descriptions of what it is we mean by *play*. Without this, how would we proceed? We could not define *play*, which means that we also could not define the basis of our curriculum. Such a description, then, is necessary to design the components of a curriculum and the criteria on which it will be evaluated.

Observational Methods, Practitioners, Researchers

Although all of this sounds simple and obvious, it often is absent from much of the research and program evaluation literature that is published. Not very often, for example, do we base components of educational programs on observations of children and teachers. All too often educators are told what to implement and how to implement various curricula. In many cases curricula are adopted by educational systems based on a packages developed by a publishing company or advocated by an educational entrepreneur who visits their school. The assumption behind many of these packaged approaches is that a good idea can be applied almost anywhere. It is developed by a group of "experts" and then sold to very different groups of users.

Although there are numerous problems with such approaches to program development, most notably that these programs often have little or no empirical basis, I argue that in order to be effective, educational programs must be localized and based on the specific characteristics of the children, their families, educators, and the immediate community. Further, the fact that the teachers themselves are generating the curriculum may have added benefits. Specifically, I think that good teaching involves teachers looking at children and figuring out a program for their specific group of children, based on the specific needs of the children and teachers; thus, packaged programs, for the most part are not applicable. When teachers do the important theoretical and empirical work of describing children and using these descriptions as bases for programs, not only are the programs better for children (to the extent that they are "tailor made") but the teachers also are empowered.

This concept of empowerment as applied to educational and family programs (see Cochran & Woolever, 1983, for an extended discussion of this issue in family programs) is similar to the notion of self-efficacy; as teachers become more confident that their work is important, they become better teachers. Thus, observational methods can be an important vehicle for teachers to develop their own curriculum based on the needs of their specific group and on their own needs.

Observational methods are an integral and basic part of the movement to empower teachers. Simply put, what children are taught should be based on what teachers know about children; this should be based on descriptions of children in areas that they find interesting and, consequently, exhibit competence. Teachers, in that they spend most time with children in schools, should have an important role in generating these descriptions and curriculum.

The extent to which instructional programs are implemented and modified, in turn, needs description. These descriptions should provide important information on the interface between individual teachers and individual children implementing educational programs. All too often educators are presented with programs to implement. Not very often, however, are we informed as to the degree to which the program is being implemented. Clearly we cannot assume that a program is being implemented in a uniform way across different teachers and schools. Observational methods provide an excellent method for this sort of process description.

Lastly, good descriptions can and should be used in evaluation of the educational program. By evaluation I mean documenting systematically the ways in which educational programs affect teachers, children, and families. Typically educators make inferences about program impact based on tests or questionnaires. A more direct method of assessment would involve using observations to complement these other forms of assessment. For example, in evaluating children's achievement it would make sense to have a variety of data, including test scores, children's work samples, and behavioral observations. Similarly, when assessing "teacher effectiveness" direct observations, should be complemented with lesson plans, student evaluations, and teacher performance tests. Given the importance of observations in schools, and the corresponding time demands, it might be helpful for school systems to provide specific training in observational methods to evaluation personnel. These ideas are discussed in greater detail in the next section.

Observational Descriptions and Educational Programs

I propose that observational descriptions of children in context should provide a basis for educational programming. This proposition is certainly not novel as it has its roots in the child study movement from the turn of the century. From at least the time of Darwin, Dewey, Piaget, and Vygotsky, and more recently to Kohlberg and Cole, the child study movement has advocated that educational programs should have, as starting points, thorough understanding of children. This is accomplished by detailed observations, which are, in turn, used as bases for program curriculum, instruction, and evaluation.

This child-centered approach contrasts with other approaches to educational programs, such as the "structure of the discipline" approach where programs for children are based on adult models of a subject matter field, like mathematics or biology. My bias is that we should not consider subject matter independent of children just as we should not consider individuals independent of context. Children as they interact in schools should be the basis of curriculum.

Observations as a Basis for Educational Programs. The traditional components of educational programs involve a needs assessment, development of materials and instructional strategies, and finally evaluation procedures. Although this framework may be useful, I suggest that we focus this process around describing children, which in turn, should be the bases of our program. In this section I outline how descriptions can be used as a basis of curriculum and instruction.

The idea I begin with is that educators should take as a starting point that which is interesting to children and, consequently, those areas in which children are likely to exhibit competence. Children are most likely to exhibit high levels of competence in areas in which they are interested, compared to those areas in which they are in minimally interested (Waters & Sroufe, 1983). If you doubt this, compare the levels of linguistic competence exhibited by some preschool children when they are engaged in fantasy play with their peer to the competence they exhibit when they are taking a standardized test. Children simply are more likely to exhibit higher levels of competence in those enjoyable situations because those situations may demand high levels in order to participate in them.

The initial job of educators is to locate those dimensions of children's lives that they find exciting and that are also intellectually challenging. This search process may be particularly important in cases in which children's home experiences differ from teachers' and schools' expected experiences. Here, obviously, is where observational methods are useful. Observational methods can be used to locate those situations that are familiar and motivating to children. Again, these ideas date at last as far back as Dewey, but it is not a trivial task to locate those important contexts which can be used as bases for educational programs. Certainly, the use of a combination of indirect and direct observational methods is a starting point. Although I have addressed in other places the way this process can work with developing mathematics (Pellegrini & Stanic, 1993) curriculum for young children, I briefly outline an example of using observational methods to locate children's indigenous mathematical competence; this competence, in turn, could be the basis of school mathematics curriculum.

Choosing to redesign school mathematics curriculum is important to the extent that American children, in comparisons to those from other nations like Japan and Taiwan, from all sectors of society have difficulty with mathematics (Stevenson & Lee, 1990). Thus, it would be useful to know where, outside of school, children exhibit mathematical competence. If we can locate these areas of competence, they could be used to complement school mathematics curriculum.

Locating competence can be accomplished in a two-step process. First, using indirect observational measures, we would want to sample where, with whom, and with what children engage in activities involving mathematical operations such as counting, making greater than and less than judgements, and one-to-one correspondences. This can be done most readily by leaving diaries with children's care givers and having them record the specified relevant information. Diary entrees are most reliable when specific information is requested. So we would specify, as in Fig. 14.1, the specific contexts of interest.

The information provided by daily diaries, or logs, could in turn, be used to identify those times and places where "live" behavioral observations should be conducted. So, taking the aforementioned information, if we want to get direct observations of children's exhibition of counting knowledge we could observe the focal children as she went up and down stairs at school. We could even use this information, later in the evaluation aspect of the process, to design a task by which to assess children's knowledge of counting.

So the indirect measures would tell us where these processes can be observed and the direct observations would tell us about the social processes involved in counting (e.g., the counting may be embedded in a song). In terms of using this information for curriculum design, we might then say that one way in which counting might be taught is by having children sing counting songs.

Date: 6 June	Child: Sarah Smith			
WHERE	WHEN	WITH WHAT	WITH WHOM	EX OF BEHAV COUNTING:
1. Stairs/school	7:30AM	Walking-up/ Mother	1,2,3 stairs	
Entered by mother				
2. Stairs/school	2:30	Down/ babysitter	1,2,3 stair	Entered by babysitter
3. His bedroom	3pm 6/6	Legos	Babysitter	1,2,3,5
Entered by baby sitter				
1:1:				
</>:				
Restaurant	7pm 6/6	Ice cream	Brother	You have more
Entered by father				

FIG. 14.1. Example of diary entree for locating mathematical competence.

Observations and Program Implementation. The next level of the educational process involves determining the extent to which programs are being implemented. That is, assume that we have an educational program that is composed of a variety of specified materials, activities, and interactional strategies. Next, we should use observational methods to determine the degree to which they are actually being implemented. We might also complement this information by identifying those processes that differentiate successful from unsuccessful implementation. The observational methods relevant to this aspect of the educational process would involve observing the degree to which individual teachers and children implement the aspects of the program. The behavioral categories would include aspects of the program specified previously, such as singing counting games, as well as other relevant aspects identified through indirect and direct methods.

This sort of "process data," or information on program implementation, is invaluable in all educational programs because it helps define what actually is implemented. The level of actual implementation is often different from the level of stated implementation. It may be helpful to think of these process data as content validity data on the program. Recall, we can claim content validity if our construct (in this case "the program") measures what it purports to measure. So, our program would be content valid if it was implemented according to the program criteria.

Too often we only have know about programs as they are stated on paper. We, generally, do not know the extent to which these stated goals corresponded to the actual implementation of the program goals. Given the variability in teachers' and children's willingness and ability to implement different programs it is very questionable that there is much correspondence between stated and actual program descriptors. That is, what goes on in most programs probably does not correspond very closely to the formal program descriptions.

A second use of process data relates to the evaluation dimension. We could explore the links between aspects of program implementation and children's achievement. For example, we might have as a goal of our program to increase children's counting games on the playground. We could identify those aspects of the program that empirically predict counting games at recess. The activities that maximize gains could be increased in the classroom whereas those that minimize gains could be phased out in favor of new ones. The new activities, of course would be derived from the first phase of this process.

Observations and Program Evaluation. Evaluation in education is currently increasing in frequency. Simultaneously, it is also under great scrutiny. Teachers and students in America and the United Kingdom, to take only two example, are under increased demand to exhibit their competence, performance, knowledge, and so forth. Traditionally, the format for students and teachers to exhibit their knowledge or skills has been paper-and-pencil tests. Performance on these tests may or may not be empirically related to the desired outcome; that is, the tests may or may not have criterion validity. For example, some states require that teachers must pass a test on their knowledge of teaching methods in order to be certified. Similarly, in other cases, children must pass a standardized test in order to be promoted from one grade to another. In most cases there is little empirical evidence to show that a specified level of performance on a test relates to desired outcome, like performance in the next grade. So, you should ask, what determines an adequate score and how are levels of adequacy determined? This type of testing, for both teachers and students, is increasing, despite such gaping problems.

There are, however, concerns being voiced in the educational community over these testing practices (e.g., Gardner, 1993). The fact that scores on these measures tell us little about actual levels of competence or performance may have something to do with the concern. For many years, standardized forms of testing have been criticized as being nonmotivating and intimidating for the test takers. Relatedly, the content and format of the test questions often do not measure the degree to which the information tested is used or can be used by the test taker.

It is in this realm that observational methods have something very important to offer. If we specify clearly what it is we want to measure, say the different types of mathematical competence discussed earlier, we could design analogue situations and then observe the extent to which children actually use these concepts in the classroom. Thus, there is little need to transfer from the assessment context to the use of the concepts in school contexts: Children are being assessed as they are using the concept. Further, the assessment situation should be minimally intimidating to children to the extent that they are being assessed in their own classrooms on familiar and interesting tasks. From a motivational perspective if we design classroom evaluation tasks with an eye on what interests children, they should exhibit maximum levels of competence on these tasks. Thus, observing children in motivating classroom situations is an ideal assessment context.

It is this concept of the motivating classroom evaluation task that also allows us to use observational methods to get at children's underlying competence, an area often claimed solely by test developers. Their argument went something like this: If we are interested in knowing how much mathematics a child knows we should ask him or her directly about those aspects of mathematics that we think are important. We should not rely on naturalistic observations of children to make judgments about children's competence because (arguments of economy of time aside, for the time being) a child may choose not to exhibit competence when he or she is being observed. To minimize this sampling of knowledge problem, test items are written to ask children about those about things that we want to know; thus, the test item is the context for children to exhibit knowledge.

The problem with the argument is that the test questions are not motivating to many children, especially young and culturally different children. This problem is partially responsible for young children being unreliable test takers (Messick, 1983). Further, observational methods can get at these elusive aspects of competence if they observe children in tasks that are motivating and, consequently, they want to exhibit high levels of competence. Is it accidental that preschool children often exhibit higher levels of language and representational processes in peer discourse events, such as fantasy play, than in more traditional assessment contexts (Cazden, 1975; Pellegrini, 1992; Vygotsky, 1978). Children exhibit higher levels of competence in fantasy play than on tests because they find fantasy motivating and want to participate in the fantasy process. Because fantasy play with peers requires high levels of linguistic and representational competence to be sustained children bring all their social cognitive processes to the fore to participate in this motivating process. So the trick is to design instructional and evaluation tasks that are meaningful, motivating, and intellectually demanding for children.

Using observational techniques for the design and evaluation of educational programs does have a downside. The down side mainly relates to economy. It should be all too evident to you, after having read this book, that conducting observations is very expensive. It takes numerous hours to gather reliable and valid information on children. Actually, this is the argument proffered by many administrators in favor of testing. Although observation is more expensive than testing, it often provides better, or at least good complementary information; it is certain less expense than school failure.

SOME THINGS TO THINK ABOUT

1. What are some indirect observational methods that could be used to answer the following questions:

A. Where do children spend most of their out of school time?

B. With whom is it spent? Doing what?

C. Where, with whom, and how do young children use reading and writing at home?

What resources are provided by these forms of literacy?

2. Who might you interview to obtain answers to these questions?

3. Write some sample questions?

4. Now that you'd gathered information on these indirect measures:

   What direct observation sampling and recording rules would you use to answer questions 1A, 1B, and 1C?

5. What are some possible classroom activities that would serve as evaluation activities?

6. How might you as a teacher get help in conducting the expensive work of direct observations?

7. How can direct observational measures be used as a replacement of traditional testing methods? How can they be used to complement traditional methods?

References and Suggested Readings

Altmann, J. (1974). Observational study of behavior: Sampling methods. *Behavior, 49*, 227–265.

American Association of University Women. (1993). *Hostile hallways: The AAUW survey on sexual harassment in America's schools.* Washington, DC: Author.

American Psychological Association. (2001, February). *APA ethics code: Draft for comments*. Washington, DC: Author.

American Psychological Association. (1999). *Publication manual* (4th ed.). Washington, DC: Author.

Animal Behaviour Society. (2001). Instructions to authors. *Animal Behaviour, 61*, ii–vi.

Applebaum, M., & McCall, R. (1983). Design and analysis in developmental research. In W. Kessen (Ed.). *Handbook of child psychology* (Vol. 1, pp. 415–476. New York: Wiley.

Archer, J., & Lloyd, B. (2002). *Sex and gender* (2nd ed.). London: Cambridge University Press.

Aries, P. (1962). *Centuries of childhood: A social history of family life.* New York: Vintage.

Babbie, E. (1998). *The basics of social research.* Belmont, CA: Wadsworth.

Bakeman, R., & Gottman, J. (1986). *Observing interaction.* New York: Cambridge University Press.

Bakeman, R., & Quera, V. (1995). *Analyzing interaction: Sequential analysis with SDIS and GSEQ.* NY: Cambridge University Press.

Barker, R. (1968). *Ecological psychology.* Stanford, CT: Stanford University Press.

Barker, R., & Wright, H. (1955). *Midwest and its children*. New York: Jossey Bass.

Bartlett, F. C. (1932). *Remembering: A study in experimental and social psychology.* Cambridge, UK: Cambridge University Press.

Bateson, P. P. G. (1991). Assessment of pain in animals. *Animal Behaviour, 42*, 827–839.

Battig, W., & Montague, W. (1969). Category names for verbal items in 56 categories. *Journal of Experimental Psychology Monographs, 80*, 1–45.

Baumrind, D. (1985). Research using intentional deception: Ethical issues revisited. *American Psychologist, 45*, 1289–1298.

Bebeau, M. (1999, July 7). *Social responsibility, scientific fraud, and reporting misconduct. Education in the responsible conduct of research.* University of Minnesota. Retrieved from http://www.research.umn.edu/ethic/curriculum.html

Bekoff, M. (1995). Play signals as punctuation: The structure of social play in canids. *Behaviour, 132*, 419–429.

Bekoff, M. (1997). Playing with play: What can we learn about cognition, negotiation, and evolution. In D. Cummins & C. Allen (Eds.), *The evolution of mind*. New York: Oxford University Press.

Bell, F. O., Hoff, A. L., & Hoyt, K. B. (1964). Answer sheets do make a difference. *Personnel Psychology, 17*, 65–71.

Bem, D. J. (1995). Writing a review article for *Psychological Bulletin. Psychological Bulletin, 118*, 172–177.

Bem, D. J. (in press). Writing the empirical journal article. In J. M. Darley, M. P. Zanna, & H. L. Roedinger (Eds.). *The compleat academic* (2nd ed.). Washington, DC: American Psychological Association.

Berenbaum, S. A., & Hines, M. (1992). Early androgens are related to childhood sex-typed toy preferences. *Psychological Science, 3*, 203–206.

Berenbaum, S. A., & Snyder, E. (1995). Early hormonal influences on childhood sex-typed activity and playmate preferences: Implications for the development of sexual orientation. *Developmental Psychology, 31*, 31–42.

Bernstein, I. (1981). Dominance: The baby and the bathwater. *The Behavioral and Brain Sciences, 4*, 419–457.

Bjorklund, D. F. (1995). *Children's thinking: Developmental function and individual differences* (2nd ed.). Pacific Grove, CA: Brooks/Cole.

Bjorklund, D. F. (2000). *Children's thinking: Developmental function and individual differences.* (3rd ed.). Belmont, CA: Wadsworth.

Bjorklund. D. F., &. Bjorklund, B. R. (1985). Organization versus item effects of an elaborated knowledge base on children's memory. *Developmental Psychology, 21*, 1120–1131.

Bjorklund, D. F., Gaultney, J. F., & Green, B. L. (1993). I watch therefore I can do: The development of meta-imitation over the preschool years and the advantage of optimism in one's imitative skills. In R. Pasnak & M. L. Howe (Eds.), *Emerging themes in cognitive development, Vol. II: Competencies* (pp. 79–102). New York: Springer-Verlag.

Bjorklund, D. F., & Jacobs, J. W. (1984). A developmental examination of ratings of associative strength. *Behavior Research Methods, Instruments & Computers, 16*, 568–569.

Bjorklund, D. F., & Jacobs, J. W. (1985). Associative and categorical processes in children's memory: The role of automaticity in the development of organization in free recall. *Journal of Experimental Child Psychology, 39*, 599–617.

Bjorklund, D. F., & Pellegrini, A. D. (2002). *Evolutionary developmental psychology*. Washington, DC: American Psychological Association.

Bjorklund, D. F., Schneider, W., Cassel, W. S., & Ashley, E. (1994). Training and extension of a memory strategy: Evidence for utilization deficiencies in the acquisition of an organizational strategy in high- and low-IQ children. *Child Development, 65*, 951–965.

Bjorkqvist, K. (1994). Sex differences in physical, verbal, and indirect aggression: A review of recent research. *Sex Roles, 30*, 177–188.

Bloch, M. (1989). Young boys' and girls' play at home and in the community: A cultural-ecological framework. In M. Bloch & A. D. Pellegrini (Eds.), *The ecological context of children's play* (pp. 120–154). Norwood, NJ: Ablex.

Block, J. (1983). Differential premises arising from differential socialization of the sexes: Some conjectures. *Child Development, 54*, 1354–1365.

Bloom, B. S. (Ed.). (1956). *Taxonomy of educational objectives. Handbook I: Cognitive domain*. New York: McKay.

Blurton Jones, N. (Ed.). (1972). *Ethological studies of child behaviour*. London: Cambridge University Press.

Blurton Jones, N. (1993). The lives of hunter-gatherer children: Effects of parental behavior and parental reproductive strategy. In M. F. Pereira & L. A. Fairbanks (Eds.), *Juvenile primates: Life history, development, and behaviors* (pp. 309–326). New York: Oxford University Press.

Blurton Jones, N., & Konner, M. (1973). Sex differences in behaviours of London and Bushman children. In R. Michaels & J. Crook (Eds.), *Comparative ecology and the behaviours of primates* (pp. 690–750). London: Academic.

Blurton Jones, N., & Leach, G. (1972). Behaviour of children and their mothers at separation and greeting. In N. Blurton Jones (Ed.), *Ethological studies of child behaviour* (pp. 217–248). London: Cambridge University Press.

Bornstein, M. H., Ferdinandsen, K., & Gross, C. G. (1981). Perception of symmetry in infancy. *Developmental Psychology, 17*, 82–86.

Borrie, A., Jonsson, G. K., & Magnusson, M. S. (2002). Temporal pattern analysis and its applicability in sport: An explanation and exemplar data. *Journal of Sports Sciences, 20*, 845–852.

Bradley, L., & Bryant, P. (1983). Categorizing sounds and learning to read—A causal connection. *Nature, 301*, 419–421.

Braunwald, S., & Brislin, R. (1979). The diary method updated. In E. Ochs & B. Schieffelin (Eds.), *Developmental pragmatics* (pp. 21–42). New York: Academic.

Broad, C. D. (1959). Bacon and the experimental method. In *A short history of science: Origins and results of the Scientific Revolution, A symposium* (pp. 27–33). New York: Doubleday.

Bronfenbrenner, U. (1979). *The ecology of human development.* Cambridge, MA: Harvard University Press.

Bronfenbrenner, U., & Mahoney, M. (1975). The structure and verification of hypotheses. In U. Bronfenbrenner & M. Mahoney (Eds.), *Influences on human development* (pp. 3–39). Hinsdale, IL: The Dryden Press.

Bruner, J. S., Goodow, J. J., & Austin, G. A. (1958). *A study of thinking*. New York: Wiley.

Bruner, J. S., Oliver, R. R., & Greenfield, P. M. (1966). *Studies in Cognitive Growth*. New York: Wiley.

Bruner, J. (1986). *Actual minds, possible worlds.* Cambridge, MA: Harvard University Press.

Brunswik, E. (1956). *Perception and the representative design of psychological experiments*. Berkeley, CA: University of California Press.

Bryk, A. S., & Raudenbush, S. W. (1992). *Hierarchical linear models: Applications and data analysis methods*. Newbury Park, CA: Sage.

Burr, W. (n.d.). *A dialectical analysis of the scientific paradigms used by family scientists*. Paper presented at the Theory and Methods Workshop at the National Council on Family Relations.

Burts, D., Hart, C., Charlesworth, R., Fleege, P., Mosely, J., & Thomasson, R. (1992). Observed activities and stress behaviors of children in developmentally inappropriate kindergarten classrooms. *Early Childhood Research Quarterly, 7*, 297–318.

Cairns, R., & Cairns, B. (1986). An evolutionary and developmental perspective on aggression. In C. Zahn-Waxler, E. Cummings, & R. Iannoti (Eds.), *Altruism and aggression* (pp. 58–87). New York: Cambridge University Press.

Cairns, R. (1986). An evolutionary and developmental perspective on aggressive patterns. In C. Zahn-Waxler, E. Cummings, & ?. Iannattir (Eds.), *Altruism and aggression* (pp. 58–87). New York: Cambridge University Press.

Caldwell, B., & Bradley, R. (1984). *The HOME Observation for measurement of the environment*. University of Arkansas at Little Rock Mimeo.

Campbell, D. T., & Fiske, D. W. (1959). Convergent and discriminate validation by the multi-trait multi-method matrix. *Psychological Bulletin, 56*, 81–105.

Campbell, D. T., & Stanley, J. (1963). *Experimental and quasi-experimental designs for research*. Chicago: Rand McNally.

Cazden, C. B. (1975). Hypercorrection in test responses. *Theory Into Practice, 14*, 343–346.

Cheyney, D., & Seyfarth, R. (1990). *How monkeys see the world.* Chicago: University of Chicago Press.

Chomsky, N. (1959). A review of Skinner's Verbal Behavior. *Language, 35*, 26–58.

Cochran, M., & Woolever, F. (1983). Beyond the deficit model: The empowerment of parents with information and informational support. In I. Sigel & L. Laosa (Eds.), *Changing families* (pp. 225–246). New York: Plenum.

Cohen, J. (1960). A coefficient of agreement for nominal scales. *Educational and Psychological Measurement, 20*, 37–46.

Cohen, J. (1988). *Statistical power analyses for behavioral sciences*. Hillsdale, NJ: Lawrence Erlbaum Associates.

Cohen, J. (1994). The earth is round ($p < .05$). *American Psychologist, 49*, 997–1003.

Coie, J. D., & Dodge, K. A. (1998). Aggression and antisocial behavior. In N. Eisenberg (Ed.), *Manual of child psychology, Vol. 3, Social, emotional, and personality development* (pp. 779–862). New York: Wiley.

Cole, M. (1993, March). *A cultural-historical goal for developmental research*. Paper presented at the biennial meetings of the Society for Research in Child Development, New Orleans, LA.

Cole, M., Hood, L., & McDermott, R. P. (1978). Concepts of ecological validity: Their differing implications for comparative cognitive research. *Newsletter of the Laboratory of Comparative Human Cognition, 2*, 34–37.

Cook, T. D., & Campbell, D. T. (1979). *Quasi-experimentation: Design and analysis issues for field settings.* Chicago: Rand McNally.

Cooper, H. (1998). *Synthesizing research.* Thousand Oaks, CA: Sage.

Corsaro, W. (1981). Entering the child's world. In J. Green & C. Wallat (Eds.), *Ethnography and language in educational settings* (pp. 117–146). Norwood, NJ: Ablex.

Crick, N. R., & Grotpeter, J. K. (1995). Relational aggression, gender, and social-psychological adjustment. *Child Development, 66*, 710–722.

Cronbach, L. J. (1957). The two disciplines of scientific psychology. *American Psychologist, 12*, 671–684.

Cronbach, L. J. (1971). Validity. In R. L. Thorndike (Ed.), *Educational measurement* (pp. 443–507). Washington, DC: American Council on Education.

Cronbach, L. (1976). *Research on classrooms and schools.* [An occasional paper of the Stanford Evaluation Consortium]. Unpublished paper, Stanford University.

Cronbach, L. (1980). Validity on parole: How can we go straight? In D. Fisk & R. Shweder (Eds.), *New directions for testing and measurement* (pp. 99–108). San Francisco: Jossey-Bass.

Cronbach, L., Glesher, G., Nanda, H., & Rajaratnam, N. (1972). *The dependability of behavioral measurement.* New York: Wiley.

Cronbach, L. J., & Meehl, P. E. (1955). Construct validity in psychological tests. *Psychological Bulletin, 52*, 281–302.

Csikszentmihalyi, M. (1990). *Flow: The psychology of optimal experience*. New York: Harper.

Dansky, J., & Silverman, I. W. (1975). Play: A general facilitator of associative fluency. *Developmental Psychology, 11*, 104.

Dansky, J., & Silverman, I. W. (1973). Effects of play on associative fluency in preschool-age children. *Developmental Psychology, 9*, 38–43.

Dashiell, J. F. (1939). Some rapprochements in contemporary psychology. *Psychological Bulletin, 36*, 1–24.

Dawkins, J. S., & Gosling, M. (1994). *Ethics in research on animal behaviour*. New York: Academic Press for the Animal Behaviour Society.

Darwin, C. (1877). Biographical sketch of an infant. *Mind, 2*, 285–294.

Dewey, J. (1938). *Experience and Education*. New York: Collier.

Dickinson, D., & Moreton, J. (1991, April). *Predicting specific kindergarten literacy skills from three-year-olds' preschool experience*. Paper presented at the biennial meetings of the Society for Research in Child Development, Seattle, Washington.

Dodge, K., Pettit, G., McClaskey, R., & Brown, M. (1986). Social competence in children. *Monography of the Society for Research in Child Development, 51*(2, Serial No. 213.).

Dooley, D. (2001). *Social research methods*. Upper Saddle River, NJ: Prentice Hall.

Driscoll, J. W., & Bateson, P. P. G. (1988). Animals in behavioural research. *Animal Behaviour, 36*, 1569–1574.

Dunbar, R. I. M. (1988). *Primate social systems*. Ithaca, NY: Cornell.

Dunn, J. (1988). *The beginnings of social understanding.* Cambridge, MA: Harvard University Press.

Dunn, J. (1993). *Young children's close relationships.* Beverly Hills: Sage.

Dworkin, M. (1999, September). *Plagiarism: Education in the responsible conduct of research.* Retrieved from http://www.research.umn.edu/ethics/curriculum.html

Eaton, W. O., & Enns, L. (1986). Sex differences in human motor activity level. *Psychological Bulletin, 100*, 19–28.

Ebinghaus, H. (1885/1964). *Memory.* New York: Teachers College Press.

Ehrhardt, A. (1985). The psychobiology of gender. In A. Rossi (Ed.), *Gender and the life course* (pp. 37–57). Hawthorne, NY: Aldine.

Elwood, R. W. (1991). Ethical implications of studies of infanticide and maternal aggression in rodents. *Animal Behaviour, 42*, 841–849.

Emerson, E. (2003). *HARCREL: Observational research programmes* [Computer software and manual]. Retrieved May 29, 2003 from http://www.lancs.ac.uk/depts/ihr/research/learning/projects/observation.htm

Erickson, F. (1986). Qualitative methods in research on teaching. In I. M. Wittrock (Ed.), *Handbook of research on teaching* (pp. 119–161), New York: Macmillan.

Evertson, C., & Green, J. (1986). Observation as inquiry and method. In M. Wittrock (Ed.), *Handbook of research on teaching* (pp. 162–213). New York: Macmillan.

Fetterman, D. M. (1998). *Ethnography*. Thousand Oaks, CA: Sage.

Fine, G., & Sandstrom, K. (1988). *Knowing children: Participant observation*. Beverly Hills, CA: Sage.

Fisher, C. B. (1993). Integrating science and ethics in research with young children and youth. *Social Policy Report—Society for Research in Child Development, 7*(4).

Fowler, F. J. (1993). *Survey research methods.* Newbury Park, CA: Sage.

Gardner, H. (1993). *Multiple intelligences: The theory in practice.* New York: Basic Books.

Goodall, J. (1986). *The chimpanzees of Gombe*. Cambridge, MA: Harvard University Press.

Gottlieb, G. (1991). Experiential canalization of behavioral development: Theory. *Developmental Psychology, 27*, 4–13.

Gottlieb, G. (1997). *Synthesizing nature-nurture: Prenatal roots of instinctive behavior.* Mahwah, NJ: Lawrence Erlbaum Associates.

Gottlieb, G. (1998). Normally occurring environmental and behavioral influences on gene activity: From central dogma to probabilistic epigenesis. *Psychological Review, 105*, 792–802.

Gottman, J., & Roy, A. (1990). *Sequential analysis.* New York: Cambridge University Press.

Graham, S., & Juvonen, J. (1998). A social cognitive perspective on peer aggression and victimization. In R. Vasta (Ed.), *Annals of child development* (pp. 23–70). London: Jessica Kingsley Publishers.

Graham, S., & Juvonen, J. (1998b). Self blame and peer victimization in middle school: An attributional analysis. *Developmental Psychology, 34*, 587–599.

Greenwood, C. R., Carta, J. J., & Dawson, H. (2000). Ecobehavioral assessment systems software (EBASS): A system for observation in education settings. In T. Thompson, D. Felce, & F. J. Symons (Eds.), *Behavioral observation: Technology and applications in developmental disabilities* (pp. 229–251). Baltimore, MD: Paul H. Brookes Publishing.

Guilford, J., & Fruchter, B. (1973). *Fundamental statistics in psychology and education.* New York: McGraw-Hill.

Gump, P. (1989). Ecological psychology and issues of play. In M. Bloch & A. Pellegrini (Eds.), *The ecological contexts of children's play* (pp. 35–56). Norwood, NJ: Ablex.

Haight, W., & Miller, P. (1992). *Ecology and the development of pretend.* Albany, NY: SUNY Press.

Haight, W. L., & Miller, P. J. (1993). *Pretending at home.* Albany: State University of New York Press.

Harris, J. R. (1998). *The nurture assumption: Why children turn out the way they do.* New York: Free Press.

Harris, P. (1990). The child's theory of mind and its cultural context. In G. Butterworth & P. Bryant (Eds.), *Causes of development* (pp. 215–237). New York: Harvester Wheatsheaf.

Hart, C., DeWolf, M., Wozniak, P., & Burts, D. (1992). Maternal and paternal disciplinary styles: Relations with preschoolers' playground behavioral orientations and peer status. *Child Development, 63*, 879–892.

Hart, C., & Sheehan, R. (1986). Preschoolers play behavior in outdoor environments. Effects of traditional and contemporary playgrounds. *American Educational Research Journal, 23*, 669–679.

Hayes, C. (1951). *The ape in our house*. New York: Harper.

Hayes, K. J., & Hayes, C. (1952) Imitation in a home-reared chimpanzee. *Journal of Comparative Physiological Psychology, 45*, 450–459.

Heath, S. (1983). *Ways with words.* New York: Cambridge University Press.

Heath, S. (with H. Chin). (1985). Narrative play in second language learning. In L. Galda & A. Pellegrini (Eds.), *Play, language, and stories* (pp. 147–166). Norwood, NJ: Ablex.

Heberlein, J. (1999, August 28). *Research data management.* Retrieved from http://www.research.umn.edu/ethics/modResearch2.html

Herbert, J., & Attridge, C. (1975). A guide for developers and users of observation systems and manuals. *American Educational Research Journal, 12*, 1–20.

Hille, M. (1991). Hand-held behavioral observations: The Observer. *Behavioral Assessment, 13*, 187–188.

Hinde, R. (1973). On the design of check-sheets. *Primates, 14*, 393–406.

Hinde, R. (1976). On describing relationships. *Journal of Child Psychology and Psychiatry, 17*, 1–19.

Hinde, R. (1980). *Ethology*. London: Fontana.

Hines, M. (1982). Prenatal gonadal hormones and sex differences in human behavior. *Psychological Bulletin, 92*, 56–80.

Hines, M., & Kaufman, F. R. (1994). Androgen and the development of human sex-typical behavior: Rough-and-tumble play and sex of preferred playmates in children with Congenital Adrenal Hyperplasia (CAH). *Child Development, 65*, 1042–1053.

Hobsbawm, E. J. (1980). The revival of narrative: Some comments. *Past & Present, 86*, 3–8.

Hollander, M., & Wolfe, D. (1973). *Nonparametric statistical methods*. New York: Wiley.

Hollenbeck, A. (1978). Problems of reliability in observational research. In G. Sackett (Ed.), Observing behavior (Vol. 1, pp. 79–98). Baltimore: University Park Press.

Hopkins, K. D., & Stanley, J. C. (1981). *Educational and psychological measurement and evaluation*. Englewood Cliffs, NJ: Prentice-Hall.

Huntingford, F. A. (1984). Some ethical issues raised by studies of predation and aggression. *Animal Behaviour, 32*, 210–215.

Hymes, D. (1980). *Language in education: Ethnolinguistic essays*. Washington, DC: Center for Applied Linguistics.

Hymes, D. (1980a). Qualitative/quantitative research methodologies in education: A linguistic approach. In D. Hymes (Ed.), *Language in education: Ethnolinguistic essays* (pp. 62–87). Washington, DC: Center for Applied Linguistics.

Hymes, D. (1980b). What is ethnography? In D. Hymes (Ed.), *Language in education: Ethnolinguistic essays* (pp. 88–103). Washington, DC: Center for Applied Linguistics.

Irwin, D. M., & Bushnell, M. M. (1980). *Observational strategies for child study*. New York: Holt, Rinehart and Winston.

James, W. (1901). *Talks to teachers on psychology: And to students on some of life's ideals*. New York: Holt.

Jensen, A. R. (1992). Scientific fraud or false accusations: The case of Cyril Burt. In D. J. Miller & M. Hersen (Eds.), *Research fraud in the behavioral and biomedical sciences* (pp. 97–124). New York: Wiley.

Joynson, R. B. (1989). *The Burt affair*. London: Routledge.

Kagan, J. (1994). On the nature of emotion. In N. Fox (Ed.), *The development of emotion regulation: Biological and behavioral considerations. Monographs for the Society for Research in Child Development, 59* (Serial #240, Nos. 1–2).

Katz, I., Achison, R., Epps, E., & Roberts, S. (1972). Race of evaluator, race of norm, and expectancy as determinants of black performance. *Journal of Experimental Social Psychology, 8*, 1–15.

Kerlinger, F. (1992). *Foundations of behavioral research* (3rd ed.). New York: Holt, Rinehart, and Winston.

Kerlinger, F. (1996). *Foundations of behavioral research*. New York: Holt, Rinehart, and Winston.

Khang, S., & Iwata, B. A. (2000). Computer systems for collecting real-time observational data. In T. Thompson, D. Felce, & F. J. Symons (Eds.), *Behavioral observation: Technology and applications in developmental disabilities* (pp. 35–46). Baltimore, MD: Paul H. Brookes, Publishing.

Klinger, E. (1999a, May). *Human subjects*. Retrieved from http://www.research.umn.edu/ethics/modHuman.html

Klinger, E. (1999b, May). *Animal subjects*. Retrieved from http://www.research.umn.edu/ethics/modAnimals.html

Kubiszyn, T., & Borich, G. (2000). *Educational testing and measurement*. New York: Wiley.

Kucera, H., & Francis, W. N. (1967). *Computational analysis of present-day American English*. Providence, RI: Brown University Press.

Kuhn, T. (1962). *The structure of scientific revolutions*. Chicago: The University of Chicago Press.

Labov, W. (1972). *Language in its inner city*. Philadelphia: University of Pennsylvania Press.

Ladd, G. (1983). Social networks of popular, average, and rejected children in school settings. *Merrill-Palmer Quarterly, 29*, 283–308.

Ladd, G., & Price, J. (1993). Play styles of peer accepted and peer rejected children on the playground. In C. Hart (Ed.), *Children on playgrounds* (pp. 130–161). Albany, NY: SUNY press.

Lancy, D. F. (1996). *Playing on the mother-ground*. New York: Guilford.

Lazar, I., & Darlington, R. (1982). Lasting effects of early education. *Monographs of the Society for Research in Child Development, 47*, 2–3.

Leger, D., & Didrichson, I. (1994). An assessment of data pooling and some alternatives. *Animal Behaviour, 48*, 823–832.

Lehner, P. N. (1996). *Handbook of ethological methods*. New York: Cambridge University Press.

Lillard, A. (1998). Ethnopsychologies: Cultural variations in theories of mind. *Psychological Bulletin, 123*, 3–32.

Linn, R. (1994). Performance assessment: Policy promises and technical measurement standards. *Educational Researcher, 23*(23), 4–14.

Lockheed, M., Harris, A., & Newcett, W. (1983). Sex and social influence: Over sex function as a status characteristic in mixed-sex groups of children? *Journal of Educational Psychology, 75*, 877–888.

Loevenger, J. (1957). Objective tests as instruments of psychological theory. *Psychological Reports, 3*, 635–694.

Lorenz, K. (1950). The comparative method in studying innate behaviour patterns. *Symposia of the Society for Experimental Biology, 4*, 221–268.

Lorenz, K. Z. (1965). *Evolution and modification of behavior.* Chicago: Chicago University Press.

Lykken, D. (1968). Statistical significance in psychological research. *Psychological Bulletin, 70*, 151–159.

Maccoby, E. E. (1998). *The two sexes: Growing up apart, coming together.* Cambridge, MA: Harvard University Press.

Magnusson, M. S. (2000). Discovering hidden time patterns in behavior: T-patterns and their detection. *Behavior Research Methods, Instruments, & Computers, 32*, 93–110.

Manne, S. L., Bakeman, R., Jacobsen, P. B., Gorfinkle, K., Bernstein, D., & Redd, W. H. (1992). Adult–child interaction during invasive medical procedures. *Health Psychology, 11*, 241–249.

Martin, P., & Bateson, P. (1993). *Measuring behaviour*. London: Cambridge University Press.

McCall, R. (1977). Challenges to a science of developmental psychology. *Child Development, 48*, 333–394.

McCall, R. (1980). *Fundamental statistics for psychology*. New York: Harcourt, Brace, Jovanovich.

Mead, M. (1954). Research on primitive children. In L. Carmichael (Ed.), *Manual of child psychology* (pp. 735–780). New York: Wiley.

Messick, S. (1975). The standard problem: Meaning and values in measurement and evaluation. *American Psychologist, 30*, 1012–1027.

Messick, S. (1983). Assessment of children. In W. Kessen (Ed.), *Handbook of child psychology*, (Vol. 1, pp. 477–526). New York: Wiley.

Messick, S. (1995). Validity of psychological assessment. *American Psychologist, 50*, 741–749.

Miller, J. F., & Chapman, R. S. (1997). *SALT: Systematic analysis of language transcripts* (Windows version 4.1): User's manual. Madison: University of Wisconsin-Madison, The Waisman Center, Language Analysis Laboratory.

Moffitt, T. E., Caspi, A., Rutter, M., & Solva, P. (2001). *Sex differences in anti-social behaviour*. Cambridge, UK: Cambridge University Press.

Morison, P. (1992). Testing in America's schools: Issues for research and policy. *Society for Research in Child Development Social Policy Report, 6*(2).

Moss, P. (1992). Shifting conceptions of validity in educational measurement: Implications for performance assessment. *Review of Educational Research, 62*, 229–258.

Munroe, R. H., Munroe, R. L., Michelson, C., Koel, A., Bolton, R., & Bolton, C. (1983). Time allocation in four societies. *Ethnology, 22*(4), 255–270.

Murray, F. (1972) Acquisition of conversation through social interaction. *Developmental Psychology, 6*, 1–6.

Murray, F. (1980). Teaching through social conflict. *Contemporary Educational Psychology, 7*, 257–271.

Neil, M., Oliver, C., & Hall, S. (2000). *ObsWin: Observational data collection and analysis* [Computer software and manual]. Retrieved May 29, 2003 from http://www.antam.co.uk/obswin/htm

Noldus, L. P., Trienes, R. J., Hendriksen, A. H., Jansen, H., & Jansen, R. G. (2000). The observer video- pro: New software for the collection, management, and presentation of time-structured data from videotapes and digital media files. *Behavior Research Methods, Instruments, and Computers, 32*, 197–206.

Norusis, M. (1988a). *SPSS/PC+ studentware.* Chicago: SPSS.

Norusis, M. (1988b). *SPSS/PC+ advanced statistics V2.0.* Chicago: SPSS.

Olson, D. R. (1970). Language and thought. *Psychological Review, 77*, 257–272.

Olweus, D. (1993). *Bullying at school.* Cambridge, MA: Blackwell.

Ottoni, E. B. (2000). EthoLog 2.2: A tool for the transcription and timing of behavior observation sessions. *Behavior Research Methods, Instruments, & Computers, 32*, 446–449.

Oxford Concise Dictionary. (1982). New York: Oxford University Press.

Patterson, G. (1982). *Coercive family processes.* Eugene, OR: Castilla.

Patton, M. (1990). *Qualitative evaluation and research methods.* Beverly Hills: Sage.

Pavlov, I. P. (1927). *Conditioned reflexes: An investigation of the physiological activity of the cerebral cortex.* London: Oxford University Press.

Pellegrini, A. D. (1988). Elementary school children's rough-and-rumble play and social competence. *Developmental Psychology, 24*, 802–806.

Pellegrini, A. D. (1989). Elementary School children's rough-and-tumble play. *Early Childhood Research Quarterly, 4*, 245–260.

Pellegrini, A. D. (1992). Ethological studies of the categorization of children's social behavior in preschool: A review. *Early Education & Development, 3*, 284–297.

Pellegrini, A. D. (1992). Kindergarten children's social cognitive status as a predictor of first grade success. *Early Childhood Research Quarterly, 7*, 565–577.

Pellegrini, A. D. (1993). Boys' rough-and-tumble play, social competence, and group composition. *British Journal of Developmental Psychology, 11*, 237–248.

Pellegrini, A. D. (1995). *School recess and playground behavior.* Albany, NY: SUNY Press.

Pellegrini, A. D. (2001, April). *Children's games as a scaffold for adjustment to primary school.* Paper in a symposium on Games in Childhood at the Society for Research in Child Development, Minneapolis, IN.

Pellegrini, A. D., & Bartini, M. (2000). A longitudinal study of bullying, victimization, and peer affiliation during the transition from primary to middle school. *American Educational Research Journal, 37*, 699–725.

Pellegrini, A. D., & Bartini, M. (2001). Dominance in early adolescent boys: Affiliative and aggressive dimensions and possible functions. *Merrill-Palmer Quarterly, 47*, 142–163.

Pellegrini, A. D., Bartini, M., & Brooks, F. (1999). School bullies, victims, and aggressive victims: Factors relating to group affiliation and victimization in early adolescence. *Journal of Educational Psychology, 91*, 216–224.

Pellegrini, A. D., Bjorklund, D. F. (1998). *Applied child study: A developmental approach* (3rd ed.). Mahwah, NJ: Lawrence Erlbaum Associates.

Pellegrini, A. D., & Bjorklund, D. F. (in press). The Ontogeny and Phylogeny of Children's Object and Fantasy Play. *Human Nature, 13*.

Pellegrini, A. D., Brody, G., & Sigel, I. (1985). Parents' book-reading habits with their children. *Journal of Educational Psychology, 77*, 332–340.

Pellegrini, A. D., Brody, G., & Stoneman, Z. (1987).Children's conversational competence with their parents. *Discourse Processes, 10*, 93–106.

Pellegrini, A. D., & Davis, P. (1993). Relations between children's playground and classroom behavior. *British Journal of Educational Psychology, 63*, 88–95.

Pellegrini, A. D., & Galda, L. (1990). The joint construction of stories by preschool children and an experimenter. In B. Britton & A. D. Pellegrini (Eds.), *Narrative thought and narrative language* (pp. **??–??**). Hillsdale, NJ: Lawrence Erlbaum Associates.

Pellegrini, A. D., & Galda, L. (1991). Longitudinal relations among symbolic play, metalinguistic verbs, and emergent literacy. In J. Christie (Ed.), *Play and early literacy development* (pp. 47–68). Albany, NY: SUNY Press.

Pellegrini, A. D., Galda, L., Shockley, B., & Stahl, S. (1995) The nexus of social and literacy experiences at home and at school: Implications for primary school oral language and literacy. *British Journal of Educational Psychology, 65*, 273–285.

Pellegrini, A. D., Hubberty, P. D., & Jones, I. (1995). The effects of recess timing on children's playground and classroom behaviors. *American Educational Research Journal, 32*, 845–864.

Pellegrini, A. D., & Perlmutter, J. (1989). Classroom contextual effects on children's play. *Developmental Psychology, 25*, 289–296.

Pellegrini, A. D., & Smith, P. K. (1998). Physical activity play: The nature and function of a neglected aspect of play. *Child Development, 69*, 577–598.

Pellegrini, A. D., & Stanic, G. M. A. (1993). Locating children's mathematical competence: Application of the developmental niche. *Journal of Applied Developmental Psychology, 14*, 501–520.

Perry, D., Willard, J., & Perry, L. (1990). Peers' perceptions of the consequences that victimized children provide aggressors. *Child Development, 61*, 1289–1309.

Phillips, S. (1976). The "silent" Indians styles of learning. In C. Cazden, V. John, & D. Hymes (Eds.), *Functions of language in the classroom* (pp. 331–342). New York: Teachers College Press.

Philips, S. U. (1972). Participation structures and communicative competence: Warm Springs children in community and classroom. In C. B. Cazden & D. Hymes (Eds.), *Functions of language in the classroom* (pp. 370–394). New York: Teachers College Press.

Piaget, J. (1962). *Play, dreams, and imitation in childhood*. New York: Norton.

Piaget, J. (1983). Piaget's theory. In W. Kessen (Ed.), *Handbook of child psychology Vol 1: History, theory, and methods* (pp. 103–128). New York: Wiley.

Pike, K. (1965). *Language in relation to a unified theory of the structure of human behavior.* The Hague, The Netherlands: Mouton.

Plomin, R., & Crabbe, J. (2000). DNA. *Psychological Bulletin, 126*, 806–828.

Popper, K. R. (1959). *The logic of scientific discovery.* New York: Basic Books.

Premack, D., & Woodruff, G. (1978). Does the chimpanzee have a theory of mind? *Behavioral and Brain Sciences, 4*, 515–526.

Roberts, W. L. (2002). *Software for observing behavior in natural settings* [Computer software and manual]. Retrieved May 29, 2003 from http://www.cariboo.bc.ca/ae/psych/roberts/homepage.htm#focal

Rubin, K., Fein, G., & Vandenberg, B. (1983). Play. In E. M. Hetherington (Ed.), *Handbook of child psychology* (Vol. 4, pp. 693–774). New York: Wiley.

Russell, B. (1959/1931). *The scientific outlook*. New York: Norton.

Rutter, M. (1967). A children's behaviour questionnaire for completion by teachers: Preliminary findings. *Journal of Child Psychology and Psychiatry, 8*, 1–11.

Rutter, M., & Garmezy, N. (1983). Developmental psychopathology. In E. M. Hetherington (Ed.), *Handbook of child psychology* (Vol. 4, pp. 775–912). New York: Wiley.

Sachs, J. (1980). The role of adult–child play in language development. In K. Rubin (Ed.), *Children's play* (pp. 33–48). San Francisco: Jossey-Bass.

Sackett, G. (1978). Measurement in observational research. In G. Sackett (Ed.), *Observing behavior* (Vol. 1, pp. 25–43). Baltimore: University Park Press.

Salkind, N. J. (2000). *Exploring research*. Upper Saddle River, NJ: Prentice Hall.

Sanders, C. (1993, November 12). Diaries show how hard dons work. *Times Higher Educational Supplement*, 1093.

Sapir, E. (1925). Sound patterns in language. *Language, 1*, 37–51.

Schrag, F. (1992, June–July). In defense of positivist research paradigms. *Educational Researcher*, 5–10.

Scarr, S. (1985). Constructing psychology: Making fact and fables for our times. *American Psychologist, 40*, 499–512.

Scarr, S. (1992). Developmental theories for the 1990s: Development and individual differences. *Child Development, 63*, 1–19.

Scarr, S. (1993). Biological and cultural diversity: The legacy of Darwin for development. *Child Development, 64*, 1333–1353.

Scarr, S. (1995a). Psychology will be truly evolutionary when behavior genetics is included. *Psychological Inquiry, 6*, 68–71.

Scarr, S. (1995b). Commentary to Gottlieb's Some conceptual deficiencies in "developmental" behavior genetics. *Human Development, 38*, 154–158.

Scarr, S., & McCartney, K. (1983). How people make their own environments: A theory of genotype x environment effects. *Child Development, 54*, 424–435.

Schlosberg, H. (1947). The concept of play. *Psychological Review, 54*, 229–231.

Schneider, W., & Weinert, F. E. (1995). Memory development during early and middle childhood: Findings from the Munich longitudinal study (LOGIC). In F. E. Weinert & W. Schneider (Eds.), *Memory performance and competencies*. Mahwah, NJ: Lawrence Erlbaum Associates.

Schwartz, D., Dodge, K. A., & Coie, J. D. (1993). The emergence of chronic peer victimization. *Child Development, 64*, 1755–1772.

Schwartz, D., Pettit, G. S., Dodge, K. A., & Bates, J. E. (1997). The early socialization and adjustment of aggressive victims of bully. *Child Development, 68*, 665–675.

Sears, R., Maccoby, E., & Levin, H. (1957). *Patterns of child rearing*. Evanston, IL: Row, Peterson.

Shadish, W. R., Cook, T. D., & Campbell, D. T. (2002). *Experimental and quasi-experimental designs for generalized causal inferences*. Boston: Houghton Mifflin Company.

Sharpe, T., & Koperwas, J. (2003). *BEST: Behavioral evaluation strategy and taxonomy flexible real-time collection and analysis of observational data* [Computer software and manual]. Retrieved May 29, 2003 from http://www.scolari.co.uk/best/best.htm

Shepard, L. (1993). Psychometricians' views about learning. *Educational Researcher, 20*(7), 2–16.

Shwreder, R. A., Goodnow, J., Hatano, G., LeVine, R. A., Markus, H., & Miller, P. (1998). The cultural psychology of development: One mind, many mentalities. In R. M. Lerner (Ed.), *Handbook of child psychology, Theoretical models of development* (Vol. 1, pp. 865–938). New York: Wiley.

Sigel, S. (1956). *Nonparametric statistics for the behavioral sciences.* New York: McGraw-Hill.

Simon, A., & Boyer, G. (Eds.). (1967). *Mirrors for behavior.* Philadelphia: Research For Better Schools.

Simon, T., & Smith, P. K. (1983). The study of play and problem solving in preschool children. *British Journal of Developmental Psychology, 1*, 289–297.

Simon, T., & Smith, P. K. (1985). Play and problem solving: A paradigm questioned. *Merrill-Palmer Quarterly, 31*, 265–277.

Skinner, B. F. (1974). *About behaviorism.* New York: Vintage.

Skinner, B. F. (1957). *Verbal behavior.* New York: Appleton-Century-Crofts.

Sluckin, A. (1981). *Growing up in the playground*. London: Routledge and Kegan Paul.

Smilansky, S. (1968). *The effects of sociodramatic play on economically disadvantaged preschool children.* New York: Wiley.

Smith, P. K. (1985). The reliability and validity of one-zero sampling. *British Educational Research Journal, 11*, 215–220.

Smith, P. K., & Connolly, K. (1980). *The ecology of preschool behaviour*. London: Cambridge University Press.

Smith, P. K., & Hagan, T. (1980). Effects of play deprivation on exercise play in nursery school children. *Animal Behaviour, 28*, 922–928.

Smith, P. K., Madsen, K. C., & Moody, J. C. (1999). What causes the age decline in reports of being bullied at school? Toward a developmental analysis of risks of being bullied. *Educational Research, 41*, 267–285.

Smith, P. K., & Sharp, S. (Eds.). (1994). *School bullying.* London: Routledge.

Smith, P. K., & Sluckin, A. (1979). Ethology, ethogeny, etics, emic, biology, culture: On the limitations of dichotomies. *European Journal of Social Psychology, 9*, 397–415.

Smith, P. K., & Whitney, S. (1987). Play and associative fluency: Experimenter effects may be responsible for previous findings. *Developmental Psychology, 23*, 49–53.

Snow, C. (1983). Literacy and language: Relationships during the preschool years. *Harvard Educational Review, 53*, 165–189.

Spitz, R. A. (1965). *The first year of life.* New York: International Universities Press.

Sroufe, L. (1979). The coherence of individual development: Early care attachment, and subsequent development issues. *American Psychologist, 34*, 834–841.

Stake, R. E. (1994). Case studies. In N. K. Denzin & Y. S. Lincoln (Eds.), *Handbook of qualitative research* (pp. 236–247). New York: Macmillan.

Stanley, J. C. (1971). Reliability. In R. L. Thorndike (Ed.), *Educational measurement* (pp. 356–442). Washington, DC: American Council on Education.

Sternberg, R. J. (2001). *Psychology: In search of the human mind* (3rd ed.). Fort Worth, TX: Harcourt.

Stevenson, H. W., & Lee, S. Y. (1990). Concepts of achievement. *Monographs for the Society for Research in Child Development, 55*(1–2) (Serial No. 221).

Stone, L. (1977). *The family, sex, and marriage in England, 1500–1800*. New York: Harper & Row.

Stone, L. (1979). The revival of narrative reflections and a new old history. *Past & Present, 85*, 3–24.

Still, A. W. (1982). On the number of subjects used in animal behaviour experiments. *Animal Behaviour, 30*, 873–880.

Stouthamer-Loeber, M., & van Kammen, W. B. (1995). *Data collection and management: A practical guide*. Thousand Oaks, CA: Sage.

Suen, H. A., & Ary, D. (1989). *Analyzing quantitative behavioral data*. Hillsdale, NJ: Lawrence Erlbaum Associates.

Suomi, S., & Harlow, H. (1972). Social rehabilitation of isolate-reared monkeys. *Developmental Psychology, 6*, 487–496.

Super, C., & Harkness, S. (1986). The developmental niche: A conceptualization at the interface of child and culture. *International Journal of Behavioral Development, 9*, 545–569.

Sutherland, K. S., Wehby, J. H., & Yoder, P. J. (2002). Examination of the relationship between teacher praise and opportunities for students with EBD to respond to academic requests. *Journal of Emotional and Behavioral Disorders, 10*, 5–13.

Sutton-Smith, B. (1967). The role of play in cognitive development. *Young Children, 22*, 364–369.

Sylva, K., Bruner, J., & Genova, P. (1976). The role of play in the problem-solving of children 3–5 years old. In T. Bruner, A. Jolly, & K. Sylva (Eds.), *Play—Its role in development and evolution* (pp. 244–261). New York: Basic Books.

Tapp, J., & Walden, T. A. (2000). PROCODER: A system for collection and analysis of observational data from videotape. In T. Thompson, D. Felce, & F. J. Symons (Eds.), *Behavioral observation: Technology and applications in developmental disabilities* (pp. 61–70). Baltimore, MD: Paul H. Brookes Publishing.

Tapp, J., Wehby, J., & Ellis, D. (1995). A multiple option observation system for experimental studies: MOOSES. *Behavior Research Methods, Instruments, & Computers, 27*, 25–31.

Tawney, R. H. (1969/1926). *Religion and the raise of capitalism*. Harmondsworth, UK: Penguin.

Terrill, R. (1973). *R. H. Tawney and his times*. Cambridge, MA: Harvard University Press.

Thompson, G. G. (1944). The social and emotional development of preschool children under two types of education programs. *Psychological Monographs, 56*(5).

Thorndike, L. (1966). Francis Bacon—A critical view. In H. F. Kearney (Ed.), *Origins of the scientific revolution* (pp. 31–35). London: Longmans.

Thelen, E. (1979). Rhythmical stereotypes in normal human infants. *Animal Behaviour, 27*, 699–715.

Thelen, E. (1980). Determinants of amounts of stereotyped behavior in normal human infants. *Ethology and Sociobiology, 1*, 141–150.

Tinbergen, N. (1959). Comparative studies of the behavior of gulls (*Laridae*): *A progress report, 15*, 1–70.

Tinbergen, N. (1963). On the aims and methods of ethology. *Zeitschirift für Tierpsychologie, 20*, 410–413.

Tizard, B., & Hughes, M. (1983). *Young children learning*. Cambridge, MA: Harvard University Press.

Tomasello, M. (1993). *First verbs*. New York: Cambridge University Press.

Tomasello, M. (1999). *The cultural origins of human cognition*. Cambridge, MA: Harvard University Press.

Tomasello, M., & Call, J. (1997). *Primate cognition*. New York: Oxford University Press.

Vandenberg, B. (1980). Play, problem solving, and creativity. In K. Rubin (Ed.), *Children's play* (pp. 49–68). San Francisco: Jossey-Bass.

Vygotsky, L. (1962). *Thought and language*. Cambridge, MA: MIT.

Vygotsky, L. (1978). *Mind in society*. Cambridge, MA: Harvard University Press.

Wachs, T. (1985, April). *Measurement of environment in the study of organism environment interaction*. Paper presented at the biennial meetings of the Society for the Research in Child Development, Toronto.

Walberg, H. J. (1984). Quantification reconsidered. In E. W. Gordon (Ed.), *Review of Educational Research* (Vol. 11, pp. 369–402). Washington, DC: American Educational Research Association.

Waters, E., & Sroufe, L. A. (1983). Social competence as a developmental construct. *Developmental Review, 3,* 79–97.

Wells, G. (1985). *Language development in the preschool years.* Cambridge, UK: Cambridge University Press.

White, D. J., King, A. P., & Duncan, S. D. (2002). Voice recognition technology as a tool for behavioral research. *Behavior Research Methods, Instruments, & Computers, 34,* 1–5.

Whiting, B., & Whiting, J. (1975). *Children of six cultures.* Cambridge, MA: Harvard University Press.

Wimmer, H., & Perner, J. (1983). Beliefs about beliefs: Representation and constraining function of wrong beliefs in young children's understanding of deception. *Cognition, 13,* 103–128.

Wright, H. (1960). Observational child study. In P. Mussen (Ed.), *Handbook of research methods in child development* (pp. 71–139). New York: Wiley.

Glossary

Abstract: The Abstract is a summary of the contents of the research report.

Actometer: A mechanical recording device, worn by participants, to measure physical activity.

Antecedent-consequence relations: When two variables, are ordered such that one precedes the other. For example, a child's infant day-care experience is antecedent to its later peer popularity.

Apparatus: Apparatus are the special material and equipment used in a study.

Applied science: Applied science takes this knowledge and applies it to everyday problems.

A priori hypothesis: Stating an hypothesis in advance.

Assent: Assent means that a child shows some form of agreement to participate in research without necessarily comprehending the full significance of the research necessary to give informed consent.

Associative hypotheses: Associative hypotheses posit a statistical relation between two variables, *a* and *b*, without specifying which variable, *a* or *b*, influences the other.

Basic science: Basic science is the quest for basic knowledge. Basic science can be descriptive, explanatory, or predictive.

Behavior setting survey: Specimen records aggregated across individuals.

Belief: A belief is a way of knowing based on faith, not a confirmation or disconfirmation; thus it cannot be considered scientific.

Beneficence: Beneficence is defined in the realm of ethics and human subjects in terms of maximizing possible benefits for and minimizing possible harm to the subjects.

Bias: When observers, experimenters, or subjects know the hypotheses of the research, which group the subjects belong to, or have additional information which results in differential treatment.

Blind and Double Blind: Blind refer to situations in which experimenters or observers are not aware of the research hypotheses. Double blind refers to situations in which neither the experimenters and observers nor the participants are aware of the hypotheses. These procedures are used to minimize bias.

Case study: Case studies can be part of ethnography or a separate mode of inquiry. Case study involves the examination of a single case. Cases can be individual children, parents, a school, an event or any other single entity. Most importantly, cases studies should be used when we want to gain very specific information about a specific cases.

Categorical variable: Categorical variables can be dichotomies, like sex (male or female) or polytomies, like the SES example.

Category/Coding system: The way in which behaviors are organized into meaningful units.

Category, exhaustive: An exhaustive category system is one that accounts for all the behaviors that are under observation.

Category, homogeneous: A category system wherein all subcomponents of the category are conceptually and empirically inter-related.

Category, mutually exclusive: A category system wherein the individual categories do not overlap such that a behavior is assigned to one and only one category.

Causal hypothesis: A causal hypotheses, on the other hand, specifies that one variable affects the other.

Checklist: A paper-and-pencil method by which we record occurrence and non-occurrence of behaviors.

Closed-ended questions: This class of items has specified responses, such as true or false; always, sometimes, or never.

Cluster sampling: Cluster sampling is defined as a sampling procedure in which we specify a relevant cluster, such as voting wards within a city or specific schools within a school district.

Cohen's *d*: A measure of the effect size in statistical results.

Collaborative research: Where the researcher and the participants, as a team, collaborate in asking questions, designing the project, interpreting results, and writing the research report.

Collective case study: This type of case study involves the aggregation of numerous cases that shed light upon a common problem. The result would be a more general picture than a single case could provide.

Confound: A confound exists when some extraneous variable unintentionally influences the independent variable.

Construct: A construct is a postulated attribute that is assumed to be reflected in form of measurement.

Construct irrelevant variance: Construct irrelevant variance is a problem when the assessment procedure has systematic variance associated with other constructs such as shared method variance, test scoring bias, or format biases.

Construct underrepresentativeness: Construct underrepresentativeness exists when our definition of a construct is too narrow and does not include important information.

Construct validity of cause or effects: Construct validity of cause or effects is a dimension of the external validity of experiments where external validity is defined as the approximate validity of our causal claims from an experiment to different people, measures, and historical time.

Context: A general term used to refer to those things that surround the person being observed (e.g., toys, peers, room size).

Context of discovery: That part of the scientific enterprise where we examine the data we have and trying to discover what the data are saying.

Context of justification: This is a context in our scientific writing when we conclude in our articles and they provide readers' with grounds for believing us.

Contiguous observations: Observation points that are next to each other (e.g., observations conducted on the same child every 2 minutes).

Continuous variable: A continuous variable is not distinct but places a measurement value along a continuum. For example, social economic status can be defined as a continuous variable by placing the number of years of education or the income of a group along a continuum.

Control: Control in experiments refers to the procedure of minimizing the influence of certain factors on experimental results. For example, the influence of the intelligence of children on experimental results can be controlled by randomly assigning children to experimental and control groups. Variables of interest are manipulated.

Convenience sampling: Samples of convenience are just that. They are chosen because they are convenient. Convenience means that the sample is readily available.

Covariation: Covariation refers to the variation, or changes, in each of two variables.

Critical Incident: A form of narrative recording that describes a specific incident.

Cross-sectional research: Examine age-related phenomena by studying different children from each of the relevant age groups.

Cybernetic: A inquiry system whereby a question is influenced by subsequent inquiry; this inquiry, in turn, becomes redefined with experience.

Data cleaning: Data cleaning refers to the process by which data are entered correctly into the computerized format. Checks should be made for omissions are inaccurate codes.

Deduction: Deduction is the logical process of moving from a general statement to a specific event.

Dependent variable: The dependent measure, y, is the consequence, or the measure being changed by the independent variable, x, in an experiment. In a medical treatment study, the severity of illness would be the dependent variable.

Descriptions by consequence: Describing a behavior in terms of what it leads to.

Description, physical: Describing in terms of physical movements.

Development, continuous: When a construct, like aggression, shows is stable across the developmental time of an individual. For example, aggression would be continuous development if it were stable in an individual across time.

Development, discontinuous: When a construct, like perspective taking, changes across developmental time. For example, perspective taking would be discontinuous if at Point 1 a child had low-level perspective taking and at Point 2 had a higher level.

Diary Method: A narrative methods whereby events and behaviors are recorded from memory.

Direct observational methods: Where observations are conducted live, in the field; contrast with indirect methods.

Deviation score: When an individual score is expressed in terms of its deviation from the score of the group in which the individual is embedded. For example, a children's score of word spoken would be expressed as his or her words—the average number of words spoken by the triad in which the target child is embedded.

Dominance: A dimension of group leaderships, especially in male groups.

Double blind: Procedures are used in experiments such that neither the researchers nor the participants know the conditions of assignment of participants or the hypotheses.

Duplicate publication: Duplicate publication involves the publication of the same or virtually the same manuscript in different places.

Duration: A measure of time where by an event or behavior is measured from beginning to end (e.g., the duration of fantasy play bouts is 3 minutes).

Ecological psychology: The study of the influence of context on behavior.

Emic perspective: Derived from phonemic wherein researchers are concerned with meaning distinction based on function. This orientation is often taken by interpretative researchers.

Empowerment: The process by which teachers and children gain a sense of worth and power in their abilities to teach and learn, respectively. Empowerment is often a result of taking an active role in charting the course of educational programs.

Environment of evolutionary adoptedness: Hunter–gather societies may represent the environment in which humans' current genetic composition evolved, the so-called environment of evolutionary adoptedness.

Epigenesis: The emergence of new biological structures and functions during the course of development.

Ethics: Relating to morals; morally correct, honorable.

Ethnography: A branch of anthropology that documents the daily life of a group from the perspective of the participants.

Ethogram: A thorough descriptions of behaviors exhibited by individuals in specific situations.

Ethology: The biological study of behavior.

Etic perspective: Derived from phonetic wherein researchers are concerned with classifying based on degree or amplitude. This orientation is often taken by empirical researchers.

Events: Behavioral episodes, contrasted with states, which are relatively short in duration (e.g., hit is an event).

Experimental control: Experimental control is the process by which extraneous influences are eliminated. By extraneous influences are influences that are not planned.

Experimental design: Experimental designs are differentiated from quasiexperimental designs in that the former employs random assignment, and the latter does not.

Experimental operational definitions: Experimental operational definitions do not address measures per se, but rather specify the procedures used in an experiment so that it can be replicated.

Explanatory statements: Statements that make causal connections between and among propositions (e.g., sugar causes children to be hyperactive).

Exploratory observation: In this initial period of an ethological study, the observer enters the field with minimal assumptions and a priori categories about the ways in which things operate.

Factor analyses: A group of statistical techniques that determine the extent to which individual behaviors, or other variables, can be group together, into larger categories. For example, we could determine, through factor analyses, the degree to which certain physical descriptions belong into distinctive categories.

Field: Refers to the real world where behaviors actually occur. For example, a field might be a classroom or a home environment.

Field notes: Observational notes where behaviors are recorded; see also Methodological, Personal, and Theoretical Notes.

Fieldwork: A generic label given to the time an ethnographer spends at the research site, using a variety of methods to understand to the culture under study. The specific field location studied and the length of time spent there will vary, as noted earlier, according to both theoretical and pragmatic concerns.

Formal channels: A channel for locating research information that are governed by rules primary researchers follow to get their information into the hands of other scholars (e.g., a journal article).

Fraud, Scientific: Scientific fraud is generally defined as fabrication or falsification of data, research procedures, or data analyses.

Frequency: A measure that indicates the number of times the target phenomenon occurred within a specified.

Generalize: The degree to which data from an experiment can be applied to explaining a similar phenomenon in the real world.

Habituation: Where participants and observers grow accustomed, to "get used" to each others' presence so they are minimally affected by each other.

Homogeneity: The degree to which the elements within composite measures are all interrelated; measured by split-half reliability.

Hypothesis: Hypotheses are conjectural statements between variables and expressed in declarative, not interrogative, form. An educated guess about what a researcher thinks will happen.

Independent variable: Independent variables in experiments are those variables that get manipulated. For example in a study comparing different drug regimens on illness, the different drug treatments would be the independent variable. The independent variable, x, is element that causes, or antecedes, the change in the dependent measure, y, in an experiment.

Indirect observational measures: Where data are collected from participants (e.g., from diaries or logs or from telephone interviews), rather than from direct observations.

Induction: Induction is defined as the logical process of reasoning from a specific to a more general level.

Informal channels: These are channels for locating research information do not have rules governing contact between the primary researcher and the person requesting the information (e.g., making personal contact with the researcher).

Informal interviews: Used as part of the ethnographic process and are a mixture of a interviews and conversations.

Instrument effects: The form of assessment can interact with personal characteristics and influence the meaning of measures. These sorts of influences are known as instrument effects.

Instrumental cases study: This form of case study is used to inform practice or theory. For example, my son's first-grade classroom and teachers were an interesting example of a cooperative social unit.

Initial/preliminary observations: Those observations contacted at the very beginning of a project. They are used to "debug" and refine the observational plan.

Intensity: A measure of behavior that indicates amplitude (e.g., vigor of exercise can be scored along high, medium, and low dimensions).

Interval data: Data categories where the distance between the categories are equal interval units, such as degrees on the Fahrenheit scale.

Intrinsic case study: This form of case study is undertaken because the researcher has intrinsic, or self motived, reasons for conducting the research. The particular case is not chosen for any specific reason; for example it may not be representative or successful, but the researcher finds the case interesting.

Informal colleges: A collection of scholars working in the same area and usually linked to each other through the work Ipsative measures measure a set of traits within individuals.

John Henry Effect: The knowledge of control group status motivates participants to reduce differences with the treatment groups. This is known as the "John Henry Effect."

Justice: The principle of justice as applied to research ethics places value on the equitable distribution of costs and benefits to participants, regardless age, race, sex, ethnicity, or social status.

Kappa: A measure of observer reliability that corrects for chance agree and is expressed from -1.0 to +1.0.

Key Informant: A key informant is a member of the culture under study who has a close knowledge of that culture. The key informant should also be willing and able to share these insights with the ethnographer.

Laboratory: This is the venue for experimental research, often an experimental playroom or classroom.

Lag Sequential Analysis: A analysis option designed to determine whether a behavior or event increases or decreases the probability of another behavior or event within the same observation session.

Latency: A measure of time from the presentation of a stimulus to a reaction (e.g., the latency is 3 seconds from when a teacher asked a question until he or she restated the question).

Latent variables: A latent variable, like a construct, is an abstract representation of an unobservable phenomenon, such as intelligence. PPVT, Stanford Binet, and productive vocabulary would all be considered manifest variables. Manifest variables are the direct measures indicative of a more general, latent variable.

Likert scale: An ordinal response scale, from example: He's happy: (1) Always; (2) Mostly; (3) Sometimes; (4) Not Often; (5) Never.

Litter effects: Where members of a group influence the score of an individual. For example, one child's social interaction score could be influenced by the social interaction of his or her peers.

Local rates: Applied to measuring intensity and is measured by noting the number of behavioral components that occur with a specific duration.

Longitudinal: This form of research is concerned with describing the process of change in the same children as they develop across time.

Macrolevel category: A category system that has a number of subcomponents; for example, aggression is a macrolevel category with microlevel components, such as hit, kick, and bite.

Manifest variable: Manifest variables are the direct measures indicative of a more general, latent variable. For example, PPVT, Stanford Binet, and productive vocabulary would all be considered manifest variables underlying the latent variable intelligence.

Manipulation: In experiments variables of interest are manipulated to determine their effect. For example, we could manipulate different toys to see their effect on children's play. Other variables should be controlled.

Measured operational definitions: These definitions describe the way in which a variable will be measured. So we can define intelligence operationally by specifying that intelligence is "operationalized" in terms of the PPVT.

Measurement: Quantification of units, often expressed in terms of frequency.

Measurement context: A measurement context can be defined as any situation in which individuals or groups are systematically assessed. These contexts typically take the form of asking individuals questions about themselves, placing them in contrived situations and having them preform, or observing them in their natural habitats.

Methodological notes: Notes made, as part of Field Notes, that help clarify issues related to method, such as logistics.

Method variance: Method variance includes the systematic effects specific to a form of assessment that are extraneous to the variable being measured. For example, in self-reports where parents are asked about their child rearing and disciplinary an extraneous influence on the response might be associated with social desirability of responses.

Microlevel category: A category system that has few subcomponents, and is often based on physical descriptions and of low inference (e.g., a microlevel category for attention might include: heart rate and gaze).

Molar: A measure that is an aggregate of molecular measures; for example, aggression has a number of molecular components.

Molecular: A measure which is expressed behaviorally in terms of minute behaviors; for example, bite, punch, and scratch are molecular behaviors that relate to the molar category, aggression.

Multistage sampling: This form of sampling is used in survey research in those circumstances when there is no way in which to sample directly from the population. It involves identifying those units in which individuals are embedded and sampling from those units.

Narrative System: Where events are described in a temporal context. Recording can be made "live" or of recalled events.

Necessary condition: A necessary condition exists when x must be present in order for there to be change in y.

Nominal data: Nominal data are categorical and unordered (e.g., they get sent to day care; to a relative, or stay home alone).

Non-participant observer: An observer who remains detached from the subject that are being observed; contrast with participant observer.

Nonprobability sampling: Nonprobability sampling does not choose based on randomized procedures. Nonprobability samples can be based on quotas, purposive, and accidental or convenience.

Normative measures: Normative measures involve comparisons across individuals. Measures are normative when individuals scores form a distribution and an individuals scores derive their meaning from relations to the distribution.

Objective descriptions: Descriptions that are low inference and, consequently, are often based on physical descriptions and not on inferences about motivation or intent.

Observational Software Program: A general term referring to a computer assisted program to aid in the collection, coding, storage, and analysis of direct observational data.

Observer drift: Where observers' scoring of the same behaviors changes across time.

Observer effects: Observer effects is another class of method variance. Observer effects can also be described as bias to the extent that observers' scoring of naturalistic observations or questionnaires is biased, or influenced, by extraneous information.

Observer fatigue: Where observer boredom or fatigue results in inaccurate scoring.

Obtrusive: Where the observer or the procedure interferes with the normal course of events that are under observation.

Occurrence/Nonoccurrence: A measure of observer reliability express as a percentage, but where the possibility of chance agreements is omitted.

Ontogeny: The study of development within a species.

Open-ended interview questions: They cannot be answered from a specified set of responses, such as yes/no or multiple choice. The respondent must use his or her own words to respond; consequently they allow for individual interpretation and response.

Operational definition: An operational definition is where a concept is defined in operations that must be performed to define it. So weight would be defined in terms of the operations necessary to measure it.

Ordinal data: Ordinal scales also involve using rule to classify phenomena, but an ordinal scale of measurement should reflect an ordered difference between categories. Ordinal scales are ordered along a single dimension, such as happy, neutral, and sad.

Participants: Participants are those individuals who take part in the research enterprise; they are the individual who are studied.

Participant mortality: Participant mortality refers to the number of participants who leave the study before it has been completed.

Participant observer: An observer who wants to get an "insider perspective" by becoming a member of the group he or she is observing; Contrast with nonparticipant observer.

Pattern: A measure of behavior that describes the way in which different types of behavior are patterned, or occur, across time; for example, children when presented with a new toy will exhibit the following pattern: exploration, play, boredom.

Patterning: Patterning is used as a measure of reliability for ethnographers. Patterns in behavior are identified and reliability exists when they recur.

Percentage of agreement: A measure of observer reliability, expressed as the percent of more than one observer agreeing.

Personal notes: Notes, part of Field Notes, whereby the observer notes his or her own reactions to the observations being conducted.

Phylogeny: The study of the development across animal species.

Plagiarism: Plagiarism is defined as presenting substantial portions or elements of another's work or data as their own, even if the other work is or data source is cited occasionally.

Pooling: Pooling refers to the use of individual observations, nor individual participants be used as the unit of analyses. For example if we have 10 children being observed 20 times, the *N*, or number of subjects should be 10, not the number of observations for each child, or 200.

Population/Universe: The whole group of people or behaviors from which we sample. A population of people could be the all the children in a particular school or state; the universe of behaviors could be all the behaviors that children exhibit.

Post hoc explanations: Explanations generated after data have been collected.

Primary sources: Sources which report original research. Primary sources are typically found in scientific journals, conference papers, research reports, and doctoral and masters theses.

Probability sampling: Probability sampling uses some form of random sampling at one or more stages in the sampling process.

Procedure section: This is the section of a research paper that details each step taken in the research study, in the order of occurrence. In this section, the research should summarize instructions given to participants, discuss the way in which groups were formed and experimental manipulations were carried out.

Process data: The descriptive information on the implementation of educational programs; for example, to what degree to teachers asks the sorts of questions specified by a program.

Project manual: Project manuals contain a record of the plan of the research, instruments used, procedures to be followed, and schedule of administration.

Proposition: A formal statement in logic and science.

Q-sort: A research technique used by observers, or participants, to form categories by putting descriptors into categories they think are relevant.

Qualitative variable: Qualitative variables are "count data" and indicate the presence or absence of a specific attribute on one or more than one category.

Qualitative research: Loosely defined as researchers following an emic perspective.

Quantitative research: Loosely defined as research following an etic perspective.

Quantitative variable: A quantitative variable, on the other hand, the amount of an attribute, rather than its presence or absence.

Quasiexperimental research designs: Quasiexperimental designs are differentiated from experimental designs in that the former does not employ random assignment and the latter does.

Quota sampling: Quota sampling is a nonprobabilistic version of stratified sampling. With quota sampling, as with stratified sampling, the researcher uses his or her knowledge of relevant dimensions of the population, such as race, sex, and social economic status.

Radio Microphone: A wireless microphone that transmits a voice to a tape recorder.

Random assignment: Random assignment means that each individual in the sample has an equal opportunity of being assigned to an experimental condition. In this way, any individual differences would be randomly distributed across conditions.

Random selection/sampling: Random selection means that all people in the population have an equal chance of being chosen. Their being chosen is based on chance. The best-case scenario would have the sample be representative of the population. This means that the sample should resemble the population.

Range: A measure of variability in a distribution of scores indicated by the difference between the largest and the smallest score.

Rating scale: A type of response item used as a questionnaire or interview where the responders gives answers in terms of degree, see Likert.

Rating scale, Cumulative points: A form of rating scale where the a responder checks one or many responses and the sum of those responses is the unit of analysis.

Rating scale, Forced choice: A form of rating scale where a responder must give only one response.

Rating scale, Graphic: A form of rating scale in which a response is displayed along a horizontal or vertical line.

Rating scale, Numerical: A form of rating scale in which one response is made and the responses lie along a continuum of degree.

Rating scale, Standard: A rating scale where the responses are along a standard criteria, for example, along criteria of percentage.

Ratio data: Data where the distance between the intervals are equal and where there is a 0 point, such as weigh.

Reactivity: Where participants being observed act "unnaturally," in reaction to their being observed.

Recency of memory: Where a responder or an interview provides information that has occurred most recently, rather than information that may be more representative.

Recording Media: Those form of technology, such as tape recorders and checklists, which are used to actually record behavioral data.

Recording rules, 0/1: Recording behavior that occurs during a specified time interval (e.g., record occurrence of smile if it occurs during a 30-second interval).

Recording rules, continuous: Recording all behaviors that occur during a specified interval (e.g., recording all the relevant behaviors of a child for 3 minutes).

Recording rule, instantaneous: Record behaviors that occur at a specified instant (e.g., score occurrence only if it is observed when a beeper sounds).

Reliability: Reliability, then, is the tendency toward consistency from one set of measurements to another. Reliability is necessary, but not sufficient for validity.

Reliability, Interobserver: The degree to which more than one observers agree on what they see.

Reliability, Intraobserver: The degree to which one observer scores consistently across time.

Reliability, Split-Half: The degree to which odd and even measures are consistent, or homogeneous.

Reliability, Test–Retest: Consistent in measures across time.

Replication: This refers to the degree to which the same results can be obtained in more than one group.

Research data: Research data are defined as the quantitative information generated through research or, more generally, recorded information generated through systematic inquiry. Research data are defined as the quantitative information generated through research or, more generally, recorded information generated through systematic inquiry.

Resolution: Changes in behavior reflected in changes in scoring.

Respect: Respect as applied to the ethics of research translates into treating individuals as autonomous beings.

Response rate graph: A response rate graph is used to track survey research responses. The graph has the days of the survey on the x axis and the number of responses for the corresponding day on the y axis.

Results section: The Results section of a research report summarizes the findings of the study. It should be organized around the research questions or hypotheses posed in the Introduction.

Retrospective Interviews: These are part of the ethnographic process and can be either structured or informal. As the label implies this sort of interview asks participants about events in the past.

Rhythmic stereotypies: These behaviors include foot kicking and body rocking and tend of peak at around 6 months of age.

Salami science: The term *salami science* is often used to refer to a related practice, that of taking many and thin slices from the same data set and publishing it in many rather than fewer places.

Sample: A sample represents the whole population or universe. For example, a sample of children would represent the whole population of a city of state. Similarly, a sample of play behaviors would represent the universe of children's behavioral acts.

Sample frame: The sample frame in research, generally, is the set of people having a chance of being selected from a given population.

Sample interval: Those time units into which the observational session is divided (e.g., a 15-minute lesson could be divided into 15 1-minute intervals).

Sample plan: A sample plan is that phase of survey research includes identifying the universe of population to be studied. Also included in a sample plan are rules covering how the sample will be drawn and its size.

Sample point: That point at the end of the sample interval.

Sampling rules, ad lib: Sampling behavior in such a way that no systematic rules are being followed.

Sampling rules, behavior/event: Choosing to observe specified sets of behaviors or events; contrasted with time sampling; for example, record all instances of aggression.

Sampling rules, focal: Sampling the behavior of individual children separately.

Sampling rules, scan: Sampling whole groups by briefly observing individuals within the group at short intervals.

Sampling rules, time: Choosing to observe based a specified time intervals; in contrast to behavioral/event sampling; for example, record behavior every 20 seconds.

Sample/Sign: Measure of behavior which index a level of abstraction where sample is an actual behavior, such as punch, and sign is an abstraction that is not directly observable, such as aggression.

Sampling with replacement: In a sampling plan we can choose to replace each number sampled.

Sampling without replacement: In a sampling plan we choose not to replace it.

Science: Science is primarily knowledge; by convention it is knowledge of a certain kind, the kind, namely, which seeks general laws connecting a number of particular fact (Russell, 1959, p. viii).

Score: A score is defined in a very general sense as any indicator of that which we say we are measuring. A score can be summarized from behavioral observations, performance on a test, or responses to questionnaires.

Secondary sources: These are the sources that discuss primary research already conducted. Secondary sources are typically found in review articles, book chapters, and text books.

Self-efficacy: Feeling of self-worth and that you can accomplish something.

Sensitizing concepts: Questions and categories that observers take with them into the field as they conduct their preliminary observations. These concepts direct them to relevant behaviors and events.

Sensitivity: The extent to which changes in behavior are reflected in measured values.

Shared method variance: Shared method variance occurs when we examine the relation between two (or more) measures derived from the same assessment medium.

Significant fact: The first step in establishing a scientific law. A significant fact is a single "instance" that is relevant to the current scientific debate.

Simple random sampling: A survey research technique where we randomly draw our sample from a population.

Smaller/larger index: A measure of interobserver reliability where two measures of the same behavior, the smaller and the larger, are compared.

Social desirability: Where interviewees giving information they think the interviewer wants to hear, rather than accurate information.

Sociological facts: Data derived from surveys. They are attributes of individuals that come from membership in some group: sex, income, education, political affiliation.

Specific questions: Interview questions used to probe the meaning of the more general information gained in the survey questions. For example, we might have a general question on where do student spend time in the dormitory.

Specimen record: Narrative descriptions of a participant's behavior in a specific context constructed by ecological psychologists (e.g., a children's school day, are described in great detail).

Stability: Similarity in measurement across time, as measured by test–retest reliability.

States: States, like response class of behaviors, refer to the transitory nature of individuals. These changes, however, are seen, as related to individuals as organisms, rather than their responses to stimuli in the environment.

Statistical conclusion validity: When we make some inferences about the relation between two variables in an experiment based on the statistical covariation between them, the validity of these statistical conclusions is referred to statistical conclusion validity.

Stratified sample: Attempts to proportionally draw a sample that reflects the population.

Sufficient condition: A sufficient condition exists when the presence of *x* means the change in *y* can occur but *y* can also occur under other circumstances as well.

Survey questions: General questions that help to define the boundaries of the study. Information on the physical setting, universe of activities, and thoughts of the participants can be gained through survey questions.

Theoretical notes: Part of Field Notes, describe that aspects of the observation that are relevant to the observer's theory.

Trait: A traits is considered to be an enduring and stable characteristic of a person.

Transaction: The reciprocal influence of two entities on each other (e.g., the influences of people and environments on each other).

Transfer: The degree to which information in one setting can be applied to another. In this chapter I discussed the degree to which information on children's knowledge as measured by a test transferred to their use of that knowledge in the classroom.

Triangulation: Triangulation is the convergence of data sources. That is, different data sources, such as observations and interviews, provide different sources of information about the same events. Validity exists when multiple data sources give the same interpretation.

Unreliability: That repeated sets of measurements never exactly duplicate themselves is what we mean by unreliability.

Validity: Generally, refers to the truthfulness of the data. Internal validity refers to the degree to which inferences from experiments are truthful and the extent to which we controlled alternative explanations. External validity refers to the degree to which we can generalize from the laboratory to a real-world context. Ecological validity refer to the degree to which similar results occur in the laboratory and the field.

Validity, Construct: The truthfulness of a nonobservable, theoretical entity, such as aggression.

Validity, Content: Where the instrument used in the measurement represents what it purports to measure.

Validity, Criterion: Composed of predictive validity (where a behavior accurately predicts something) and concurrent validity (where a behavior is related to a similar measure, taken contemporaneously).

Variables: Symbols to which we attach numerical values. For example, we could have a variable, x, which represent social economic status (SES).

Vigor: An intensity measure of physical activity; for example, higher heart rate is a measure of vigor.

Author Index

Subject Index